INTERNATIONAL DEVELOPMENT IN FOCUS

Alternative Paths to Public Financial Management and Public Sector Reform

Experiences from East Asia

Sokbunthoeun So, Michael Woolcock, Leah April,
Caroline Hughes, and Nicola Smithers, Editors

WORLD BANK GROUP

Contents

Acknowledgments

The editors and authors are grateful to James Brumby (Director, Governance Global Practice, East Asia and Pacific, Latin America and the Caribbean, and South Asia), Fily Sissoko (Practice Manager, Governance Global Practice, Myanmar, Pacific, and Vietnam), Arturo Herrera Gutierrez (Practice Manager, Governance Global Practice, China, Indonesia, and Singapore), George Addo Larbi (Practice Manager, Governance Global Practice, Bangladesh and the Philippines), and Robert Taliercio (Practice Manager, Governance Global Practice, Latin America and the Caribbean, Public Sector and Institutions) for their overall guidance in the development of specific chapters and this whole edited volume. We also thank colleagues from the Global Delivery Initiative for the inputs provided during the early phase of concept preparation. Our gratitude also goes to all our government counterparts for their collaboration and contribution to this book. We thank our peer reviewers Verena Maria Fritz (Senior Public Sector Specialist) and Davide Zucchini (Senior Public Sector Specialist) for all their useful comments for refining this report. We also thank Sodeth Ly for his inputs into the Cambodian case study and Linna Ky for her excellent assistance. The team is also grateful to numerous individuals whose names are not mentioned here for their inputs into each case study.

This edited volume emerges from an international workshop on experimental approaches to Public Financial Management (PFM)/Public Sector Reform for Sustainability of Results, held in Cambodia in September 2017. Our special thanks go to the Cambodia Ministry of Economy and Finance for co-organizing the workshop with the World Bank. A multidonor trust fund supported by Australia, the European Union, and Sweden for the PFM reform program in Cambodia, which financed the workshop and the documentation of these different countries' reform experiences, is gratefully acknowledged.

List of Contributors

Leah April
Senior Public Sector Specialist for the Latin America and the Caribbean Region of the World Bank.

Erwin Ariadharma
Senior Public Sector Management Specialist of the World Bank Governance Global Practice based in Indonesia.

Pike Pike Aye
Public Sector Management Specialist of the World Bank Governance Global Practice based in Yangon, Myanmar.

Kok Hong Chea
Deputy Director of Macroeconomic and Fiscal Policy Department of Cambodia Ministry of Economy and Finance. He is directly involved in the monitoring and evaluation of the implementation of Revenue Mobilization in Cambodia.

David Craig
Senior Governance Specialist of the World Bank Governance Global Practice based in Papua New Guinea.

Atul Deshpande
Senior Public Sector Specialist of the World Bank Governance Global Practice based in Yangon, Myanmar.

Jeevakumar Govindasamy
Public Sector Specialist of the World Bank Governance Global Practice based at the Global Knowledge and Research Hub in Malaysia.

Caroline Hughes
Rev. Theodore Hesburgh CSC Chair in Peace Studies, Kroc Institute for International Peace Studies, University of Notre Dame.

Kai-Alexander Kaiser
Senior Economist with the World Bank's Governance Global Practice with the World Bank in Hanoi.

Meng Foon Lee
Senior Management Consultant based in Malaysia. Lee was a former Deputy Director and Head of the Leadership Centre of the National Institute of Public Administration, and Administrative and Diplomatic Officer in Malaysia.

Prathna Maun
Director of Information Technology Department of Cambodia Ministry of Economy and Finance. He is also the Project Manager for the Financial Management Information System (FMIS) in Cambodia.

Bernard Myers
Senior Public Sector Management Specialist in the World Bank's Kuala Lumpur Office.

Phuong Anh Nguyen
Public Sector Specialist of the World Bank Governance Global Practice based in Vietnam.

Pisith Phlong
Change Management Consultant at the World Bank Country Office in Cambodia.

Hari Purnomo
Senior Public Sector Specialist for the Governance Global Practice of the World Bank in Jakarta, Indonesia.

Thanapat Reungsri
Senior Consultant on Public Financial Management of the World Bank based in Bangkok, Thailand. He was formerly a Budget Analyst at the Thai Bureau of Budget.

Nicola Smithers
Practice Manager for Anglophone Africa in the Governance Global Practice of the World Bank.

Sokbunthoeun So
Public Sector Specialist of the World Bank Governance Global Practice based in Phnom Penh, Cambodia.

Saysanith Vongviengkham
Public Sector Specialist of the World Bank Governance Global Practice based in Vientiane, Lao People's Democratic Republic.

Fanny Weiner
Senior Public Sector Management Specialist of the World Bank Governance Global Practice based in Vientiane, Lao People's Democratic Republic.

Michael Woolcock
Lead Social Scientist in the World Bank's Development Research Group based in Washington, DC.

Abbreviations

ABS	Activity Budget Sheet
APMF	Activity Performance Management Framework
BFR	Big Fast Results
BoB	Bureau of the Budget
BoT	Bank of Thailand
BR	Bureaucracy Reform
BRISA	Bureaucracy Reform Implementation Self-Assessment
BRO	Budget Review Officers
BSC	Balanced-Scorecard
CACC	Central Agencies Coordinating Committee
CAT	Computer Assisted Test
CBM	Central Bank of Myanmar
CGD	Comptroller General's Department
CM	change management
COTS	commercial-off-the-shelf
CPMC	Central Performance Management Committee
CUEPACS	Congress of Unions of Employees in the Public and Civil Services
DDA	District Development Authorities
DE	development expenditure
DEMPA	debt management performance assessment
DG	Director General
DoF	Department of Finance
DOLA	Department of Local Administration
DPL	Development Policy Loans
DPLGA	Department of Provincial and Local Government Affairs
DSIP	District Services Improvement Program
DTP	Directorate for Treasury Transformation
EAP	External Advisory Panel
EFD	External Financial Department
EoDB	Ease of Doing Business
EPU	Economic Planning Unit
ERT	Executive Reform Team

ETP	Economic Transformation Program
FMCBP	Financial Management Capacity Building Project
FMIS	Financial Management Information System
FMWG	FMIS Project Management Working Group
FRR	Financial Rules and Regulations
GAAP	Generally Accepted Accounting Principles
GDB	General Department of Budget
GDCE	General Department of Customs and Excise
GDT	General Department of Taxation
GFIS	Government Financial Information System
GFMIS	Government Financial Management Information System
GFMRAP	Government Financial Management and Revenue Administration Project
GNI	gross national income
GoV	Government of Vietnam
GTP	Government Transformation Program
HR	Human Resources
IA	implementing agencies
IC	Implementation Committee
ICT	information and communications technology
IFMIS	Integrated Financial Management Information System
IFMS	Integrated Financial Management System
IPF	Investment Project Financing
IPSAS	international public sector accounting systems
IRBM	Integrated Results-Based Management
IRD	Internal Revenue Department
ISR	Implementation Status and Results Report
ITAS	Integrated Tax Administration System
JDPBPC	Joint District Planning and Budget Priorities Committee
JPAC	Joint Public Accounts Committee
KIT	Khmer Information Technology
KPI	key performance indicator
LAO	Local Administrative Organizations
LDC	least developed country
LLG	Local Level Government
LMA	line ministries and agencies
LTO	Large Taxpayer's Office
M&E	monitoring and evaluation
MBS	Modified Budgeting System
MEB	Myanmar Economic Bank
MEF	Ministry of Economy and Finance
MES	Ministry Executive Summary
MoF	Ministry of Finance
MOPF	Ministry of Planning and Finance
MOU	memorandum of understanding
MPFM	Modernization of Public Finance Management
MPI	Ministry of Planning and Investment
MTEF	Medium Term Expenditure Framework
MTO	Medium Taxpayer Offices
NBO	National Budget Office
NBOS	National Blue Ocean Strategy

NDC	National Decentralization Committee
NEFC	National Economic and Fiscal Commission
NGPES	National Growth and Poverty Eradication Strategy
NKRA	National Key Result Area
NOSC	National OBB Steering Committee
NPM	New Public Management
NUTP	National Union of the Teaching Profession
OAG	Office of the Auditor General
OAS	Official Assessment System
OBB	outcome based budgeting
OCSC	Office of the Civil Service Commission
OE	operational expenditure
ONDC	Office of National Decentralization Committee
OPDC	Office of the Public Sector Development Commission
PAP	priority action plan
PBB	Performance Based Budgeting
PBS	Program Budget Sheet
PDMO	Public Debt Management Office
PEFA	Public Expenditure and Financial Accountability
PEMANDU	Performance Management and Delivery Unit
PEMNA	Public Expenditure Management Network in Asia
PFM	Public Financial Management
PFMRP	Public Financial Management Reform Program (in Cambodia)
PFMSP	Public Financial Management Strengthening Program
PGAS	Papua New Guinea Accounting System
PI	performance indicator
PIM	Public Investment Management
PIU	project implementation unit
PLSSMA	Provincial and Lower Local Services Management Authority
PMS	performance management system
PPBS	Program Performance Budgeting System
PPMF	Program Performance Management Framework
PRSO	Poverty Reduction Support Operation
PS	Permanent Secretary
PSD	Public Service Department
PSI	Public Sector and Institutional
PSMRP	Public Sector Management Reform Plan
PSTF	Public Service Transformation Framework
PSTL	Public Service Transformation Labs
PT	provincial treasuries
QA	Quality Assurance
RIGFA	Reform of Intergovernmental Financing Arrangements
RLT	Resource Leaders Training
RMP	Revenue Management Program
RTC	Rural Transformation Centers
SAO	State Audit Organization
SAS	Self-Assessment System
SBL	State Budget Law
SEE	State Economic Enterprises
SOP	Standard Operating Procedures
SPAN	Sistem Perbendaharaan dan Anggaran Negara

TABMIS	Treasury and Budget Management Information System
TADAT	tax administration diagnostic assessment tool
TAO	Tambon/Sub-district Administrative Organizations
TAPL	Tax Administration Procedures Law
TSA	Treasury Single Account
TTP	Treasury Transformation Program
UTC	Urban Transformation Centers
VST	Vietnam State Treasury

1 Introduction

ALTERNATIVE APPROACHES TO REFORMING
THE PUBLIC SECTOR: EAST ASIAN
EXPERIENCES IN PUBLIC FINANCIAL
MANAGEMENT AND PUBLIC SECTOR REFORM

**MICHAEL WOOLCOCK, SOKBUNTHOEUN SO, NICOLA SMITHERS,
LEAH APRIL, and CAROLINE HUGHES**

Reforming public sector organizations—their structures, policies, processes and practices—is notoriously difficult, in rich and poor countries alike (Grindle and Thomas 1991; World Bank 2012). Even in the most favorable of circumstances, the scale and complexity of the tasks to be undertaken are enormous, requiring levels of coordination and collaboration that may be without precedent for those involved. Entirely new skills—for example, learning to use sophisticated software—may need to be acquired by tens of thousands of people. Such reforms are often premised on the need to "modernize" prevailing administrative systems, with the long-run payoff being enhanced efficiency and effectiveness in the collection, management and allocation of public resources, all in pursuit of top-priority national strategy objectives. But these payoffs may take many years to fully materialize, requiring sustained commitments from senior officials as setbacks, delays and confusion threaten to sap morale and momentum. High turnover, competing distractions and inherent uncertainty can compromise the necessary focus.

Compounding these logistical challenges, however, is the pervasive reality that circumstances are often not favorable to large-scale reform: partisan interests, ideological commitments and institutional incentives (e.g., career preservation, risk aversion, obligations to key supporters, powerful unions) can combine to undermine the change process or block it entirely, even when the societal gains from reform are unambiguous and popular (World Bank 2016b). The challenges can be especially difficult in low-income countries, where leaders may face contradictory pressure from domestic constituencies and international agencies, finding themselves caught between proposed reforms they regard (rightly or wrongly) as onerous impositions by outsiders, yet also needing to show "progress" and "results" consistent with global standards (to sustain their legitimacy and ensure an ongoing flow of vital external resources). Such pressures can create a dynamic whereby enacted "reforms" have the allure or appearance of change without fundamentally altering underlying structures and performance capability (Andrews 2013; Bridges and Woolcock 2017; see also World Bank 2017), thereby leading to cynicism about the very possibility and desirability of reform. Passing anti-corruption legislation, for example, but remaining unwilling (or just unable) to seriously enforce it, is one way in which leaders can appease demands for reform while otherwise maintaining the status quo (Andrews et al. 2017). Upgrading administrative technology and conducting extensive "capability building" exercises[1]—as necessary as these may sometimes be—is another familiar way in which vast sums can continue to be spent without raising either organizational performance or the ire of independent watchdogs.

Over the last few decades, increasing attention has been given to devising analytical frameworks and practical strategies that forge a more constructive understanding of these dynamics while also charting a potentially more promising path forward. How can particular "binding constraints" to public sector reform be more readily identified and resolved? What specific external assistance can be offered to domestic reformers who are "willing" but not (yet) "able" to enact change? When should national leaders borrow effective reform strategies from abroad? How can they optimally adapt them to suit local realities? A range of approaches have sought to respond to such questions. For example, one approach involves adopting the type of reform strategies and incentives systems (score cards, key performance indicators, etc.) used in the private sector (an approach often referred to as New Public Management); another seeks to create dedicated teams ("delivery units"[2])—embedded within ministries but reporting directly to the president or prime minister—solely focused on enhancing the implementation of designated reforms; and a third calls for remaining cognizant of global "best practices" (and associated professional standards) but ultimately working to adapt these to the local context in response to problems that have been locally nominated and prioritized (thereby leading to the crafting of "best fit" solutions).

Variants within this third "adaptive" category are discussed in more detail below, since they have emerged most recently (and thus have yet to fully cohere into discrete work programs) while also attracting considerable attention, not only among public sector reform specialists but among development professionals more broadly. The cases presented in this volume exemplify this third approach in action, even if, importantly, most of them were not initially undertaken as an explicit instantiation of a particular analytical tradition. For the most part, rather, reformers took a decidedly pragmatic approach, working within the political space afforded them to find workable and supportable solutions to the challenges at hand. In this volume we thus work inductively from the cases studies to the broader theories, doing so to forge an informed dialogue between practitioners and researchers about the conditions under which key factors align to sustain public sector reform. More specifically, and for direct operational purposes, our goal here is not to identify a new or universal set of "lessons" for public sector reformers, but rather to encourage those tasked with such work to engage in the iterative process of "finding and fitting" context-specific solutions to context-specific problems. In this sense, the task of successful reformers is less that of the dutiful functionary assessed by the extent of their compliance with a standard "script" than that of the creative and diligent bureaucratic entrepreneur crafting solutions that blend professional principles with local realities. If there is a general lesson from the cases in this volume, it that such behavior should be required, recognized and rewarded.

The opportunity to prepare this volume stems from an increasing recognition that many public sector reform challenges are deeply idiosyncratic—that is, that different kinds of problems and contexts require different combinations of solutions, even if the broad principles and objectives of the reform process are relatively similar. Beyond recognizing the importance of strong leadership, sustained political commitment and effective inter/intra-agency coordination, public sector reform strategies need to be customized to fit the particular sectoral and country characteristics in which they are being undertaken, then carried out in such a way that imbues the reform process (which will inevitably generate some level of contention) with local legitimacy and durability. Since the very complexity and uncertainty of the reform "journey" means that it is impossible to pre-identify all the challenges and contingencies that will be encountered, it is equally important to use real-time feedback mechanisms and administrative instruments that will enable any necessary mid-course corrections to be made.

Actually, doing all of these tasks is itself extremely complex, and is thus a reason why, even in seemingly favorable circumstances, many public sector reform efforts struggle to fully realize their objectives. Many, but by no means all. This volume brings together a range of experiences with public sector reform initiatives across eight countries in the East Asia region, a region where the very success of broader development strategies—sustained growth, enhanced well-being, expanded education access, reduced poverty—has created fresh demands on the public sector to undertake incrementally more complex tasks, at scale, for all. In several of these countries, a public sector that successfully managed a transition from low to middle income status now seeks to identify and enact strategies that will take them to high income status in the coming decades. But these new strategies are unlikely to amount to mere "upgrades" of earlier versions. For example, a society in which people expect to live until 65 (or longer) has qualitatively different health concerns than a society where life expectancy is 45; it also requires the construction of pension systems for retirees (itself a newly created phase in life) and assisted living facilities for those who cannot be cared for by their families (which are smaller and more dispersed than in the past). More complex and specialized economies require workers with correspondingly more sophisticated skills, which in turn requires a vastly expanded education system focused on promoting lifelong learning (as opposed to merely requiring attendance through primary school) (World Bank 2018). An economy more integrated into global trading and financial networks requires a clear, equitable and effective justice system capable of regulating powerful companies, upholding environmental standards, enforcing safe working conditions and safeguarding contractual agreements. And so on. The challenges facing the public sector, in short, just keep getting harder, not easier, as the development process itself successfully unfolds.

The eight country cases from East Asia presented in this volume explore *how* recent reforms have been undertaken in public financial management (PFM) and the public sector more broadly. Most of them would qualify as "successes." Some could be considered as "mixed outcomes" and even "failure." However, for present purposes the most insightful and "useable" lessons come from examining in more detail the variable outcomes associated with particular *aspects* of the reform process—even if a given reform is deemed to have been "moderately successful" overall, for example, there are likely to be certain aspects that worked quite well, others that muddled through, and still others that were clearly unsuccessful. In such circumstances, the key analytical task is identifying and explaining this variation; accordingly, our focus here is less on formally "demonstrating" success (or not) per se than on documenting the processes by which the array of outcomes was achieved. Put differently, that most of the cases discussed here are mostly "successful" instances of reform should not be interpreted as meaning that all aspects of the reform went smoothly or according to plan; the cases have been selected and prepared precisely because there were *always* serious design and implementation challenges that were met with variable degrees of success and failure along the way.

As such, a central focus of the processes discussed in the cases is to highlight innovative decision-making and implementation strategies on the part of those responsible for leading the reforms—certainly in the country context itself, where the political and bureaucratic space for deviating from standard approaches is often considerably constrained. In such circumstance, being "innovative" means—by definition—*not* holding unwaveringly to predetermined plans and *not* insistently using standard techniques in standard ways. As such, the primary purpose in presenting these cases is to document how the space (more formally, the authorizing environment) for innovative reform strategies was created and sustained, how and through whom such space was implemented, and how emergent implementation challenges were addressed.[3] Importantly, the approaches deployed in these cases, and the conclusions we derive from them, are not presented as a new list of universal "best practices" that those undertaking similar reforms should now adopt, but rather as ideas and inspiration that they might consider. In other words, they are cases of how "best fit" strategies in combination with "best practice" approaches were crafted and implemented—of how general principles became specific applications in particular places in response to idiosyncratic problems.

ARRAYING "ADAPTIVE" APPROACHES TO PUBLIC SECTOR REFORM: A FRAMEWORK

When analysts seek to account for the broad range of outcomes associated with public sector reform, and in particular the long list of efforts that achieved far less than what was envisioned, there are essentially three key factors around which they weave an explanation: (a) the technical quality (including correct "sequencing" and "coherence") of the reforms; (b) the willingness of senior management and leadership teams to inspire and sustain the necessary actions, and/or to exert the necessary pressure (including positive incentives) to overcome active resistance; (c) the implementation capability of staff at all levels to actually carry out the day-to-day tasks required to implement the reforms, their ability to adapt the reform in response to implementation trial and error, and to overcome numerous (often unexpected) implementation challenges. Carefully designed reforms that enjoy adequate political support and are implemented by competent, motivated staff are likely to succeed; weaknesses in any one of these domains, however, are likely to compromise the reforms or halt them entirely.

Different analytical traditions, however, tend to focus on one of these factors rather than all three. From an orthodox public administration standpoint, the central concern is ensuring the technical content and merit of the "policy" (or the fuller "policy package") that is to be reformed, and identifying entry points for professional tools to help realize them.[4] For political economy specialists, the fate of public sector reforms turns on the balance of power between competing interest groups (including citizens), and the effectiveness of strategies deployed by the leaders of constituent coalitions as they seek to promote or block reform (or selected aspects of it); for these analysts, the material incentives at stake, prevailing social norms and the rhetorical framing of the respective claims are key to understanding how prevailing institutional "equilibria" are created, sustained, and (potentially) shifted (World Bank 2016a).[5] Those stressing the importance of organizational capability for implementation success (Andrews et al. 2017) point to whether designated staff—specifically teams, as opposed to particular individuals—can actually do the (often) complex, high-stakes, time-consuming, discretionary work associated with learning new ways of doing things; and if they cannot, discerning what can be done to help them acquire it.

These analytical traditions have rather different histories, scholarly foundations and preferred ways of engaging with complex policy issues, thus rendering it difficult to forge an erstwhile "consensus" between them. Thus, even if one might readily concede that all three of the key factors cited above—policy reform design, leadership and political support, implementation capability—"matter" when explaining the success/failure of particular public sector reform efforts, it is rare to see them given equal attention in any given case.

For present purposes, the chapters that follow have relatively little to say about how the reforms' technical quality influenced the likelihood with which the reforms would be taken up—not because we think such matters unimportant (quite the contrary), but because the reform processes in these cases were conducted over many years and shaped by input from an array of specialist individuals and organizations, including the World Bank, thus rendering it highly likely that the technical quality of the proposed PFM/PS reforms met professional standards. However, one key aspect of technical quality that can be noted is the "Pace and Coherence of Reforms," that is, the extent to which reforms were to be undertaken incrementally or focused on a singular transformative moment (a "big bang") at the design phase.

The chapters do, however, discuss in detail the nature and extent of the political support the reforms enjoyed (though without formal recourse to the theory and nomenclature of political economy analysis), and whether the sophistication of the proposed reforms matched or overwhelmed the prevailing skill levels of those charged with implementing them. The largest space is given to the ways specific reformers sought to adapt and iterate along the way—because (a) in the transition from broad principles to specific applications, the very complexity of what was being proposed was often unable to be fully pre-specified or the associated challenges anticipated;[6] and (b) staff themselves had to learn how to do this *kind* of work, many having never before engaged in a public sector reform process of this nature, magnitude or intensity. Iterating itself, however, can require high levels of capability if the task at hand is sufficiently complex and contested; as the Papua New Guinea chapter in particular stresses, insisting that staff "iterate" is no panacea—indeed, in a situation characterized by inexperienced staff, an insufficiently robust authorizing environment, and/or unclear process guidelines, it may only intensify confusion.

Within the broad "Political Support" space, but at a more granular analytical level, one can usefully array our eight country cases across two principal sub-components. The first of these we call "Consensus Leadership": the extent to which leaders of the reform process actively sought to build a shared understanding of problems and solutions among the various stakeholders. The second sub-component is "Communication Practices": the extent to which regular, clear and constructive guidelines were provided from senior managers to everyday staff. In the "Implementation Capability" space, a different set of two sub-components can be identified. First, "Design Adaptation": the extent to which attempts were made to modify international best practices to fit local circumstances; and second, "Experimentation and Real-Time Adjustment": ways in which innovative responses were sought for emergent/mid-course implementation challenges and improvement opportunities.

Table 1.1 arrays our eight cases across these five domains (Pace and Coherence of Reform, Consensus Leadership, Communication Practices, Design Adaptation, Experimentation and Real-Time Adjustment), thereby highlighting the key similarities and differences between them.

Beyond offering ex post explanations of reform outcomes, the analytical traditions outlined above can also be deployed to offer broader practical insights on how to enhance the effectiveness of public sector reforms. Technical design, including how reforms are sequenced, can be informed by approaches such as the platform approach and technical interdependencies. Applied political economy analysis, for example, can be undertaken to document context-specific political realities, the better to focus on understanding how power is structured and sustained,[7] thereby helping those seeking to identify potentially fruitful (or especially unlikely) spaces for initiating reform.[8] Similarly, the tools of "positive deviance" have been used to locate those sub-national places where, holding policies and institutions "constant," superior performance within the current system has been obtained (see Brixi, Lust, and Woolcock 2015). Still other approaches seek to proactively engage with reform-minded teams within public agencies to build their collective capability to implement a reform agenda, partnering alongside them as they pragmatically address specific implementation problems that they themselves (as opposed to external "experts") have nominated and prioritized. In ways akin to learning a musical instrument or a second language, such reform strategies endeavor to help teams work iteratively towards higher levels of performance capability—beginning with where they are "at" and building steadily from there through practical exercises in "learning by doing." Beyond acquiring new technical skills, an important first step in this process is building strategic networks: that is, finding and partnering with those people who have important knowledge, resources or leverage to move the agenda forward.[9]

The analytical framework we have developed for this book, however, offers its own particular insights and "lessons." These are spelled out more formally in the concluding section, but a focus on five key areas outlined above—"Pace and coherence of reforms," "Consensus leadership," "Communication practices," "Design adaptation," and "Experimentation and real-time adjustment"—and the conditions under which they become salient and actionable, seems to us a fruitful analytical entry point for constructive in-country conversations about how to manage the public sector reform process.

Pace and coherence of reform entailed adequate understanding of priorities of the governments (stated and unstated) and the country context and appropriate design. For example, appropriate design adaption tailored to the country context and well sequenced platform approach to PFM reform in Cambodia has helped to bring about substantive results in revenue mobilization and FMIS implementation.

TABLE 1.1 **Specific elements addressed in the eight country cases**

MALAYSIA	INDONESIA	THAILAND	CAMBODIA	VIETNAM	MYANMAR	LAO PDR	PAPUA NEW GUINEA
1. Design quality: pace and coherence of reforms							
Mixed approach: Budget reform built around existing budgeting culture: Evolution rather than revolution Public Sector Reform: Sought "big results fast" while adopting a pragmatic approach to implementation such as short-term initiatives/ quick wins	Incremental approach: Gradual rollout of bureaucratic reform to central govt agencies—completed in 3 waves IFMIS—SPAN based on international good practice with some modifications to fit local context	A "big bang" approach to reform Tight timelines on performance-based budgeting and GFMIS but more gradual and experimental with fiscal decentralization	"Best fit" well-designed platform approach; adapt international best practice for specific reform implementation Some policies introduced after result achieved	Classic top-down reform Follow good practice—starting with laws and policy; piloting; and scale up as results materialized or abandoned as pilot failed	Flexible approach to introducing wholesale reform drawing heavily from international experience rather than best international practices	First-generation reforms focused on establishing a basic PFM framework using international experience as examples	Experimentation and "home grown" solution Extensive and open review, legislation, implementation of IFMS, changes to procurement, and human resource management innovation
2. Leadership and political support: consensus leadership and communication practices							
Strong leadership; clear national development plan and key result areas Regular communication with relevant organizations	Strong leadership support (post-Asian Financial Crisis) Multiple communication channels	Strong leadership support (post–Asian Financial Crisis)	High level support for overall PFM reform; strong ownership Communication was inadequate, revigorated with FMIS	Strong leadership support for PFM reform in the context of post Doi Moi reform	Strong leadership during transition Strong PFM sector working group for Development partners	Political commitment largely personality-driven; fluctuating levels of support Champion led communication to help facilitate reform	High-level support and trusted leadership for reform
3. Implementation capability: "Design Adaptation" and "Experimentation and Real-Time Adjustment"							
High adaptability as innovation and experimentation allowed (particularly under public service transformation) Clear timeline plan monitored by delivery unit Innovation; creativity; experimentation allowed	Best fit built in with feedback after 2 years implementation for Civil Service Reform IFMIS reform: Strong open discussion and agreement on what change is needed Lack of space for building flexibility and little time for experimentation	Combined "best practices" from other countries Classic top down reform, rapidly scaled up, and inadequate time for experimentation and adjustment in the case of PBE and GFMIS Decentralization reforms more bottom up, gradual	No specific up-front decision on what kind of change shall be made; Incremental and gradual, yet substantive; whole system focus with clear objectives under each platform Implicit authorized environment allowed experimentation to work; implementation adjusted over time	Gradualist, piloting, and expansion as results emerged Gradualism plus adequate support generated satisfactory results	Incremental approach putting in place reforms where possible and adapting and adjusting timeframe and complexity to suit realities on the ground	Classic case of adopting international best practice without full consideration of local context Space for significant experimentation limited	Adaptation of best practice through experimentation. Gradual approach to decentralization, resulting in fragmentation between and across levels of government

Consensus leadership is not the same as leadership understood as generic "political will" but more about being resolutely committed, reliable, and an effective communicator to and navigator of the prevailing political landscape, such that meaningful change is sustained over time. A strong political push for reform can help bring about speedy policy decisions, for example, but these may not necessarily be efficient or conducive to forging the desirable long-run outcome of enhanced institutional functioning. The "big bang" approach to performance based budgeting (PBB) in Thailand, supported by strong push from top leadership, resulted in the budget being presented in two formats (performance based budget and traditional line time budget) to parliamentarians. It took effective communication to clear up tensions and retain a clear vision throughout the reform. In the case of Indonesia, the FMIS SPAN project spanned across three presidents, six finance ministers, and various changes in director generals of budgets and treasuries. Effective communication practice helped reformers stay the course towards the reform objectives. Further, the presence of a robust authorizing environment for innovation, experimentation, and adjustment was critical to the success of public service transformation in Malaysia.

EAST ASIAN EXPERIENCES WITH PUBLIC FINANCIAL MANAGEMENT AND PUBLIC SECTOR REFORM: AN OVERVIEW

In the eight chapters that follow, country and sector specialists discuss the ways in which major reforms—in PFM and public sector reform (PSR)—have been undertaken. Beyond describing the rationale, the key design features of the reforms, and the sequence of steps by which they were enacted, the central focus is on *how* and by whom these were carried out, in particular on how challenges that emerged during the implementation process were navigated—mostly successfully, but not always. This Introduction constitutes chapter 1; in the paragraphs that follow, we provide a brief summary of each of the subsequent substantive chapters so that readers with particular interests in specific aspects of the reform process can direct their energies accordingly.

Chapter 2 focuses on two public sector reform experiences in **Malaysia**: (a) Outcome Based Budgeting (OBB), which is Malaysia's approach to PBB; and (b) Strengthening Public Service Delivery, a strategic reform initiative which seeks to improve the efficiency of government and to facilitate business- and public-related services to address citizens' needs. Both the OBB reform and the public service delivery transformation combined elements of international good practices with local adaptation, innovation, and experimentation. A key common feature is the presence of a robust authorizing environment for innovation and experimentation that facilitated the identification of specific solutions suited to the Malaysian context. Both cases of reform started with experimentation of specific solutions, followed by further scale-up with success of initial results, and/or a scaling down or re-assessment of the strategy on the basis of lessons learned from setbacks along the way. However, the level of achievement varies in the two initiatives owing to the complexity of each reform endeavor, and the extent to which strong leadership could be sustained throughout the reform period.

Chapter 3 focuses on two reform experiences in **Indonesia**: (a) public expenditure management through the introduction of an Integrated Financial

TABLE 1.2 **Overview of country coverage and areas of reform explored**

COUNTRY CASES	BUDGET MANAGEMENT[a]	BUREAUCRACY REFORM	FINANCIAL MANAGEMENT INFORMATION SYSTEM	REVENUE MOBILIZATION	PUBLIC INVESTMENT MANAGEMENT	DECENTRALIZATION
Malaysia	✓	✓				
Indonesia		✓	✓			
Thailand	✓		✓			✓
Cambodia	✓		✓	✓		
Vietnam			✓		✓	✓
Myanmar	✓			✓		
Lao PDR	✓					
Papua New Guinea			✓			✓

Note: Blank cells in table=not covered in respective case study.
a. Including budget formulation, program budgeting, performance-based budgeting.

Management Information System (IFMIS); and (b) Bureaucracy Reform. Indonesia represents a case where reform emerged from the context of a devastating financial crisis, economic recession and regime change (from autocracy to democracy). Consequently, there were strong political pressures promoting change, and successive leaders from different parties exemplified this in driving reform forward through personal intervention and sponsorship. The reform program was highly ambitious, and reformers were able to mobilize significant funding to support the reform including, for example, providing salary supplements to reform minded agencies. To a great extent, the challenges that arose were the result of over-ambition: the original PFM reform program had to be significantly scaled back from its original objectives. A key feature of the program was the use of dedicated change management experts, who were able to deal with some of the problems of sequencing and capacity building that resulted from the scope of the program. The Indonesian case shows how, even where the political context for reform is very supportive, care needs to be taken in designing the technical aspects of the program to ensure that reforms do not become the unmanageable victim of their own momentum.

Chapter 4 explores three reform experiences in **Thailand**: (a) PBB; (b) Government Financial Management Information System (GFMIS); and (c) Fiscal Decentralization. Two different approaches were observed across these experiences. Both PBB and GFMIS reform adopted "best practices" from other countries and started off with a piloting/experimenting approach, but this was hastily implemented in "big bang" fashion to expedite the reform process, with strong leadership commitment to push it through; in so doing, however, this approach created new challenges for implementation readiness and overall capacity to adapt to new practice. The decentralization reform was implemented through a more systematic but gradual implementation approach with relatively successful outcomes, but it also highlights the importance of understanding the capacity of stakeholders to embrace change. The Thailand case shows how political commitment facilitates speedy adoption of reform policy and creates the necessary conditions for reform to progress. However, understanding the public-sector context is also important: the combination of a limited institutional capacity among ministries and agencies, overly complicated measures, and overly short time horizons can adversely impact the reform's prospects.

Chapter 5 focuses on three areas of PFM reform efforts in **Cambodia**—(a) revenue mobilization; (b) budget execution through implementation of the FMIS; and (c) program budgeting—and Cambodia's approach to implementing these reforms, namely experimenting with best fit strategies under platform approach. This approach involved a combination of standardized "best practice" and customized "best fit" solutions and was ideally suited to the PFM reform strategy that envisioned improvements to PFM systems as a series of platforms, each of which make a significant improvement in what PFM systems can achieve while providing a stepping stone to the next. The three described interventions illustrate well this approach, one in which reformers provide space for experimentation, reflection and recalibration of strategies and processes. Empowering the tax department, for example, to introduce new incentive schemes accelerated a cultural shift to a more customer-oriented focus; introducing a comprehensive change management approach for the FMIS implementation helped build buy-in for the system and changed the way staff conduct their daily work; and recalibrating an overly ambitious budget reform strategy to better reflect the pace of other key reforms needed to achieve the intended budget reform objectives assisted the government in keeping the reforms on track over the requisite number of years.

The **Vietnam** case study, conveyed in chapter 6, explores three reform experiences: (a) Treasury and Budget Management Information System (TABMIS); (b) fiscal decentralization; and (c) Public Investment Management (PIM). All three are classic instances of top-down gradualist interventions that incorporate international standards and good practice with customization to the evolving Vietnam context. Out of the three reform experiences, TABMIS was considered successful while the other two (fiscal decentralization and PIM) were considered "mixed." Reforms to fiscal decentralization and PIM were guided by formal laws without much support to facilitate the transition to the Vietnamese context. Adoption of specific laws was useful but did not translate into automatic compliance by concerned stakeholders, who needed to be guided and trained in how to implement new practices. Gradualism coupled with an appropriate plan and adequate support was important to the success of TABMIS. The TABMIS implementation in particular illustrates how project implementation for similar systems needs to be phased in early in the project to achieve significant outcomes such as good budgetary control and cash management.

Chapter 7 illustrates **Myanmar**'s "best suited" reform approach to introducing transformational PFM reforms in a country context that, at the time, had little exposure to international "good practice" and little experience to fully understand, absorb and adapt such practices and concepts. Two specific examples highlighted in this case, budget formulation and strengthening tax administration, illustrate well how Myanmar followed the "best suited" approach to PFM reform rather than the best practice internationally. The approach was to be flexible and draw from international experience and lessons, rather than seeking to import best international practices. It sought to employ international experience to not only improve individual processes but to link them together as part of the whole PFM cycle. The thinking at the time was that reforming wholesale existing systems and process with outside solutions would not have suited Myanmar given its unique system, shaped in part by its isolation. Furthermore, the system that existed had many positive aspects that were working well. As a result, the incremental, iterative approach to reforming certain processes, building on what already existed and learning from international experience, helped and continues to sustain the momentum, space, and support for Myanmar's ongoing PFM transformation.

The Lao People's Democratic Republic PFM reforms discussed in chapter 8 can be characterized as two distinct phases or generations of PFM interventions, with the first phase largely promoting international good practice and laying the foundation for what is possible in the second. It is a cautionary tale of moving forward to implement "best practice" without full consideration of local context. The design of the first-generation reforms was focused on establishing a basic PFM framework using international experience as examples; upon reflection, however, this approach did not provide sufficient space for significant experimentation or country adaptation. It also did not consider fully the implications of introducing such practices in a government context where awareness and knowledge on PFM principles had not been sufficiently developed. The centrally controlled and planned environment, with little exposure to international practices and ideas, was often at odds with the reform agenda being undertaking. Such transformative endeavors require time, patience and a substantive adaptation period for the government staff involved to foster an environment conducive to implementation. The case also underscores the importance of high-level government leadership and coordination, and what can happen when that support evaporates for a significant period of time. Adapting and adjusting reforms, including their sequencing and implementation time frame, to the country context—as is taking place now in the second generation of PFM reforms—could have put the country on a steadier, more sustainable path.

Chapter 9 considers two significant public sector reforms carried out in **Papua New Guinea** between 2014 and 2017, and their potential combined significance in strengthening "Public Financial Management for Service Delivery": (a) PFM/Budget Execution (including an Integrated Financial Information System (IFMS), in reforms driven principally by the Department of Finance (DoF); and (b) Public Sector and Institutional (PSI) reform, including decentralization and local service delivery, in reforms driven by the Department of Provincial and Local Government Affairs (DPLGA). Both are presented in their early, current forms, as examples respectfully of translation of "best practice" (the PFM reforms) and "best fit" (the PSI decentralization and service delivery) approaches. But it also proposes that for either reform to succeed, both will need to find ways to bring Papua New Guinea capabilities and international experience together. This, all the more so because of the sheer scale of challenges the country faces as a highly diverse, heavily resource-dependent economy and society, which creates distinctive challenges, choices and opportunities for these important PFM and PSI reforms.

IMPLICATIONS FOR REFORMERS AND DEVELOPMENT PRACTITIONERS

Some key lessons emerge from the eight East Asian country case studies presented here. Some of these "lessons" are familiar (e.g., the importance of strong and sustained leadership), though they bear repeating (since they seem to be so frequently overlooked), while others, we hope—for example, explicitly creating and protecting the space and time needed for international practices to be adapted to the idiosyncrasies of local contexts—are more original, insightful and broadly applicable, especially to "emerging economies" inexorably facing rising pressures to embark upon their own PFM/PSR journey.

The analyses of these case studies have been organized around three key areas: design quality; leadership and political support; and implementation capability. In drawing out the implications of the case studies for these three areas of consideration, an overarching theme emerges: that in public sector reform, the journey is as important as the destination. Issues of authorized environment to embark on reform, timing, sequencing, monitoring, communication, flexibility in making necessary adjustment, and management of reform project/programs (including procurement where relevant) are vital areas that need to be as carefully designed and managed as the final outline of the reform. Even where the goal of the reform is to achieve greater standardization with international best practice—as in the case of many of the PFM reforms described here—there is huge scope for tailoring the journey to the particular exigencies of each case. This can ensure not only that the reform is delivered as effectively as possible, but also builds morale, positive working practices and reform appetite within public service agencies.

A further issue that emerges from the analysis here is the interaction between the different aspects that we consider. The three areas of design quality, political leadership and implementation capability are not independent of one another. Good quality design can attract and strengthen political support, whereas poor design can prompt loss of consequence. Political commitment can lead to higher capability implementing staff being allocated or attracted to a reform area. Conversely, a capable team can boost political commitment by showing results and can make up for any initial shortfalls in design. Our case studies draw out the dynamic relationship between the three areas as this developed over the reform journey.

Finally, the cases suggest strongly that reform is as much an art as a science. There are frequently pros and cons for any approach. For example, increasing the pace of reform may promise quick wins that strengthen political commitment but strain implementing capacity. Slowing it down may allow more time to bring everyone on board, but lose the advantage of momentum. Allowing local innovation may be essential in ensuring a workable outcome, but may also allow loopholes that can be exploited by recalcitrant staff or contractors that an international "best practice" package would have closed down. These are genuine trade-offs, and resolving them is genuinely a case-by-case judgement call. The case studies presented show how those judgement calls have played out, for better or for worse, and here we draw these together for comparative purposes.

Design quality

Design quality involves the ability to judge an appropriate program and pace of reform at an early stage. Well-designed reform that is appropriately sequenced to country context is crucial to the implementation process. High capability teams will only be able to do so much with a badly designed reform. Well-designed and appropriately sequenced reform help countries undertaking reform to progress at their own pace.

Our case studies cluster around two different approaches to the pace and coherence of reforms. Indonesia and Thailand both embarked on large scale reforms in the aftermath of financial crisis. In the case of Indonesia, regime change and democratization prompted far-reaching and ambitious approaches to reform, led in particular by the Ministry of Finance which had been at the center of coping with the aftermath of the crisis. In Thailand, the crisis occurred alongside the implementation of a new constitution and the emergence of a new party system. The result of these changes was the emergence of a new regime in which the executive was more powerful than in the past, and was able to push through a raft of rapid changes in the context of political and economic turmoil.

In Thailand, the "big bang" approach, and in Indonesia, the sheer scale of the FMIS project, led to difficulties, confusion and delays. Political determination to implement wholesale changes in the way that budgeting and PFM were done, without adequate preparation of civil service capacities, caused confusion and the continuation of parallel systems. This was exemplified in the fact that in the end the budget was presented to parliamentarians in two forms—a traditional line item budget *and* the performance based budget introduced in the reform—rather than one supplanting the other. The more gradualist approach taken with respect to decentralization proved much more manageable. In Indonesia, ambitions to fundamentally restructure the whole of government following the fall of the Suharto regime proved to be unachievable, and had to be scaled back in order to succeed.

Political environment

With respect to the political environment, emerging factors of significance included the extent to which a political consensus on reform existed at leadership level and the extent to which leaders worked to build and expand this consensus in lower levels of government and with stakeholders outside the leadership group. A further pertinent feature of the political environment was the nature and effectiveness of communication practices between reform leaders and other key actors.

Part of the interest of the case studies offered here is their location in the dynamic South East Asian region, which over the past 40 years has seen rapid economic growth and social transformation but also financial crisis and regime change. Our set of case studies includes two upper middle-income countries (Malaysia and Thailand) and six lower middle-income countries (Indonesia, Cambodia, Vietnam, Lao PDR, Myanmar and Papua New Guinea). Of these, Vietnam, Cambodia, Lao PDR, Myanmar and Papua New Guinea achieved middle income status in the last 10 years, while Malaysia, Thailand and Indonesia all developed rapidly during the 1980s before suffering a severe financial crisis in 1997–98. Three of the countries in our set—Thailand, Indonesia and Myanmar—have undergone recent periods of political instability, conflict and/or regime change, while Vietnam, Cambodia and Lao PDR have fundamentally reoriented their political and economic systems in the past 25 years (i.e., since the end of the Cold War). The rapidity of economic, social and political change in these countries sets the scene for any discussion of the political environment for public sector reform.

A common feature of the countries in the set is a pronounced shift in the 1990s and 2000s away from state-directed economic policies and towards an open and market-based approach to economic development. Precipitated for some countries by the end of the Cold War and for others by the Asian Financial Crisis, this shift has entailed rapid integration into the regional and global economy. At the same time, improving living standards and rising expectations have prompted the need for states to respond to citizens' demands for better services and more effective administration, putting pressure on bureaucracies and budgets. This context explains a common theme in all of our case studies: an appetite for reform at the highest political levels.

However, the case studies also show that a broad-brush "political will" for reform is not the same as committed, reliable and effective political leadership. In some cases, the extent of pressure from public opinion or from political leaders threatened to overwhelm the capacity of the bureaucracy to deliver reform. In both Thailand and Indonesia, in the aftermath of the Asian Financial Crisis, strong political pressures to change how things were done led to the design of enormously aspirational reform programs which in some ways proved overly-ambitious.

A further emerging lesson from these cases is that changeability in political support over time, or a relatively narrow leadership consensus, is an important issue affecting reform prospects. In Indonesia, despite numerous changes of personnel at the top of the Ministry of Finance, a consistently pro-reform message was propagated, underpinned by the politics of regime change, a strong legal footing for reforms, and the politics of Indonesia's relationship with key donor agencies after the economic crash. Indonesia's FMIS project spanned across three Presidents, six Finance Ministers, and some changes with the Director Generals of Treasury and Budget officials.

Similarly, in Myanmar, in the context of a political transition and ongoing ceasefire negotiations, political support for reform appeared fairly constant and in line with the broader objectives of the transition, and was combined with close attention to the appropriacy of international best practice solutions to the Myanmar context.

Other case studies differed. In Vietnam, Lao PDR and Cambodia, public sector reform is conducted in a public sector culture which is very different from that envisaged by standard liberal prescriptions. This means that even quite limited reforms can require radical changes in mindset for public servants. In Lao PDR, changing priorities within government and the need for reformers to negotiate with other stakeholders led to a more variable pace of change with a period of almost no activity. Similarly, both the Cambodian and Vietnamese governments, although committed at the highest level to improved management of public finances, balanced this priority with a strong concern for stability in the context of strongly hierarchical bureaucracies. In both cases this produced an incremental "evolution, not revolution" or gradualist approach, that at times more closely resembled a "stop-start" pace. This approach reflected the need for political leaders to conduct complex negotiations with powerful constituencies internal to the state and party structures, which had the power to significantly affect the reform. In Cambodia, the introduction of a change management team tasked specifically with assisting and advancing these negotiations was ultimately successful in advancing progress in FMIS, a key element of the country's PFM reform.

Where reform constituencies are relatively small, expanding the reform consensus requires effective means of communication. These case studies suggest that the ability to communicate strategically and effectively was central to successful reforms. However, different forms of communication were needed in different cases. In the Malaysian and Indonesian civil services, mass communication strategies designed to bring civil servants generally on board with reform programs, through demonstrating the benefits to them of enthusiastic embrace of change, were highly effective. In other contexts, the key to reform breakthrough was achieved by targeted strategies to bring particular actors together, often across institutional boundaries. In Cambodia, specific strategies to improve the functioning of a cross-agency steering group was necessary to promote reform. In Papua New Guinea, high levels of local autonomy between fragmented districts and parallel systems for disbursing money mean that a dearth of national-level information is a key constraint on government functioning. Communication strategies to try to link and consolidate a complex range of distinct and idiosyncratic information flows are central to any public sector reform.

Institutional environment

The institutional environment is significant particularly in terms of the capacity of public service officials and other relevant stakeholders to carry out the reforms. Key issues affecting this factor identified in these case studies include design adaptation at the outset and the ability to experiment and adjust along the way. This involves individual and institutional capacity; sophistication and experience in innovation; and the authorizing environment for internal discussion of reforms. Our case studies differ sharply in these regards. Malaysia represents a case where a strong and effective public sector has been central to the country's economic success for decades; Vietnam, Lao PDR, Cambodia, Indonesia, Myanmar and to an extent Thailand are all cases where the basis of public sector functioning has transformed radically within a generation; while Papua New Guinea represents a case where the central bureaucracy is limited in the face of pressure from other agencies of government.

In our case studies, we found a diversity of situations with regard to the design adaptation of reform to local conditions. In some cases, this issue was a high priority for reformers. In both Malaysia and Myanmar, governments set a high premium on tailoring international practice to the particular needs of the local context, using international study tours as a means to learn about international experience before embarking on program design. As described in the case studies, these approaches fit with the political approach of determined but measured reform in a context where leaders paid attention to widening the consensus for reform through carefully designed communication strategies, and allowed latitude for experimentation and innovation.

In other contexts, particularly those where reform momentum emerged out of crisis, such as in Thailand and Indonesia, international solutions were initially adopted, and adaptations were found to be necessary at a later stage. In both of these cases, the latitude offered to civil servants for innovation and adaptation varied over time and between reform programs. In Thailand, the strong focus of the Prime Minister on e-government entailed little latitude for experimentation, while a less intense approach to decentralization allowed more of this. In Indonesia, the construction of an extremely powerful anti-corruption agency in the wake of regime change prompted a mood of excessive caution within the civil service. This prompted some initial reluctance to embrace reform, through fear of making mistakes that might be construed as corrupt practices, but this fear was overcome through clear communications from the central leadership that gradually rebuilt confidence among civil servants.

With respect to highly technical information systems, such as IFMIS-SPAN in Indonesia, TABMIS in Vietnam and FMIS in Cambodia, an important attraction of the reform is the enhanced functionality of the system. The introduction of advanced software makes new business practices possible and old ones redundant and therefore the software itself can be used as a tool to promote more imaginative thinking about the prospects for change. In these contexts, the introduction of an alien international system took time and was highly disconcerting for a range of stakeholders who feared the consequences for their jobs. However, once the software was in place, the information that it began to generate offered opportunities for experimentation that appear to have been quickly grasped by civil servants involved. With that in mind, as pointed out in the discussion of Papua New Guinea, excessive customization of the system may reflect efforts to resist rather than promote change. Strong leadership and clear communication strategies may provide a means to ease initial fears until civil servants can get their hands on the system and start to realize its potential in the local context.

Overall, the case studies suggest that the three areas outlined above are linked together in specific ways in each different reform context. Particular configurations of leadership produce particular approaches to change, and these relate in different ways to capacities, attitudes to risk and pace of change in different reform programs. This varies not only across countries, but also between programs within countries in our case studies. These eight cases suggest that neither political will, nor technical design, nor capacity can be seen in isolation, but as multiple strands of a single reform effort, interacting in dynamic ways across the reform journey. Understanding the complexity of these interactions implies that external funders, partners and supporters of reform need to be just as ready to take an iterative approach to their assistance strategies as reformers do in implementing their reform programs.

CONCLUSION

It is inherently difficult to carry out major reforms in the public sector generally, and to PFM systems in particular. The enormity and importance of these challenges, however, despite their seemingly "modest" record of success, should not be grounds for resignation. Indeed, whether one is a high middle-income country (Malaysia) or a decidedly poor and fragmented one (Papua New Guinea), *not* embarking on reform is no longer an option (if ever it was); the question, rather, is *how* reform will happen—that is, how optimal design characteristics, robust political support for them, and enhanced organizational capability to implement and adapt will be forged over time. As the cases presented here amply demonstrate, implementing public sector reforms is a highly complex (and inherently contentious) task; but precisely because of their great difficulty, decision-makers undertaking public sector reforms should draw renewed energy and inspiration from identifying and learning from those countries, sectors and sub-national spaces where substantive (not merely cosmetic) change has, and has not, been achieved.

NOTES

1. On the (often) perfunctory and performative nature of "capacity building" activities, especially when done at scale, see Swidler and Watkins (2017, chapter 9).
2. The most prominent of these 'delivery units' was pioneered in the United Kingdom during the Blair Administration (see Barber 2015) but Malaysia's PEMANDU unit—explicitly

modeled on the UK's—has also been influential within and beyond its borders (it is actively engaged in Uganda, South Africa and India, among others). Strictly speaking, delivery units are also concerned with improving the implementation of *current* policies (although doing so often entails enacting concomitant 'reforms'). For a recent assessment of the performance and generalizability of PEMANDU-style delivery units, see Kunicova (2017).

3. See Fritz (2017) for an excellent overview of broader approaches to public sector reform undertaken by those seeking to 'do development differently'.

4. Such tools include Public Expenditure Reviews (PER), Public Expenditure Tracking Surveys (PETS), Public Expenditure and Financial Accountability (PEFA), Performance Budgeting, etc.

5. Cognizant of the importance of 'getting incentives right', some approaches to public sector reform in this tradition (e.g., performance-based budgeting) advocate reforms in which funding levels are directly linked to anticipated programmatic outcomes (see Moynihan and Beazley 2017). Whether this is a reasonable strategy to routinely deploy in low-income countries, where implementation capability and program efficacy are inherently likely to be highly variable, is much less clear. Several of the cases in this volume do showcase attempts to use performance-based budgeting in such countries, however, making the 'lessons' from them all the more salient.

6. See Kaufmann (2016) for a rich discussion of engaging with processes that have inherently uncertain outcomes.

7. For example, 'Thinking and Working Politically' (Booth and Unsworth 2014); some political economists (e.g., World Bank 2016a) have also sought to account for variations in reform success using the tools of game theory, behavioral norms and electoral incentives. See also Fritz, Verhoeven and Avenia (2017).

8. See Hughes et al. (2017) for further examples of successful change management in 'challenging environments'.

9. See Andrews, Pritchett, and Woolcock (2017) on public sector efforts to promote direct foreign investment in Sri Lanka, where the importance of building such networks was a vital part of (what became) a successful effort to attract sizeable new levels of foreign investment (into solar energy).

BIBLIOGRAPHY

Andrews, Matt. 2013. *The Limits of Institutional Reform*. New York. Cambridge University Press.

Andrews, Matt, Duminda Ariyasinghe, Amara S. Beling, Peter Harrington, Tim McNaught, Fathima Nafla Niyas, Anisha Poobalan, Mahinda Ramanayake, H. Senavirathne, Upatissa Sirigampala, Renuka M. Weerakone, and W. A. F. Jayasiri Wijesooriya. 2017. "Learning to Improve the Investment Climate for Economic Diversification: PDIA in Action in Sri Lanka." Center for International Development Faculty Working Paper 337, Cambridge. Harvard University.

Andrews, Matt, Lant Pritchett, and Michael Woolcock. 2017. *Building State Capability: Evidence, Analysis, Action*. New York: Oxford University Press.

Barber, Michael. 2015. *How to Run a Government*. London: Allen Lane.

Booth, David, and Sue Unsworth. 2014. *Politically Smart, Locally Led Development*. London: ODI.

Bridges, Kate, and Michael Woolcock. 2017. "How (Not) to Fix Things That Matter: Assessing and Responding to Malawi's History of Institutional Reform." Policy Research Working Paper 8289, World Bank, Washington, DC.

Brixi, Hana, Ellen Lust, and Michael Woolcock. 2015. *Trust, Voice and Incentives: Learning from Local Success Stories in Service Delivery in the Middle East and North Africa*. Washington, DC: World Bank.

Fritz, Verena. 2017. "Doing Development Differently: Understanding the Landscape and Implications of New Approaches to Governance and Public Sector Reforms." In *Transformation, Politics and Implementation: Smart Implementation in Governance Programs*, edited by Renate Kirsch, Elke Siehl, and Albrecht Stockmayer, 75–97. Frankfurt: GIZ.

Fritz, Verena, Marijn Verhoeven, and Ambra Avenia. 2017. *Political Economy of Public Financial Management Reforms: Experiences and Implications for Dialogue and Operational Engagement*. Washington, DC: World Bank.

Grindle, Merilee, and John Thomas. 1991. *Public Choice and Policy Change: The Political Economy of Reform in Developing Countries*. Baltimore, MD: Johns Hopkins University Press.

Hughes, Caroline, Sokbunthoeun So, Erwin Ariadharma, and Leah April. 2017. "Change Management that Works: Making Impacts in Challenging Environments." Policy Research Working Paper 8265, World Bank, Washington, DC.

Kaufmann, Stuart. 2016. *Humanity in a Creative Universe*. New York: Oxford University Press.

Kunicova, Jana. 2017. "Driving Performance from the Center: Malaysia's Experience with PEMANDU." World Bank Knowledge and Research Hub, Kuala Lumpur.

Lawson, Andrew. 2012. *Evaluation of Public Financial Management Reform in Burkina Faso, Ghana and Malawi 2001–2010* (Final Synthesis Report). Stockholm: SIDA.

Moynihan, Donald, and Ivor Beazley. 2017. *Toward Next-Generation Performance Budgeting: Lessons from the Experiences of Seven Reforming Countries*. Washington, DC: World Bank.

Swidler, Ann, and Susan Cotts Watkins. 2017. *A Fraught Embrace: The Romance and Reality of AIDS Altruism in Africa*. Princeton, NJ: Princeton University Press.

World Bank. 2012. *Better Results from Public Sector Institutions*. Washington, DC: World Bank.

———. 2016a. *Making Politics Work for Development: Harnessing Transparency and Citizen Engagement*. Washington, DC: World Bank.

———. 2016b. *World Development Report: Digital Dividends*. Washington, DC: World Bank.

———. 2017. *World Development Report: Governance and the Law*. Washington, DC: World Bank.

———. 2018. *World Development Report: Learning to Realize Education's Promise*. Washington, DC: World Bank.

2 Malaysia
ADAPTATION, INNOVATION, AND EXPERIMENTATION TO ADDRESS EMERGING PUBLIC SECTOR CHALLENGES

BERNARD MYERS, JEEVAKUMAR GOVINDASAMY, and MENG FOON LEE

INTRODUCTION

Malaysia is an upper middle-income country which has embarked on reform initiatives centered on boosting economic growth in a more inclusive and sustainable manner, as well as supported by efforts to make the government bureaucracy for citizen-centric and performance based. The country has a long history of national development planning, with the 5-year Malaysia Plans as the primary medium-term planning mechanism while the national budget as the primary annual planning mechanism.

Malaysia's economic growth over the last 50 years has enabled it to virtually eliminate extreme poverty, and focus on addressing relative poverty (i.e., improving the well-being of the bottom 40 percent). Moreover, Malaysia aspires to avoid "the middle-income trap" and become a high-income advanced country by 2020.[1] As the country has sought to reach this goal, it has faced various challenges. Malaysia is a relatively open economy, and is easily affected by developments in global environment, including movements and shocks in the economy and financial markets, fluctuation in commodity and energy prices, changes in the pattern/flows of foreign direct investments. The rise of globalization, the advancement of science and technology, increasing expectations and demands of citizens, and a changing workforce have added further complexity to the challenges that Malaysia faces.

A new set of national initiatives were introduced in 2009 to push for reforms in the economic and government front. Among them are the National Transformation Program (NTP), which was launched in 2010 with the goal of addressing Malaysia's key development challenges. The NTP has two main components: the Economic Transformation Program (ETP) and the Government

This chapter is composed of two main sections. The section on Performance Based Budgeting was written by Bernard Myers and Jeevakumar Govindasamy and was extracted from a recently published World Bank report "Budgeting for Performance in Malaysia" produced by the Malaysia Knowledge and Research Hub in Kuala Lumpur. The section on public service delivery and public service transformation was written by Meng Foon Lee.

Transformation Program (GTP). The implementation of the ETP and the GTP were coordinated and monitored by the Performance Management and Delivery Unit (PEMANDU) which was established in September 2009 as a unit within the Prime Minister's Department (Economic Planning Unit 2017; PEMANDU 2010, 2011).

The ETP's main aim was to "elevate the country to developed-nation status by 2020, targeting GNI per capita of US$15,000."[2] The GTP was introduced as a reform effort to radically transform the way the government worked in order to improve and strengthen the public service delivery system, and to put the public's needs first. The GTP served as a mechanism to promote a more performance-oriented, accountable and responsive system of government. It comprised a set of initiatives aimed at achieving rapid and meaningful improvements in service delivery in six National Key Result Areas (NKRAs): reducing crime, fighting corruption, improving student outcomes, raising living standards of low income households, improving rural basic infrastructure, and improving urban public transport (PEMANDU 2010).

This chapter focuses on two reform experiences in Malaysia namely Performance Based Budgeting (PBB) and strengthening public service delivery, which are two reform initiatives the Malaysian government has paid closed attention. Outcome based budgeting (OBB) is the Malaysian government's approach to PBB and is a critical part of this strategic reform initiative. Public service reform initiative is aimed at improving the efficiency and effectiveness of the public sector as well as its service delivery, in tandem of the country's economic and social aspirations.

PERFORMANCE BASED BUDGETING

Issues

Malaysia was an early leader in Asia in applying performance management to annual budgeting, starting in 1969 with the introduction of its Program Performance Budgeting System (PPBS). This system drew inspiration from the United States' approach to program budgeting first pioneered in the 1960s. It recognized the shortcomings of a traditional line-item, input-control approach to budgeting and instead introduced a program-structure approach, with dedicated indicators related to specific managerial responsibilities. Activities were measured and used as an indicator of performance. PPBS brought with it more explicit prioritization of budget items, modernization of the accounting system from strict cash to a modified cash basis, and harmonization of budget codes and classification across agencies. This provided a foundation for future budget reforms.

Responding to the limitations of PPBS and global trends around "New Public Management," Malaysia introduced in 1989 a new system called the Modified Budgeting System (MBS). During the late 1980s, government was growing in size, but retained highly centralized controls, which inhibited responsiveness, accountability, and flexibility. As such, a primary objective of MBS was to devolve managerial and spending powers away from the center and towards program and project managers, improving flexibility and responsiveness. With this devolution came the need to hold managers accountable for results and to define measurable targets. These results chains were articulated through program agreements between line agencies and the MOF, which specified inputs and outputs at the ministry level and the activity level. The MBS also featured a set of expenditure targets, with the objective of improving selectivity of spending, while also imposing a degree of fiscal discipline. In practice, MBS perpetuated a focus on input utilization; program managers were more likely to draw attention if they failed to meet financial targets for budget execution.

Reform intervention

The above issue was addressed with the Prime Minister's decision to adopt a more outcome-based approach to national development planning. This decision became the driver for MOF to begin looking at ways to update the annual budget process. The 10th Malaysia Plan (2011–15) was designed to be outcome compliant, establishing a development vision for Malaysia linked to the achievement of outcomes across various national key results areas. To strengthen the linkages between policies, planning and budgeting, the MOF determined that the annual budget should therefore be outcomes focused as well. Six key transformation levers were identified to guide the development of the new budgeting system: (a) focus on outcomes, (b) vertical alignment of national priorities and ministry programs and activities, (c) managing cross-cutting initiatives, (d) coordination of development and operating expenditure, (e) accountability for results and authority over resources, and (f) a systematic monitoring and evaluation (M&E) mechanism.

OBB was designed to address some specific shortcomings recognized by MOF in the implementation of MBS. The primary shortcoming was a perceived focus on input utilization and outputs at the expense of performance and results. Additionally, MBS did not adequately support clear linkages between government policies, national planning, and the annual budget process. Ministries could claim that budget activities supported ministerial strategies, but there was no means to link these to the broader national strategies outlined in the 5-year plan. Therefore, MBS did not function effectively as a strategic planning tool, as program agreements were not based on top-down strategic planning. Without good information on results from line agencies, Budget Review Officers (BROs) continued to focus on line items rather than accountability for results. Under-execution of one's budget allocation could be more easily assessed than performance outcomes.

OBB has created an integrated results framework at every level of the budget process. Under OBB, the program structures are reviewed and refined through an integrated program-activity structure, which provides hierarchical linkages of ministry programs and activities, and systematically aligns them to national priorities. It also establishes a logical structure on how program information is strategically collected and utilized for planning, budgeting, and M&E. Each program under OBB is an intervention aimed at addressing a specific problem, compared to programs under MBS, where many were institutional in nature. Activities are a common unit for under MBS and OBB, but they can only be mapped to one specific program, even where they may contribute to achieving multiple program outcomes. This helps to create a one-to-one match between the administrative and program-activity structures to preserve accountability and line of sight. Outcome objectives, along with relevant KPIs, are defined at all three levels of ministry, program, and activity. As the budget book is still approved by program, the activity level detail is used for internal management purposes within the ministry.

OBB was also designed to better integrate development and operating expenditure processes under a unified results framework. Like many countries in Southeast Asia, Malaysia has an institutional separation between the budgeting functions for capital or development expenditure (DE), which fall within the Economic Planning Unit (EPU) under the Prime Minister's Department, and the budgeting functions for operational expenditure (OE), which fall within the National Budget Office (NBO) at the Ministry of Finance (MoF). This institutional separation can sometimes create issues such as poor alignment between policy objectives under different types of spending or inadequate resourcing of operational costs for new development projects. Thus, OBB was designed to help manage this issue by requiring spending agencies to coordinate and prepare both operational and development budget submissions under a single, unified results framework. Doing so was intended to eliminate redundancy in funding and promote better value for money through improved coordination of DE and OE.

Conceptually, the OBB system is grounded in a results framework involving top-down strategic planning and alignment, followed by bottom-up budgeting and reporting. The national level strategies and priorities are guided by the 5-year national development plan. OBB in turn links the different levels—national strategies, ministerial outcomes, program outcomes, and activity outcomes—through an integrated results framework. While the budget is formulated at the activity level based on agreed outputs, each activity must be mapped to a specific program. National strategies are comprised of national key results areas or key focus areas, as well as national key performance indicators (KPIs). KPIs are in turn defined at each of the subsequent levels of outcomes—ministry, program, and activity. Each program is comprised of individual activities, each with its own results framework, specific outcome areas, KPIs, and outputs. The budget is built at the activity level, aggregated up to the program level, and finally consolidated at the ministry level, based on the performance agreement for the budget year.

Performance agreements capture the target outcomes and establish the institutional accountability for their achievement at all levels. Performance agreements at the activity level, namely the Activity Performance Management Framework (APMF), are accompanied by the Activity Budget Sheet (ABS). At the next level up, the Program Performance Management Framework (PPMF) displays the agreed outcomes and KPIs for each program, and it is accompanied by the Program Budget Sheet (PBS). The Ministry Executive Summary (MES) summarizes the Ministry's overall Results Framework and total inputs required for the implementation of all its programs and activities. Figures 2.1 and 2.2 detail the conceptual framework for OBB. In summary, each results framework, starting with the activity level, forms the basis of a performance agreement that is rolled up into the ministry-wide executive summary agreement.[3]

Ministries justify their new programs, following transmission of the budget circular in January, using an online analytical framework called the Program Logic and Linkages model (ProLL).[4] Senior managers use ProLL to identify and outline program objectives. They are required to begin with a demand analysis, which helps to identify clients/stakeholders, what their problems and needs are, and which policies will best address these problems and needs. In principle, it is from this demand analysis that a program is defined with preliminary outcomes to be achieved. Using ProLL, strategies for achievement of outcomes are also identified with short-, medium- and long-term actions. This strategic planning exercise helps lay out a clear results chain from inputs all the way to outputs,

FIGURE 2.1
Results framework and performance agreement under OBB

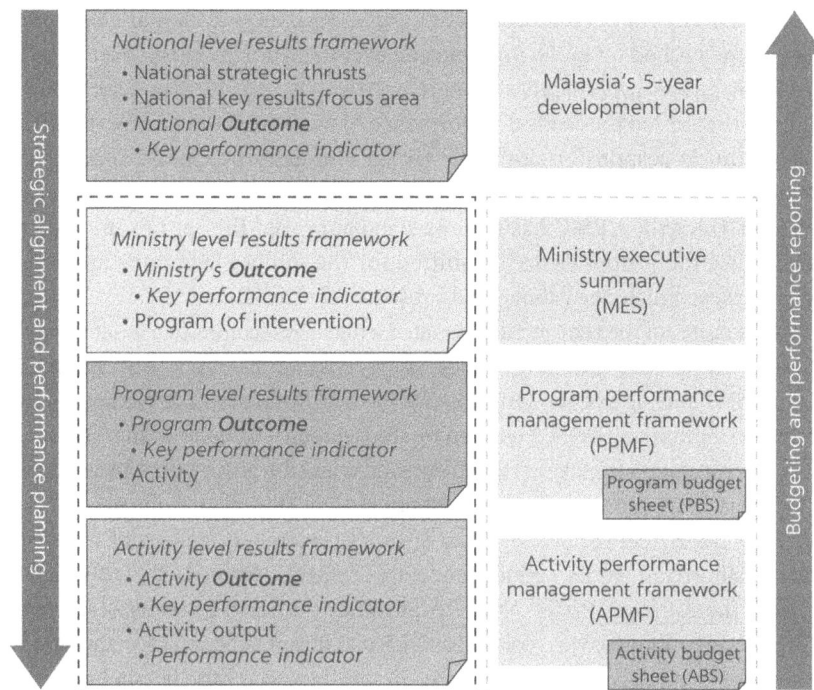

Source: Adapted from National Budget Office.
Note: OBB = Outcome based budgeting.

FIGURE 2.2
Budget building under OBB

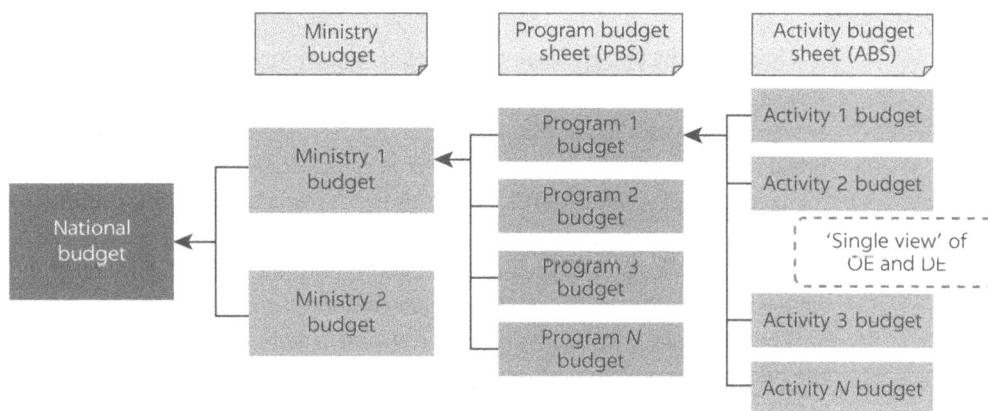

Source: Adapted from National Budget Office.
Note: OBB = Outcome based budgeting; OE = operational expenditure; DE = development expenditure.

outcomes and impact. Of course, in the transition from MBS to OBB there was already a substantial legacy of programs that had a set of pre-defined beneficiaries and a set of existing performance indicators. What MOF gained from OBB was a fresh opportunity to revisit that existing structure of budget programs, validate their consistency with the higher-level strategic priorities, strengthen the results chain between outputs and outcomes, and enhance the quality and relevance of KPIs. OBB also created the opportunity to strengthen the focus of organizational accountability more directly on the program manager.

After results frameworks have been developed at the ministry, program, and activity levels, spending units begin to develop budget submissions from the bottom up. The inputs required to undertake various activities are budgeted for, and then rolled up to the program and eventually the ministry level. Ideally by March, budget proposals are submitted to the NBO, which then disseminates budget proposals to the Central Performance Management Committee (CPMC). The CPMC is responsible for reviewing all ministry proposals and results frameworks, and for performing a challenge function against the ministerial requests. Once the CPMC has reviewed and approved the various ministries' allocations, the proposals are submitted for the Budget Director's approval, before proceeding to the cabinet and subsequently Parliament.

At the outset of the reform, MOF created a high-level committee to set the policy, steer the process, and study possible approaches for the new system. In preparation for the design of the OBB, the MOF in 2010 created the National OBB Steering Committee (NOSC) chaired by the Secretary General to the Treasury, with representation from key stakeholders including the NBO, EPU, MAMPU, the Public Service Department (PSD), the National Audit Department, the Accountant General's Department of Malaysia, the Attorney General's Chambers of Malaysia, and the Ministry of Works. An independent unit was also formed—the OBB team—to act as the secretariat to the NOSC and to study the budget systems of interest. A high-level committee was required as OBB was meant to address two important challenges faced during the MBS phase. Firstly, there was little buy-in by implementing entities on any reform initiative driven by the NBO. It was seen as a budget preparation requirement mandated by the NBO for its own purpose.

The OBB team drew on both local and international experience to expand on the foundation provided by MBS. For example, the OBB team made benchmarking visits to Canada, New Zealand, and Singapore. They also recruited a team of international consultants to assist in developing the OBB conceptual framework and the design process. The initial framework, which drew heavily on the MBS, was developed by a local research institution called the Center for Development & Research in Evaluation, which later upscaled to meet the requirements of the Integrated Results-Based Management (IRBM) system. The OBB team had a broad range of activities to coordinate: conceptual design, outreach and change management programs, developing training materials, providing training to BROs and line ministries, setting the OBB implementation strategies, handholding the pilot agencies on implementation coordination, and developing the MyResults system to support OBB implementation.

The OBB team had the institutional freedom to work full-time on developing the reform. Recognizing the challenges of undertaking reform while also managing core daily tasks, and in line with the Treasury Transformation Program (TTP), the OBB team was moved to the NBO in 2014 to form a new wing called the Performance Management and Evaluation Sector. This team is responsible for supporting, coordinating, and managing the implementation of OBB. This sector is also tasked with developing a systematic M&E framework to complete the full strategic cycle of OBB, as well as with maintaining continuous engagement and capacity building at the NBO and line ministries.

The OBB team organized their work around three dimensions of the budget transformation system. These dimensions were: (a) the budget model and framework—program-activity structure, vertical and horizontal linkages; (b) the people and stakeholders involved in the budget process—change management, capacity building, enhanced accountability through greater empowerment to the

CEOs; and (c) the management information system to complement M&E, as well as the Decision Support System through which OBB is applied and managed. Specific requirements and strategies were identified for each of these dimensions. For example, model development was guided by strong vertical alignment between policies, programs, and activities, with horizontal linkages between related programs, as well as by an integrated approach to budget preparation and review. An OBB policy framework and guidelines were required to ensure the model's consistent application across the public sector. People and stakeholder strategies were informed by the principles of accountability at all levels, a comprehensive training and capacity building program, special sessions with senior management, and a carefully constructed communications strategy. The information technology system strategies focused on development of a robust online system for budget submission and review, with modules for performance monitoring and reporting.

Changes to the budget system were driven administratively, rather than through changes to the legal framework governing the budget process. Malaysia's organic budget law (Financial Procedures Act of 1957) serves as the foundation for its management of public finances. However, the move to the OBB system was accomplished through administrative channels, rather than through changes to the underlying legislation. The OBB roll-out was accompanied by an MOF circular to spending agencies. This circular described the OBB concepts, detailed the process and regulatory changes necessary for implementation of OBB, and outlined the new responsibilities of spending agencies with regards to preparation and submission of results frameworks, as well as performance monitoring and reporting. This allowed for a smoother and more efficient transition where civil servants could drive change within an existing legal framework.

Result/Implementation progress

The first 2 years of the transition period were devoted to design of the reform, communication with key stakeholders, and development of a pilot program. From 2010 to 2012, the OBB team was engaged in developing the conceptual framework for the OBB, creating the necessary training materials to support the reform, and visiting the ministries and departments to give talks and run forums whereby line agency input could be incorporated into the design. Five ministries were chosen to participate in a pilot program for OBB, with another joining voluntarily. Ministries were chosen for specific reasons, with a view to testing OBB across a range of different stakeholders. For example, MOF was chosen as a core central ministry; the Public Works Department was chosen to test OBB in a setting with significant DE; the Ministry of Transportation and Ministry of Human Resources were chosen as ministries with very specific mandates; and the Ministry of Education was chosen as a large, complex ministry; and the Ministry of International Trade and Industry volunteered based on its recognition of the importance of OBB as a strategic planning tool.

Initial success with the pilot ministries led to an attempted full roll-out in 2013, which was subsequently scaled back as being too ambitious. After successfully testing the OBB with the original 5 + 1 pilot ministries, the OBB team attempted to roll the system out across the whole of government. However, it quickly became apparent that there was a low level of understanding about the details of performance budgeting. The results frameworks that were submitted were of poor quality, with significant confusion between inputs, outputs, and preliminary, intermediate, and tertiary level outcomes. Concluding that more individual training and capacity building was necessary, the OBB team rolled back the scope to focus on three "champion ministries" with whom they could have detailed discussions on how to develop appropriate results chains. The demonstration effect of OBB being effectively used as a strategic planning tool in the three champion ministries led to additional ministries volunteering in subsequent years.

The OBB team has since focused on providing specific training and capacity building on a ministry-by-ministry basis to ensure good understanding of the principles of performance management and support the development of quality results frameworks. At the central agency level, resource leaders were identified, comprising all the BROs at the NBO, desk officers at the EPU who are overseeing development budgets for line ministries, and desk officers at the PSD who are responsible for public sector organizational development. Resource leaders serve as reference points to give advice on OBB matters to line ministries (since the OBB team has a limited number of staff and is mandated to focus on more complex issues and advancing the OBB agenda). Continuous Resource Leaders Training (RLT) is being conducted by the OBB team to provide the resource leaders with the necessary conceptual and technical knowledge on OBB.

A key feature of Malaysia's change management strategy was the extensive program of training and awareness-raising across all levels of stakeholders. At the national level, the OBB team employed a multi-faceted approach with a combination of awareness briefings, forums and seminars, structured training programs, and information sessions on the MyResults portal (See figure 2.3). In addition to the national level training, the OBB communication strategy focused on agency specific training at various levels. These included targeting top management as champions and sponsors of the reform, working with activity heads

FIGURE 2.3

Web page from the first My Results module

Source: https://www.myresults.gov.my/portal/.

to establish technical activists at the "user" level, liaising with human resource units to leverage trainers as OBB coaches, and identifying focal persons and end users, typically at the deputy director/assistant head of department level. Training and communication materials were developed and delivered domestically through collaboration between members of the OBB team and the domestic think tank which worked on the conceptual framework. In addition, the team used a "training of trainers" approach to develop expertise within ministries.

Some institutional challenges that were evident during the period of MBS could still be constraints to OBB implementation now, despite a significant increase in performance information available to MOF. Even when ministries of finance are able to obtain substantial amounts of data on program results—that is, reporting against agreed indicators—it may not lead to improvements in service delivery. Many factors could affect how data generated from PBB reforms gets used, and whether it helps generate a change in budget culture or changes in policy design and implementation. The World Bank's 2011 review of public expenditure management in Malaysia highlighted challenges to performance management that are still potentially relevant today: (a) Quality and completeness of the performance reports submitted by ministries; (b) Technical capacity of the MOF to use performance information effectively in the annual budget process; (c) Encouragement for program managers and senior officials to draw on performance information and to take actions based on it; and (d) The level of authority and freedom of managers to deliver on performance agreements.

Approach to reform

Malaysia's OBB provides an excellent example of how strategic planning processes can be linked effectively with budget programs through an integrated results framework. OBB built on the program budgeting structure that was in place under MBS, and improved on it by emphasizing national development outcomes and mapping the contribution of the budget to them. OBB strengthened the focus on outcomes by driving it down to all levels of the central government—from the national level to the ministry level, then to ministry programs and finally to activities. OBB also reinforced the accountability for outcomes by establishing performance agreements at ministry, program, and activity level. Although budget planning is still based around specific activities, these must be able to show their contribution to the 5-year national plan. In principle, these programs are comprised of both OE and DE allocations and will facilitate greater coordination among the two institutions responsible for the planning of both budgets.

These formal linkages established under OBB have the potential to help policymakers validate the relevance of long-standing activities to the achievement of national strategies. While IT systems facilitate this mapping of programs and activities to national strategies, the story of OBB has more to do with the NBO's policy guidance than the IT system. Nevertheless, the current modules of MyResults provide the facility for ministries to plan the results chain to justify the creation of new programs and activities. It also enables BROs to see more clearly the range of programs and activities across ministries, and to identify potential overlaps that may exist.

Managing the change process was at the forefront of OBB implementation and was addressed by MOF from multiple angles. From the start, MOF recognized the challenges inherent in implementing a complex reform process and created a dedicated unit to manage OBB implementation. It then gave this unit access to both international and local consultants to help backstop staff during the development process. Communication and outreach to stakeholders across government figured prominently in the change management plan, and substantial time and effort were devoted to developing a training-of-trainers approach to build capacity in developing results frameworks. Although there were some initial starts and stops, officials learned to pace the reform roll-out in line with their capacity to work with line ministries on their results frameworks.

The design of a comprehensive IT system to support OBB reflected foresight, although actual implementation has been slower than expected. Substantial work remains to realize the vision that was laid out for the MyResults system. However, if the remaining modules are fully developed and rolled out as planned, MOF will have succeeded in creating a single online system for ministries to input their budget submissions, plan expenditures during the year, and report on non-financial performance.

Systematic reporting and evaluation of performance information are not yet well-developed; thus, the eventual impact of OBB on service delivery is still to unfold. Quarterly reporting against KPIs began only in January 2018, and it will require time to assess the compliance and the impact of such. There are no requirements in place to compel ministries to report on their achievement of performance agreements. Nor are there any mechanisms in place to validate the accuracy of the information or to parse which data are most useful to analyze. Capacity to evaluate performance information will understandably take time to build. The pace of capacity building, however, could be affected by the degree to which senior policy makers or Parliament demand performance evaluation as an input to their decision-making and oversight, respectively.

The most challenging part of any PBB reform is to create and sustain demand for performance information. Demand can be reflected at multiple levels within the government, as well as external to the government. Presenting information in new ways that are informative and useful for each audience is part of the equation, and potentially could be developed over time in Malaysia. But human resource and career management practices can also help encourage a performance orientation among managers and directors. In Malaysia, as in many other countries, human resource policies are generally set centrally and not driven by MOF. While OBB makes program managers directly responsible for program performance, it did not usher in major changes to the reward or recognition systems of government. Such changes can contribute to program performance, the quality of performance information, and, in turn, to the sustainability of the demand for such information.

PUBLIC SERVICE DELIVERY AND PUBLIC SERVICE TRANSFORMATION

Issues

Beside budget management challenge, Malaysia also faced other challenges that reduce the efficiency of public service provision. Among some of the challenges which affect the public service are centralization of power; bureaucratic red tape and hierarchical reporting; inadequate strategic work competency; silo mentality and insufficient consultation and collaboration among public agencies; complacency from being in a comfort zone; lack of awareness and responsiveness to external requirements; and a lack of mentoring and coaching support for staff development (Public Service Department 2013). Also, for the nation to remain competitive globally and to achieve its national vision, Vision 2020, there was an urgent need for public sector human resource management to be strengthened. Various reform efforts were initiated under Dr. Mahathir Mohamed, Malaysia's third Prime Minister (1981–2003), to improve efficiency and performance of the public sector as well as the private sector. However, challenges in delivering efficient public services remained (see Iyer 2011; McCourt 2012; Siddiquee 2014).

Reform intervention

Efforts to undertake reforms on the economic and government front through the NTP also catalyzed and shaped reforms in the public service. A comprehensive framework on public service transformation effort was put in place in 2013. Following extensive engagement and consultations with various stakeholders, the PSD developed a Public Service Transformation Framework (PSTF) to guide government ministries and agencies in their transformation efforts to overcome challenges confronting the public service. The PSTF aimed to address the following:

- Enhance strategic competency
- Reduce centralized authority
- Eliminate bureaucratic red tape
- Delayer the reporting hierarchy
- Improve the level of responsiveness and awareness to external requirements
- Encourage breaking out of the comfort zone
- Deal with rising expectations and requirements of all stakeholders
- Break the silo mentality and increase consultation
- Improve mentoring and coaching

The PSTF, which placed human resources and talent at the center stage of transformation, was first developed in May 2013 to build the capacity of the PSD to deliver the transformation of the public service. It was subsequently expanded beyond the PSD to be a public-service wide framework (Public Service Department 2013).

Apart from consultative sessions with stakeholders, the PSD's internal expertise also carried out comparative studies and benchmarked with best practices from several countries in order to develop the PSTF. This "outside-in" and "inside-out" approach was adopted to enable the PSD to formulate a framework according to its own objectives and identity without incurring additional costs. Several buy-in initiatives, including change management programs, were also conducted for all PSD personnel to gain their confidence and cooperation, and to strengthen their sense of ownership, esprit de corps, and break down the silos during the organizational transformation process (Public Service Department 2013).

As indicated earlier, the PSTF was introduced to support the implementation of the NTP, with the overall goal of developing a high performing, trustworthy, dynamic and citizen-centric public service (Public Service Department 2013). Its goal was to develop and retain talent in the public sector; strengthen public sector organizations; improve public service delivery by becoming citizen-centric; intensify engagement, collaboration and inclusiveness among government agencies; and inculcate patriotism and integrity among public servants. In order to provide better service delivery, the public sector had to be less bureaucratic, leaner and more productive, facilitative, skilled, efficient and innovative. As the Chief Secretary to the Government, Ali Hamsa, put it, "We have to prioritize the demand and needs of the *rakyat* (citizens), transform and equip ourselves with the right skills, knowledge and expertise in order to compete in this rapidly changing world" (Ali Hamsa 2013b).

In 2013, the PSD set up a Working Committee Taskforce for Managing Change and Driving Transformation to operationalize its transformation programs. Information regarding the concepts and principles from the PSTF was disseminated to all levels of PSD personnel. The PSD also carried out activities such as *Expression Week, Transformation Showcases* and other transformation activities to ensure that all PSD personnel fully understood and appreciated the concepts and principles contained in the PSTF. Information regarding the PSD transformation process was also shared with the Congress of Unions of Employees in the Public and Civil Services (CUEPACS), and at the National Consultative Joint Meetings. Social media was also used to share information regarding the PSD transformation process. A better understanding and appreciation of the essence, spirit and purpose of the public service transformation agenda was facilitated through consultation with and involvement by all PSD personnel and stakeholders (Public Service Department 2013).

The PSTF was approved by the Special Cabinet Committee on Salary and Establishment for the Public Sector in July 2013 for public service-wide adoption, after it had undergone several revisions based on feedback from the engagements and consultations with various stakeholders. The PSTF served as the official guide for every public agency to implement public service transformation in their respective organizations. It was widely disseminated to all ministries/agencies and each ministry/agency would develop and implement their own transformation plan in line with PSTF, as announced by the Prime Minister during his 2014 Budget Speech on 25 October 2013 (Public Service Department 2013).

The Transformation Plan for each organization was to be aligned to the vision, mission, values and corporate strategy for that organization. Subsequently, the meeting of the Chief Secretary to the Government (KSN) with Secretaries-General of Ministries and Heads of Services in February 2014 agreed that all ministries/agencies would take the initiative to implement their transformation by presenting their transformation plans at the meetings. Public Service Transformation Labs (PSTL) were then conducted by the PSD with all the ministries/agencies to guide them in the development of their transformation plans based on the PSTF (Public Service Department 2013). The PSTL were conducted from April to June 2014 and in November 2014.

The Public Service Transformation Plan was a tool to implement the PSTF and served as an implementation planning document to accomplish organizational change from the existing state ("as is") to a desired state ("to be") for every public agency (Public Service Department 2013). In developing the Transformation Plan for each agency, the agency's Organization Strategic Plan (PSO) and the OBB documents served as the main reference points for the plan's development. This shows that there was a conscious and concerted effort to align the PSTF with the PSO and OBB at the design stage (see figure 2.4).

The Public Service Transformation Plan adopted the Big Fast Results (BFR) methodology of the GTP to facilitate quick and impactful transformation of the

FIGURE 2.4

Alignment of PSO and OBB with agency's transformation plan

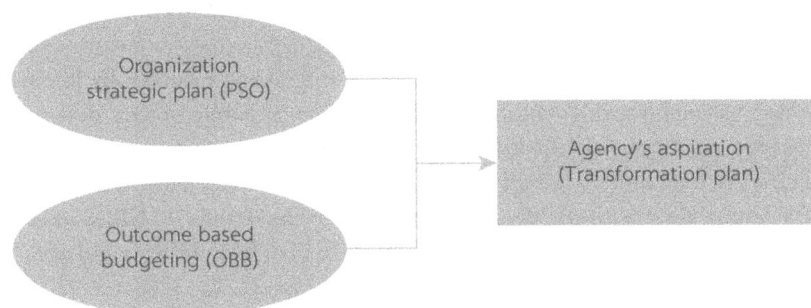

Source: Public Service Department 2013.

public service. The PSTF was a comprehensive guide for all agencies to quickly deliver tangible results in order to develop a high-performing public service which is trustworthy, dynamic and people-oriented. Strategic thrusts and measures were developed to address public service challenges and key priorities for the *rakyat* on a medium and longer-term basis. Each agency focused on its public service delivery effectiveness, development of competent public servants and efficient and adaptable organization structures, and involvement of all stakeholders to instill shared values of patriotism and integrity. The "quick wins" were short term public sector-wide and agency-wide initiatives to achieve success within 6 months or less. Since the quick wins involved initiatives that had significant impact which could be measured and monitored by KPIs, they were effective in enhancing confidence, participation and commitment of the agency and its staff and stakeholders to support its transformation programs (Public Service Department 2013).

In line with the 11th Malaysia Plan (2016–20) and the NTP's objective of making Malaysia a high-income developed nation by the year 2020, the PSD was given the mandate to lead the transformation of the public service. On March 11, 2013, the Chief Secretary to the Government announced that the public service transformation agenda would be spearheaded by two central government agencies namely the PSD and the MoF.

Further, innovation and creativity for addressing public service delivery problems was encouraged under the National Blue Ocean Strategy (NBOS).[5] NBOS is one of the responses for a creative avenue for innovative solutions to address various economic and social concerns—what has been termed a blue ocean shift to break public sector convention and agency silos to enable the exploration of new approaches and methods for national development. Adapted from Kim and Mauborgne's *Blue Ocean Strategy* diagnostic model (2005),[6] the NBOS initiative aimed at delivering high impact, low cost, and rapidly executed initiatives as part of the NTP. Through the NBOS, more than 80 organizations from the public sector, including the police and military, higher learning institutions, NGOs, youth groups and the public have worked more collaboratively towards reforming the public service delivery using innovative approaches of the blue ocean strategy. Under the NBOS Innovative Public Service Delivery impact area, several initiatives were implemented to reduce the distance between the government and the *rakyat* by providing improved access to government agencies and resources for health, training and community needs.

Result/Implementation progress

There was strong buy-in by various ministries to developing and implementing transformation plans. In 2014, 22 Ministries had generated 847 transformation initiatives for the public sector.[7] Since 2013, the PSD has successfully implemented various transformation initiatives as part of public service delivery enhancement. It started off with 25 strategic measures of quick wins. From the quick wins, a total of 94 initiatives were proposed to be implemented in 2013 (JPA Annual Report 2013). Meanwhile, since 2009, more than 90 NBOS initiatives had been successfully implemented by more than 80 ministries and agencies to address a wide range of economic and social issues. The implementation of the NBOS has torn down silos, an example being police-military collaborations in crime prevention. The police force and armed forces shared training facilities as well as conducted joint patrols. That resulted in government savings of almost $188 million from 2010 to 2015 (Ali Hamza 2016a, 2016b).

The processes and structures of public institutions were re-engineered to eliminate redundancies and duplication in order to make the government lean, consultative and delivery-focused (PEMANDU 2014). Sixty-six public agencies have become matrix-based organizations from delayering and restructuring exercises to streamline functions, manpower and funding. The public service had also been right-sized for better productivity. Right sizing involved not having more civil servants than the positions available. Apart from doing away with 29,000 positions that were not needed, the PSD also reassigned the affected civil servants to other sections. For example, in order to achieve the crime reduction objective under the NKRA, 7,000 police personnel could patrol the streets because the PSD had redeployed 4,200 civil servants to perform their administrative work. Multi-skilling had been introduced to improve the overall performance in the public service.[8] Malaysian ringgit (RM) 195 million in remuneration payments has been saved from the abolishment of 38,051 posts. An Exit policy had been implemented since 2015 through PSD Service Circular no. 7, 2015 to remove the non-performers in the public sector and to ensure a high performing public sector with integrity (see Tenth Malaysia Plan 2011–2015).

The usage of online public services was expanded and strengthened to provide greater accessibility and convenience for the *rakyat* with 77 percent (10,369) of public services provided online out of a total of 13,483. Multiple channels of delivery focusing on mobile platforms were deployed and cyber security protection in critical online transactions was strengthened. 708 e-payment services from 7,122 online services have been provided by 339 public agencies. Urban Transformation Centers (UTCs) (See box 2.1) and Rural Transformation Centers (RTCs) have been established since 2012 to provide multiple clusters of frontline services to the *rakyat* under one roof (Tenth Malaysia Plan 2011–2015). In 2015, the PSD set up 1 Malaysia Customer Service of Civil Servants (*1 SERVE*) and 1 Malaysia Civil Service Retirement Support (*1 PESARA*) counters to provide multiple services for civil servants at one focal point for the welfare of serving and retired civil servants (Marzuki 2016).

Human resource and talent management in the public sector has been strengthened through a series of measures. They include contract appointments for top talents in critical fields through flexible pay structures and outcome-based KPIs. Flexible work arrangements were also introduced to maximize productivity as well as to retain talent and provide work-life balance. Public agencies have been empowered to customize their talent management through a bottom-up

BOX 2.1

Urban Transformation Centers

The Urban Transformation Centers (UTCs) is an innovative and creative initiative under the NBOS to provide multiple clusters of frontline services from the public and private sectors for the urban community at a one-stop center or in one building, from 8.00 am to 10.00 pm, seven days a week. Existing underutilized buildings are swiftly renovated and modified to save construction time and cost without compromising quality.

The UTC provides services from the National Registration Department, Road Transport Department, Inland Revenue Board of Malaysia, Immigration Department, Postal Services, Banking Services, Healthcare Services etc. The rakyat is able to perform multiple transactions under one roof, thereby saving time and money for them. The UTCs have reduced government spending in terms of its own facility and staffing costs.

Since its inception in 2012, a total number of 48.5 million people have utilized services from various government agencies at 18 UTCs throughout the country. For the rural community, such services are provided by Rural Transformation Centers (RTCs) and for the remote parts of the country, by Mobile Community Transformation Centers (MCTCs).

A customer satisfaction survey involving 40 respondents at the UTC Kuala Lumpur was conducted in 2015 using convenience sampling to gauge customer satisfaction with respect to counter service, customer service, facilities and support services (Jalil, Malek, and Choy, 2015). 80 percent of the respondents rated the counter service as good and 20 percent rated it as satisfactory. 57.5 percent rated the customer service as good and 42.5 percent rated it as satisfactory. 65 percent rated the facilities as good and 25 percent rated it as satisfactory. 67.5 percent rated support services as good and 32.5 percent rated it as satisfactory. No one had rated counter service, customer service and support services as being not satisfactory.

approach in talent development and performance evaluation. 613,743 public servants have benefited from improved career advancement in 81 schemes of services. Public sector training has been upgraded to improve on relevance and impact, focusing on developing leadership skills and functional specializations. A fast track program was introduced to identify high potential public servants to be placed in leadership positions (Public Service Department 2017).

In the implementation of the PSTF and public service transformation, there are several key challenges. First, there was the need to secure buy-in from relevant public sector agencies and public servants at central and local levels for the transformation of the public service. This was overcome through engagement of public service unions from the outset, PSD road shows, interactive sessions with the PSD and participation in PSD's PSTL. The PSD built on the strong institutional channels for consultation that already existed, notably with the public service unions, to engage and bring these key stakeholders into the design and implementation of the PSTF. The voice of public servants throughout the process was important for building the legitimacy and ownership of reforms. By 2014, all ministries/agencies had developed their respective transformation plans. The agency transformation plans were presented at the monthly meetings of the Heads of Agencies. The PSD had also established an online monitoring system, JPA-Monitor, to oversee the implementation progress of agency transformation initiatives in a transparent and accountable manner. JPA-Monitor sought to ensure public accountability by monitoring the implementation of agency initiatives according to agency delivery targets, outputs, outcomes and KPIs (JPA Transform 2014).

Second, complexity arose due to the need to focus on high impact initiatives and on the broader horizon for transformation efforts. Thus, planning initiatives focused on results and outcomes, as part of the daily work of public agencies. A time frame and KPIs had to be set for all projects to measure the impact of the changes implemented. A progress chart for each planned project had to be provided for regular monitoring and reporting purposes. Monitoring and reporting at all levels played a key role in ensuring the successful implementation of all planned projects in the transformation process.

Finally, the biggest challenge was to "shape an institutional culture that supports the new service delivery model of the *Rakyat serving and giving their best for the Rakyat*" (Public Service Department 2013, 5). There was a need to shape a high performing, high integrity, dynamic and citizen-centric public service. To address such a challenge, the public service transformation process emphasized the need for regular and continuous engagement sessions among members of the organization, as well as engagement sessions with customers and stakeholders. Commitment of top management was vital and cooperation by all members of the organization was needed to ensure success. Work in silos was reduced and collective and informed decisions at all levels inculcated a sense of ownership and helped to ensure the smooth implementation of the transformation agenda. Inclusiveness of the reform agenda was promoted with 88 engagement sessions held with various stakeholders, including public sector worker unions. They included CUEPACS and NUTP (National Union of the Teaching Profession of Malaysia), and the Police and the Army. Significant investment was made in the road shows, sessions and labs to enable this engagement. After each PSTL, the PSD also followed through with handholding sessions to further refine the Transformation Plans of the agencies. The Digital Malaysia Initiative had helped to leverage on digital technology for staff and citizen engagement. Social media had been used extensively to obtain relevant ideas from the public (Marzuki 2016).

Approach to reform

The PSTF was developed through the identification of local problems, experimentation and benchmarking with best practices from other countries (e.g., Singapore; Hong Kong SAR, China; New Zealand; Australia; The United Kingdom; Canada; The Republic of Korea; Japan; India; and other ASEAN counterparts). Although international best practice was used for benchmarking purposes, the problems and challenges confronting the Malaysian public service were identified locally by the PSD and its stakeholders, including the country's political leadership. The PSD was given the mandate by the country's political and administrative leadership to experiment and find solutions to achieve the new policy agenda of "1 Malaysia: People First, Performance Now" and to support the national transformation agenda to achieve Vision 2020. Substantial effort was undertaken to think through the design of the program, drawing in international experience as appropriate and adapting this to the Malaysian public service context. While the PSTF sought "big results fast," a pragmatic approach to implementation was adopted that included short term initiatives and quick wins to initiate the public service transformation process for each strategic measure (JPA Transform 2013, 2014, 2015; Public Service Department 2013).

Readiness to change required effective consultation, communication and dissemination of information to all members of the public service. The change management process in the PSD focused strongly on human development through communication, learning experiences, inclusiveness and active participation by all members of the organization. Change was facilitated by building shared goals and perspectives in the public service. Extensive consultation with key stakeholders from the Ministries and the general public were held through a series of ministerial retreats, surveys, town hall meetings, open days, online polls, and expert consultations to identify eight NKRAs that needed urgent redress. NKRAs were a combination of short term priorities to address urgent public demands, and medium and long-term issues and challenges that required government prioritization and attention (PEMANDU 2010, 2011).

Buy-in from public sector agencies and public servants at central and local levels for the transformation of the public service was achieved through engagement of public service unions from the outset. The PSD built on the strong institutional channels for consultation that already existed, notably with the public service unions, to engage and bring these key stakeholders into the design and implementation of the PSTF. The voice of public servants throughout the process was important for building the legitimacy and ownership of reforms.

Furthermore, the involvement and consultations of all public-sector agencies in the experimentation process from 2013 to 2015 not only ensured that the transformation initiatives would be legitimate, relevant and practical but also encouraged ownership of and commitment for the reform agenda. It also enabled continuous learning by the PSD, stakeholders and public agencies involved.

Innovation and creativity were encouraged in the transformation process. The PSD-led innovation resulted in nationwide adoption of PSTF. Numerous innovative and creative initiatives were produced and shared in the PSTLs and brainstorming sessions between the PSD and its stakeholders. The PSTL was pioneered by the PSD as a new approach for effective engagement in the public sector. After going through PSTL, the PSD also followed through with hand-holding sessions to further refine the Transformation Plans of the agencies. By 2014, all ministries/agencies had developed their respective transformation plans. The agency transformation plans were presented at the monthly meetings of the Heads of Agencies. The PSD had also established an online monitoring system, JPA-Monitor, to oversee the implementation progress of agency transformation initiatives in a transparent and accountable manner. JPA-Monitor sought to ensure public accountability by monitoring the implementation of agency initiatives according to agency delivery targets, outputs, outcomes and KPIs.

A combination of the "outside-in" and the "inside-out" approach was adopted to reap maximum benefits for the transformation process. As one retired senior civil servant observed, "Malaysia has developed a reform culture since Mahathir's time with many best practices from abroad but relevance to the local context is more important, for success." The biggest challenge for the transformation of the public service was to shape an institutional culture that would support the new public service delivery model of "People First, Performance Now."

CONCLUSION AND LESSON LEARNED

Both the OBB reform and the public service delivery transformation in Malaysia saw elements of international good practices, local adaptation, innovation, and experimentation. A key common feature is the presence of an authorizing environment for innovation and experimentation in search of specific solution to the country's problem. Both cases of reform start with small-scale experimentation of specific solution; further scale-up with success of initial results; and/or scale down/re-strategize with lesson learned from draw backs along the way. However, level of achievement varies in the two reform initiatives owing to the complexity of each reform endeavor.

Performance based budgeting

OBB is the Malaysian government's approach to PBB. While Malaysia has not yet realized the full benefits of its OBB initiative, a stronger foundation on which to build OBB has been put in place through a series of measures adapted from good practices, innovation, and experimentation that led to a significant upgrade in the budget system. PBB is generally a complex reform to implement in most countries regardless of income level, and there is no single best practice that exists globally. Experimentation and adaptation to the national context are especially essential for building incentives for performance management.

Malaysia's experience with OBB also resonates globally. The establishment of performance agreements and the requirement to report on performance under PBB aimed to motivate program managers in a positive manner; however, there is traditionally a lack of clear rewards or sanctions for performance in many countries. In the long-run, if outstanding performance and poor performance are not addressed through the system then there is a risk that ministries and departments will lose interest and view PBB as only another reporting burden placed upon them. Additionally, demand from Members of Parliament and Budget Committees is rarely in proportion to the volume of information that is at their disposal from PBB initiatives. Even demand from government ministers may need to be cultivated by presenting the information at an appropriate timing and format that meets their particular needs in the policy process.

Many countries—at different levels of economic development—have introduced elements of PBB in order to develop better links between budget allocations and performance of individual programs. The reasons are understandable. First, PBB offers the promise of a more evidence-based rationale for making budget decisions across an array of competing policy and program areas. Second, it offers a framework for linking medium term national plans and strategies with the annual budget process. Third, the program logic structure gives a more transparent view of what activities are undertaken than a traditional line item budget. Ultimately, PBB holds out the allure of improving public sector performance and the quality of service delivery.

Despite the compelling reasons to introduce PBB, the reality has often failed to live up to expectations—but why? Is this a case of a country trying to adopt an international "best practice" approach, rather than a "best fit?" Not necessarily. The nature of national budgeting processes is that they reflect political processes as much as technical (i.e., accounting) processes. Moreover, for performance management to be effective requires involvement of other stakeholders beyond merely ministries of finance (e.g., prime ministers and PSDs).

The struggles to maximize the benefits of PBB, therefore, may reflect a more complex set of factors, including unrealistic expectations from those who champion it. The past decade of experience from OECD countries suggests that many of these high capacity governments are still learning lessons and adapting PBB to better fit their administrative reality and capacity. Rather than abandoning PBB altogether, they have been progressively taking stock of what has worked and what has not, and applying those lessons to a new generation of PBB.

Public service transformation

Conventional boundaries that had existed across public and private organizations in Malaysia were reconstructed under the Public Service Transformation. Costs were lowered by breaking down silos across the ministries/agencies to unlock underutilized resources. This transformation can be attributed in part to the effective and innovative plan that reflect local reality and was authorized to implement to generate "big results fast" with direct involvement and support by the top leadership in all phases of the transformation process.

Malaysia's PSTF was developed through the identification of local problems, experimentation and benchmarking with best practices from other countries. Intensive and extensive consultations with stakeholders through transformation labs and consultation sessions had produced a wide variety of innovative ideas and practical solutions for problems on the ground. Cooperation, communication and understanding by all stakeholders was important to the success. The implementation process was supported by strong change management in respective organizations. This helped to secure buy-in and to ensure that all public servants understood and appreciated the purpose and benefits of the public service transformation agenda.

Engaging with various parties at all levels (given cross-sectoral nature) and the right actors at the outset was mission critical. The engagement of the central body of public services unions, CUEPACS, from the outset was a critical success factor. Consultations and personal involvement in transformation activities contributed significantly to the understanding and support by the PSD staff, CUEPACS and public service unions, and other stakeholders for the implementation. Engagement sessions were also crucial in generating a better understanding of the public service transformation agenda at grassroots level where feedback from the target groups was important to ensure successful implementation of public programs.

NOTES

1. As of 2016 per capita GDP was more than US$ 9,500.
2. See http://etp.pemandu.gov.my/About_ETP-@-Overview_of_ETP.aspx.
3. The ministry agreements are shared with the MOF for their purposes; they are not published or shared with the Parliament.
4. ProLL © 2010, Arunaselam Rasappan and Jerome Winston CeDRE International
5. Blue Ocean Strategy is a business theory, which advocates that companies will perform better by searching for ways to create 'blue oceans' of 'uncontested market space' instead of competing with similar companies especially when supply exceeds demand in a market (Kim and Mauborgne 2005).
6. See Ali Hamsa 2013a; JPA Transform 2015; Kim and Mauborgne 2005; Najib Tun Razak 2016.

7. 21% of the initiatives were for strategic thrust 1 (revitalizing public servants); 22% of the initiatives were for strategic thrust 2 (re-engineering public organizations); 27% of the initiatives were for strategic thrust 3 (enhancing service delivery); 16% of the initiatives were for strategic thrust 4 (inclusiveness and ownership); and 14% of the initiatives were for strategic thrust 5 (enculturing shared values). 69 initiatives were for quick wins (0–6 months); 269 initiatives were for short-term (>6–12 months); 169 initiatives were for medium term (>12–24 months); and 183 initiatives were for long term (>24 months). 157 initiatives did not indicate any specific time frame (JPA Transform 2014).
8. A junior staff of a line ministry commented: "We help in the activities of other units besides our own work so we have learnt new skills but sometimes we are very busy."

BIBLIOGRAPHY

Ali, Hamsa. 2013a. "National Blue Ocean Strategy: Low Cost, High Impact, Rapidly Executed Initiatives." *New Straits Times*, May 20.

———. 2013b. "Speech Delivered at 13th Civil Service Premier Assembly (MAPPA)." *Kuala Lumpur*, 11 March, (accessed September 2, 2017), http://www.jpa.gov.my.

———. 2016a. "Malaysia to Showcase Blue Ocean Achievements." *The Star*, July 14.

———. 2016b. "Running like Clockwork, Malaysia 2016." VIP Interview with the Hon. Tan Sri Ali, Hamza, Malaysia's Chief Secretary to the Government by *The Business Year*, (accessed September 2, 2017) https://www.thebusinessyear.com/malaysia-2016/running-like -clockwork/vip-interview.

Iyer, D. 2011. "Tying Performance Management to Service Delivery: Public Sector Reform in Malaysia, 2009–2011." *Innovations for Successful Societies*, Princeton University (accessed September 3, 2017), http://www.princeton.edu/successfulsocieties.

Jalil, N. H. A, J. A. Malek, and E. A. Choy. 2015. "Urban Transformation Centre (UTC) as One-Stop Services Centre: A study of customer satisfaction with the Kuala Lumpur UTC." *Malaysian Journal of Society & Space* 11(1): 143–57.

JPA Annual Report. 2013. *Public Service Transformation*. Putrajaya: Jabatan Perkhidmatan Awam Malaysia.

JPA Transform. 2013. *Gerbang Transformasi Anda*. Edisi Pertama. Putrajaya: Jabatan Perkhidmatan Awam Malaysia.

———. 2014. *Gerbang Transformasi Anda*. Edisi Keempat. Putrajaya: Jabatan Perkhidmatan Awam Malaysia.

———. 2015. Gerbang Transformasi Anda: Edisi Kelima. *Putrajaya: Jabatan Perkhidmatan Awam Malaysia.*

Kim, W. C., and R. Mauborgne. 2005. *Blue Ocean Strategy*. Boston, MA: Harvard Business School Press.

Malay Mail Online. 2017. "Urban Transformation Centre Is a World Class Product, DPM Says. May 18, 2017." (accessed October 28, 2017), http://www.themalaymailonline.com/malaysia /article/urban-transformation-centre-is-a-world-class-product-dpm-says.

Marzuki, J. 2016. "Transformation in the Public Sector: Malaysia's Perspective." Keynote Address. Putrajaya: Public Service Department.

McCourt, W. 2012. "Can Top-down and Bottom-Up Be Reconciled? Electoral Competition and Service Delivery in Malaysia." *World Development* 40 (1): 2329–41.

Najib Tun Razak. 2013. "Speech delivered at 13th Civil Service Premier Assembly (MAPPA)." *Kuala Lumpur*, 11 March 2013 (accessed September 2, 2017), http://www.jpa.gov.my.

———. 2016. "Keynote Address at the International Conference on Blue Ocean Strategy 'Transforming Nations Through Creativity and Innovation'." *Kuala Lumpur*, 16 August 2016 (accessed October 28, 2017), http://www.bernama.com.

PEMANDU. 2010. *Government Transformation Program: Annual Report, 2010*. Putrajaya: Prime Minister's Department.

——. 2011. *Government Transformation Program: Annual Report, 2011.* Putrajaya: Prime Minister's Department.

——. 2014. *Government Transformation Program: Annual Report, 2014.* Putrajaya: Prime Minister's Department.

Public Service Department. 2013. *Guidelines for Developing a Transformation Plan.* Putrajaya: Public Service Department.

——. 2017. *Transform: Our Achievements.* http://www.jpa.gov.my (accessed September 1, 2017).

Siddiquee, N. A. 2014. "Malaysia's Government Transformation Programme: A Preliminary Assessment." *Intellectual Discourse* 22 (1): 7–31.

Government of Malaysia. "Tenth Malaysia Plan, 2011–2015." Putrajaya: Prime Minister's Department, Economic Planning Unit, Malaysia (accessed September 5, 2017), http://www.epu.gov.my/en/rmk/tenth-malaysia-plan-10th-mp.

3 Indonesia

LEVERAGING BEST PRACTICES AND EXPERIMENTATION IN PUBLIC FINANCIAL MANAGEMENT AND PUBLIC SECTOR REFORMS IN POST–ASIAN FINANCIAL CRISIS CONTEXT

ERWIN ARIADHARMA and HARI PURNOMO

INTRODUCTION

Indonesia was one of several Asian countries severely hit by the Asian financial crisis of 1997–98. The financial crisis caused the Indonesian economy to contract by over 13 percent of GDP in 1998; government debt rose dramatically, reaching almost 100 percent of GDP by 1999; the Rupiah exchange depreciated by around 400 percent, unemployment spiked, while many national banks collapsed and liquidated. The crisis highlighted the lack of efficiency, transparency and accountability in the management and use of public resources. At the same time, the recovery process following the crisis involved structural adjustment packages through which international donors worked with the government to design new institutions on the basis of international best practice.

The crisis caused the fall of the New Order regime which had ruled Indonesia for three decades, and the protest movement that toppled the regime made anti-corruption a key watchword in Indonesian politics. For successive presidents operating in an environment of free media and competitive elections, the need to improve services and tackle corruption has been pressing. Strengthening public sector governance and performance was thus a key imperative following the collapse of the New Order. During the early years of democracy, particularly between 1998 and 2004, Indonesia embarked on several ambitious and wide-ranging reform programs to quickly transform the old authoritarian New Order system of governance into one supporting democracy and open market economy. These reform efforts included amending the constitution, promoting electoral reform, anti-corruption initiatives, public expenditure and revenue management reforms and decentralization, to name a few of the most important areas. Many new laws were passed and new regulatory and monitoring institutions, required in a democracy and market economy, were established including a powerful Anti-Corruption Commission (KPK). This paper focuses on two main areas of reform—Public Financial Management (PFM) and Civil Service Reforms—central to governance and public sector performance.

PUBLIC FINANCIAL MANAGEMENT REFORM

Key issues in PFM

Indonesia's PFM systems were characterized by major weaknesses such as inadequate accountability, lack of control on state money, overlapping audit institutions, abuse of system and low capacity human resources (HR). Shrinking budgetary resources due to the crisis and rising public expenditure needs made it imperative to seek out for new ways of using public resources wisely, prudently, and transparently. Fragmented and overlapping structures in the Ministry of Finance (MoF) were also a major constraint, leading to inadequate fiscal discipline, poor resource allocation and unreliable fiscal reporting.

Reform intervention

Recognizing the need for reform, the MoF established in 2001 the Financial Management Reform Committee; it comprised leading bureaucrats, practitioners, politicians, and academics in Indonesia, and was tasked with guiding public financial management (PFM) reforms. The committee's tasks included providing guidance to the MoF in dealing with each of the many aspects related to the improvement of PFM in the government, facilitating dialogue with the Parliament, and recommending improvements to the business processes, organizations, and systems. It also played a critical role in promulgating the MoF's 2002 White Paper on Indonesian PFM.

The 2002 White Paper articulated the need for comprehensive PFM reforms covering budget preparation and execution, revenue administration, public accounting and auditing and accountability for results to the Parliament and the people. The White Paper also described the rationale for changes proposed to the legal and institutional frameworks of the PFM process and timetable for reform implementation. Further, the segregation of roles between the finance ministry and line ministries was clarified to support transparency and professionalism in public expenditure management.

The White Paper laid the foundation for enacting various laws to modernize the country's financial management system at the central government level, in particular:

(a) The State Finances Law 17/2003, which detailed the provisions for the budget process, mandates specific milestones and dates for the preparation and adoption of the budget, general principles and authorities for the management and accountability of state finances, and the financial relationship between the central government and other institutions.

(b) The State Treasury Law 1/2004, which outlined the responsibilities of the State Treasurer, articulates the creation of revenues and expenditures treasurers in government ministries and agencies, together with general principles on the management and accountability of public funds.

(c) The State Accountability and Audit Law 15/2004, which paved the way to more accountable and transparent government institutions, obligating each of them to submit a financial report to be audited by Supreme Audit Institution (BPK) before being presented to the Parliament. The law establishes the operational foundation for the BPK as an external auditor to audit the management of and responsibility for state finance.

Soon after the issuance of those PFM legal and regulations, MoF in 2004 initiated a suite of business process reengineering and capacity building initiatives to improve efficiency and effectiveness in the management of the state finances. Recognizing that managing change of the magnitude of PFM reforms envisioned in the finance related laws would require high-level support and attention, dedicated human resources, sustained technical assistance support and a strategy that goes beyond the medium term, the MoF approached a variety of development partners (including the World Bank) and international donor countries for support to ensure the realization of the envisioned long-term PFM reform goals.

Since the beginning of the PFM reform process, the World Bank has provided an array of financing instruments to assist the improvement of PFM systems in Indonesia, including Development Policy Loans (DPL), the Investment Project Financing (IPF), the grants funded by multi-donor trust funds (PFM MDTF), and its own administrative budget to finance technical assistance for policy advice when needed to back up its policy reform proposals. The World Bank also provided assistance to help sub-national governments improve transparency, accountability and public participation practices. On December 22, 2004, the MoF signed with the World Bank a package of loan, credit and grant agreements for the "Government Financial Management and Revenue Administration Project" (GFMRAP). The GFMRAP Phase I operation was financed through a combination of US\$55 million IBRD loan, SDR 3.14 million (equivalent to US\$5 million) IDA credit, US\$5 million PHRD Japan Grant, about US\$12 million of the Public Finance Management Multi Donors Trust Fund (PFM MDTF) financed by the EU, the Netherlands, Switzerland, Canada, and USA, and around US\$15 million in government's own resources.

The GFMRAP was intended to provide support on the overall PFM landscape of the widespread reform areas, including the PFM reform agenda in the fiscal policy development capacity, budget planning, budget execution, accounting and reporting, procurement, revenue administration, legislative scrutiny of budgets and audit reports, and governance accountability. It had various components within MoF (DG Treasury, DG Budget, DG Tax, DG Customs and Excise, Fiscal Policy Office, IT Center, Inspectorate General, and Secretary General) and outside the MoF (Tax Court, Parliament, and Planning Ministry-Bappenas). While the project's ambitious design with broad scope of coverage responded to the government's need to lock in major PFM reforms, it took time for the reforms to take place. Pockets of resistance were identified upfront but building consensus among a large group of stakeholders took time.

The GFMRAP's key indicators were:

(a) Improved national government policy priorities reflected in a Medium-Term Expenditure Framework and annual budgets;
(b) Reduced leakage in expenditure flows to end-users, as measured by Public Expenditure Tracking Surveys;
(c) Automated treasury payment system to enable better financial reporting, more efficient use of cash balances and reduced corruption;
(d) Improved customs revenue performance and time-for-release performance;
(e) Demonstrable evidence of improved transparency and performance of tax and customs collection.

Initially, GFMRAP was planned to include three phases to be implemented over 12 years, tackling both public resource management and revenue generation. Phase 1, which comprised the creation and roll-out of a new Financial Management Information System, called SPAN, was initially scheduled to take 4.5 years, but eventually took 11 years, due to delays in procurement and development of the IT software. Consequently, Phases II and III, dealing with revenue generation, were dropped halfway through, to focus on Phase 1 only.

Result

In March 2009 when the GFMRAP project was first restructured, the core focus of the project was scaled down by focusing more on the deployment of an Integrated Financial Management Information System (IFMIS) which is called the "Sistem Perbendaharaan dan Anggaran Negara (SPAN)." SPAN was envisaged as an integrated state treasury (Perbendaharaan) and budget preparation (Anggaran) system (See figure 3.1 for SPAN project structure). The SPAN contract was worth around USD 58.9 million, of which USD 46.9 was funded by the World Bank to mostly finance the supply and installation costs, while the remaining USD 12 million was paid from the government's own funds to finance 5 years of post-warranty and recurrent costs. SPAN is currently fully operational and the backbone of the PFM systems in Indonesia. The launch of SPAN by Indonesia's President Joko Widodo in April 2015 at the Presidential Palace reflected the importance of SPAN as a landmark achievement for the country to improve its public finance management. Since then, SPAN has been used by the MoF at the DG Budget and DG Treasury headquarters, in addition to the 182 Treasury local services offices (KPPNs) and 33 Treasury regional offices (Kanwils) all over Indonesia. Over 4,000 user's licenses serve over 24,000 spending units of the central government agencies located across the country.

The full implementation of SPAN and accrual accounting in 2015, along with the Treasury Single Account since 2010 and the rollout of the management revenue concentration system (MPN-G2) in 2016, have contributed to quality and timely financial reporting. This was reflected in the "unqualified" audit opinion awarded to the 2016 Financial Report of the Central Government (LKPP) by the Supreme Audit Agency (BPK) in May 2017, reflecting a "clean bill of health" for central government reports. This is the first unqualified audit opinion the central government has received since the beginning of reforms in 2004.

Key achievements of PFM reforms include:

(a) Curbing opportunities for corruption by reducing the opportunities for discretion and informality that are more common in manual, paper-based systems. A key reform was the consolidation of cash balances from thousands of government bank accounts into a Treasury Single Account.

(b) Improving transparency in payments through electronic transfers to suppliers and employees replacing manual checks.

(c) Improving predictability of budget execution and reductions in payment errors. Annual budget ceiling data is integrated with SPAN so spending units cannot disburse beyond this limit, helping strengthen expenditure control.

These reforms improved efficiencies. Consolidation of balances into the Treasury Single Account reduced the number of idle cash balances generating higher interest. Automation of payments allowed increased efficiency whereas although government budget and expenditure increased threefold over this

FIGURE 3.1
SPAN project structure

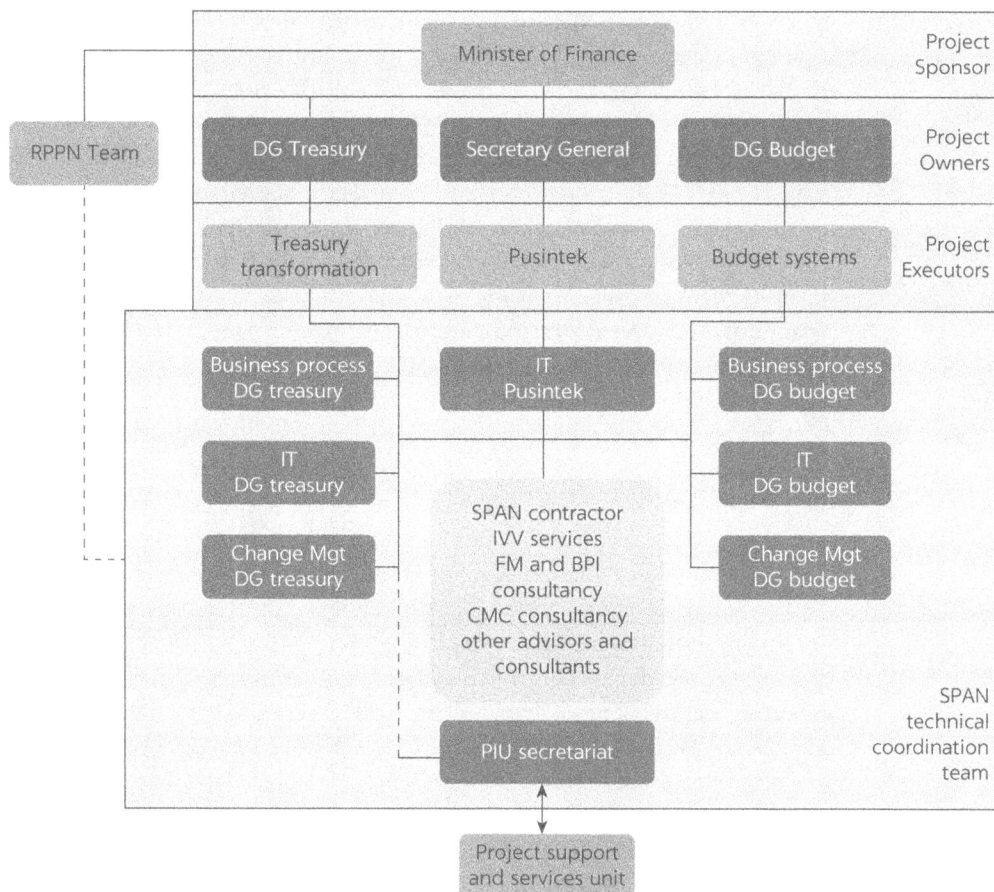

Source: GFMRAP document.
Note: DG = director general; IVV = independent verification and validation; FM = financial management; BPI = business process improvement; CMC = change management and communications; PIU = project implementation unit; RPPN = State Budget and Treasury Reform; SPAN = Sistem Perbendaharaan dan Anggaran Negara.

period, the number of Treasury officials remained the same and many of them were able to shift their time to working more on analytical than administrative tasks. SPAN also greatly improved access to information, allowing not only the senior government officials to make better decisions about their program implementation but also for the line ministry spending unit staff to see their budget execution progress both on-line and in real time. In time, SPAN has benefited the general public through the improvement of the quality of audited financial statements to reflect better transparency and accountability of the state's finances.

Approach to PFM Reform/FMIS implementation and lesson learned

Indonesia SPAN was implemented based on good practice with some modifications to fit the local context. DG Treasury has set an ambitious vision "to be a world-class state treasury manager" in implementing its mission to: (a) achieve prudent, efficient and optimum cash and fund investment management; (b) support timely, effective, and accountable budget execution; (c) achieve accountable, transparent, and timely state finance accounting and reporting; and (d) develop reliable, professional and modern treasury support systems.

Positive features of this ultimately successful reform include the strong and continuous commitment from top leadership. There have been three Presidents, six Finance Ministers, and some changes with the Director Generals of Treasury and Budget officials over the life of SPAN Project since 2004 to now. When initially conceived in 2003–04, the project began with good support from the top management. As the project progressed and delays started to occur for various reasons, the support also kept on varying and it was a difficult challenge to keep the high level of support from the top, especially following changes of government. However, a collective belief that failure was not an option persisted and continued commitment from the political as well as bureaucratic levels remained strong enough to complete the project. Ultimately political will was the key to keeping the reform moving forward.

A further positive aspect was the strong involvement of the MoF Internal Auditor (Inspectorate General) during the project implementation. This assisted in resolving problems of risk aversion in a climate where civil servants were afraid of making decisions because of tough anti-corruption measures. The inclusion of the MoF Internal Auditor helped senior management understand issues and suggest appropriate solutions, identifying risks and providing advice for solving problems before they were flagged up as irregularities by external auditors. A well-defined and efficient governance structure with clear lines of reporting and frequent stakeholder consultation was also essential to success. However, these elements of success also brought their own problems: political and project pressure to speed up implementation reduced the time available to experiment with solutions to unforeseen issues, jeopardizing the coherence of overall project planning and sequencing.

Change management and adequate communication was also important to the outcome of SPAN. Multiple communication media and Change Agents networks were used to help disseminate needed information about SPAN. The SPAN "Change Agents" program was designed to serve as the bridge of communication and coordination between SPAN project team and the stakeholders. "Change Agents" (Duta Span) were formally recruited and trained to act as information providers and opinion leaders within their work units, keeping their colleagues updated on implementation. Other communication channels included a SPAN website, SPAN newsletters, email blasts, promotional gimmicks such as pens and mugs, and SPAN roadshows, attended by the Minister or by Echelon 1 Ministry staff in key regions. Key messages were tailored different audiences and the effect of messages disseminated was continuously monitored to check for understanding by recipients (Hughes et al. 2017).

Attention was also made to ensure the availability of dedicated full-time staff to manage and implement the SPAN. In 2008, a new Echelon II unit called the Directorate for Treasury Transformation (DTP, later to be renamed as the Directorate for Treasury Technology and Information System, or SITP) was established as a project implementation unit (PIU) within the DG Treasury. Its task was to oversee all activities related to the development and implementation of SPAN and to champion the SPAN reform project effort. Headed by an Echelon II level official and staffed with about 100 dedicated staff picked for their qualifications and energy, the DTP unit was given the mandate to manage the SPAN project, recommend the necessary changes in the Treasury's business processes, draft the implementing regulations, and oversee the work of all contractors and consultants involved with the project. The roles and responsibilities of government officials assigned to this unit were also geared towards developing, testing, and rolling out the SPAN system. Unit staff had no other duties besides implementing SPAN, a departure from normal World Bank projects managed by civil servants who are often part of the PIU but still have regular functional responsibilities. Within the PIU, staff were divided into Project Work Streams, who worked with external consultants (described below), produced analytical studies, provided recommendations for management, and implemented the project. The Unit reported weekly progress to the Finance Minister's advisor and presented issues for decision to a high level steering committee chaired by the Finance Minister who was a strong and influential champion of the program. The active involvement of top leadership in the implementation process helped to push the reforms forward.

In spite of this orderly arrangement, the actual implementation was not without its challenges. The first challenge was long delays in the procurement process which took almost 5 years to complete. The procurement of a commercial off-the-shelf (COTS) IT system is a complex activity, and the MoF teams had no prior experience of it. The process designed for SPAN included a two-stage bidding process where the procurement team also had little knowledge or experience of doing this process. Different interpretations between the MoF procurement team and the World Bank task team of the bidding documents and Bank guidelines took a long time to resolve. In fact, rigorous fiduciary safeguards and mitigation measures built into procurement processes to manage the high risk of the project had the effect of slowing down the procurement process. This was a particularly acute problem given the high level of risk aversion among civil servants to take a decision, fearful of newly established and powerful anti-corruption agencies within the Indonesian state.

A second challenge was elaborating the requirements for the development of the IT system. This caused delays of 7 months. The problem here was that SPAN was supposed to assist in the implementation of better business processes built under a ready to use COTS application, but regrettably the ideas about new business processes was not finalized long before the software application developer started to work. Ideally, the new improved business processes should have been designed before developing the software application. However, in fact, business process improvements were being drafted at the same time as the requirements were being developed in SPAN, which created complex challenges of timing and sequencing. The supplier of SPAN proved to be unable to provide qualified and experienced assistance to the MoF on this. These issues suggest that business processes need to be designed first and then frozen while the software development takes place. Close collaboration between the consultant designing new business processes and the software developers/suppliers is therefore essential.

Further delays were experienced in developing and rolling out the software. Initially, the supplier produced a single over-arching project schedule that could be used to measure the progress of the project. The supplier provided training of all stakeholders in the quality assurance (QA) processes to be used to track progress. A comprehensive project charter document was prepared at the start of the project with a detailed project schedule that integrated the project activities across all teams. However, because of delays at earlier stages, the project schedule quickly became irrelevant. Political pressure to make up for lost time led to frequent compromises which lowered the quality standard criteria that needed to be passed at each of the life-cycle milestones. Furthermore, training provided to project stakeholders was not sufficiently thorough to gain full understanding. This situation resulted in fragmented project schedules, often with unrealistic due dates and a snowballing of further delays as corrective action needed to be taken, including restructuring the project team.

A further problem was significant underestimation of the server capacity required, partly due to greater demands imposed by new business processes and partly because of wrong assumptions in the initial estimates. Even with the availability of future projections at the time of bidding, the actual conditions during implementation could differ drastically from the assumptions during bidding; scope for this needed to be built into the program, including opportunities for recalculating system requirement at a late stage in the process.

This leads to a broader point: a structured and disciplined QA methodology must govern all decisions on a project. A single overarching plan is required to integrate activities and tasks and map interdependencies and all stakeholders must be conversant and compliant with it. But this must incorporate flexibility. The complexity of the SPAN project was such that all contingencies were unlikely to be foreseen, but allowance for this was not built into the initial schedule. Even though this project was a program employing a COTS international solution, the embedding of the solution into the local specific context required a degree of experimentation and trial-and-error that was not initially anticipated and factored into the plan. Pressure to make up for accumulating delays further compounded this problem, particularly since the SPAN contract was made in a turn-key manner such that any additional costs for delays had to be borne by the supplier. A key lesson is that realistic assessments of resource constraints are essential. Equally, although high level political support is vital to the success of the project, political and project pressures must not interfere with precise planning regarding sequencing. New interdependencies that become apparent need to be identified and incorporated into the plan. Teams should include Solution Architects whose task is specifically to deal with such problems. Milestone requirements that are needed to maintain high quality should never be compromised, and unless necessary tasks have been completed in their entirety, project team must not be allowed to progress to any follow-on activities and/or tasks.

CIVIL SERVICE REFORM

Key issues in indonesia civil service

Civil service reform was slow to get off the ground following the start of Indonesia's transition from authoritarian to democratic rule. The old regulatory body under the New Order civil service law from 1974 prevailed and very little changed in practice. That means that the government structures and the people in them, who were supposed to implement all the new, fundamental reforms, never became targets of corresponding change ambitions. Therefore, the Indonesian civil service largely continued to operate as it had under the New Order regime, which implied structures guided by military influence as well as fragmentation, red tape and people recruited and managed based on patronage rather than on professional considerations. Although small in international comparison, most of the Indonesian civil service continued to operate as a bloated, non-professional body prone to corruption several years into democratization.

Reform intervention

Civil service reform was an area of difficulty for post-New Order governments. The government issued a new civil service law in 1999 (Law No. 43 Year 1999) as part of the comprehensive package of reform laws during the transition of the country but it was never followed up with necessary secondary, implementing regulations. Lack of national civil service reform engagement led to a piecemeal approach to reform, pushed by dedicated leaders in some central and regional institutions, within or alongside the unreformed national regulatory framework.

Initial pilots in the MoF provided the basis for an ambitious government-wide strategy which has been implemented over the past decade. Indonesia made extensive use of international expertise and barometers to manage its program, in a context characterized by intense political pressure for reform. The format of adopting and trialing international best practice, with assistance from expert consultants, and then taking time to experiment with local innovation afterwards, has proven successful.

The most comprehensive reform concept at this time was the Bureaucracy Reform Initiative, initiated in late 2006 in the MoF. This became known as the first wave of Bureaucracy Reform (BR), and lasted from 2006 to 2009. BR in MoF was aiming at addressing both corruption and efficiency and performance shortcomings through organizational restructuring, improved business processes, introduction of new Standard Operating Procedures (SOP) for critical public service delivery, as well as modernized Human Resources (HR) policies and practices. In addition, the Supreme Audit Institution (BPK) and the Supreme Court (MA), neither of which was a government institution under the reformed Constitution, were in 2007 mandated by the Parliament to implement BR as originally designed by MoF.

As part of the reform incentives, in 2007 officials in MoF and BPK began to receive an additional allowance called Performance Allowance or BR Allowance. Different from basic salary and legally defined allowances, which are tied to rank and seniority, the BR allowance is tied to the job. Job analyses were carried out in MoF and BPK and new job descriptions were developed determining the complexity, scope and accountability of the job. The new job descriptions then became the basis for conducting Job Evaluations to determine the worth of the job and hence the amount of the allowance.

Based on the successful impact of initial BR in both MoF and BPK, the government of Indonesia decided in 2008 to further roll out BR among central government institutions and subsequently to move the responsibility for BR implementation to the center of government, i.e., to the then Ministry for Administrative and Bureaucratic Reform (abbreviated as MENPANRB). In MENPANRB, an intensive work program for developing the BR concept, policy and implementation guidelines commenced and a schedule for its roll-out was prepared. The second wave of BR intervention, from 2010 to 2014, was more specific and ambitious (see table 3.1).

In late 2009, the BR Steering Committee (KPRBN), chaired by the Vice-President of the Republic of Indonesia, was established together with the National BR Team (TRBN), chaired by the Minister of MENPANRB and the National BR Management Unit (UPRBN), chaired by a Deputy Minister for MENPANRB in charge for BRs. In addition to these new structures, two other teams were established—the Independent Team and the Quality Assurance

TABLE 3.1 **First and second waves of bureaucracy reform**

FIRST WAVE OF BUREAUCRACY REFORMS (2004–09)	SECOND WAVE OF BUREAUCRACY REFORMS (2010–14)
Nature:	**Nature:**
Institutional	National and institutional
Objective:	**Objective:**
Good governance	1. Clean government and free form corruption, collusion and nepotism
	2. Improved public service delivery
	3. Improved capacity and accountability of civil servants
Areas of change:	**Areas of change:**
1. Organization	1. Organization
2. Organizational culture	2. Business process
3. Business process	3. Regulations
4. Regulation-deregulation	4. Human resources management policies and practices
5. Human resources management policies and practices	5. Supervision
	6. Accountability
	7. Public service delivery
	8. Mind-set and working culture

Source: World Bank and Ministry of Administrative and Bureaucracy Reform 2013.

Team (QA Team)—and tasked with, respectively, providing independent advice and evaluation, and with providing assurance on the quality of BR implementation. The new program developed the concept of BR, added new reform areas beyond the MoF, and incorporated a requirement for Quick Wins.

The implementation schedule envisaged a gradual implementation up to 2014 when all 76 central government institutions should be implementing BR. In 2010, the BR Grand Design 2010–25 (under Presidential Regulation No. 83 Year 2010) and the BR Road Map 2010–14 (under Minister of MENPANRB Regulation No. 20 Year 2010) were issued defining reform vision, objectives, key reform areas and guiding the implementation process. The Road Map clearly defines nine BR programs to be done at institutional level, namely: (a) Change Management; (b) Realignment of Laws and Regulations; (c) Realignment and Strengthening of Organizations; (d) Improvement of Business Processes; (e) Improvement of Human Resources Management; (f) Strengthening of Internal Supervisory Mechanisms; (g) Strengthening of Performance Accountability; (h) Improvement of Public Service Quality; and (i) Monitoring and Evaluation. In 2011, nine books with detailed implementation guidelines were issued under ministerial regulations by MENPANRB to support these reforms. The BR Road Map also delineated the Indicators and Targets of the BR program, evaluated both by internal government agencies and by external indices such as the Corruption Perceptions Index and the Ease of Doing Business (EoDB) index. At the beginning of 2012, MENPANRB endorsed a new initiative to speed up the reform process called "Nine Bureaucracy Reform Acceleration Programs." This added specificity to the program addressing issues of civil service management, remuneration, professionalization, recruitment and promotion. It also incorporated better evaluation of organization management; improved efficiency, including through e-government initiatives; reduced red tape in licensing and regulation of businesses; and more transparency. After 4 years of implementation, more than 60 line ministries and central agencies have received additional allowances of between 70 percent and 100 percent, depending on their progress with BR.

A third wave of reform was initiated in 2014, when the government introduced a new Civil Service Law (Law No. 5 Year 2014 on Civil Service Apparatus) which brought significant changes to the civil service landscape, specifically in its institutional and human resources management policies. Indonesia is unusual in that civil service reform was driven, not by a concern to cut costs, but by concern to reduce corruption and improve service delivery. In 2007, the OECD reported that only 27 percent of Indonesian people trusted their government. Although the law has been passed, a significant number of regulations are still awaiting approval in support of this reform. In early 2015, a new BR Road Map was issued by MENPANRB under a ministerial regulation focusing on three areas: clean and accountable bureaucracy; effective and efficient bureaucracy; and quality of public service delivery.

Result

The Indonesian government experimented with two different systems of monitoring and evaluation. One system used a framework of checklists and scores to evaluate the ability of agencies to meet reform targets; the other system focused on using evaluation tools to identify relationships between enabling factors and results. The second system was intended to promote learning and innovation, as institutions were encouraged to identify cause and effect relationships. However, after 2 years of experimentation with this, the government integrated it back into the original approach. Although the framework of enablers and results was retained, the checklist and scoring system was brought back to allow a ranking of agencies on which the disbursement of the BR Allowance would depend.

Review of these evaluations suggests that BR has achieved more success at central level than at regional level, and that reform appears more successful when measured by internal government indicators—e.g., Supreme Audit Board's Opinion, Public Service Integrity and Accountable Government Organization—than in external indicators such as the World Bank's EoDB and Corruption Perception Index of Transparency International (See figure 3.1).

Specific achievements of the reform include:

(a) **Streamlining and restructuring of government institutions:** In 2011–12, the government introduced civil service moratorium and performed reviews of 16 government institutions. Four Ministries and agencies were restructured, and a further review resulted in the liquidation of 10 agencies in 2014.

(b) **New recruitment system in place:** In 2013, the government introduced a new recruitment system using Computer Assisted Test (CAT) in central and regional governments. The new system brought transparency and accountability in the recruitment process which was previously prone to corruption, collusion and nepotism.

(c) **Open promotion:** a new "open bidding" process replaced the previous closed-door system in selected ministries from 2012 to promote transparency. It was subsequently widely applied in line ministries and agencies

(LMA) at central level and is expected to remove the glass ceiling between the subnational and central civil service.

(d) **New Civil Service Law and new regulation on HR Management for State Apparatus:** To accommodate and institutionalize the reforms, the government introduced a new legal framework including the Civil Service Law of 2014 (Law No. 5 Year 2014 on Civil Service Apparatus/ASN Law) and a new Government Regulation on HR Management for State Apparatus (Government Regulation No. 11 Year 2017) to support the implementation of the Law. Changes in the Law include:

- **Institutional and structural changes:** Establishment of the State Civil Service Apparatus Commission (KASN) reporting directly to the president to implement a meritocratic selection and appointment system for high ranking officials; development of a new, separately managed Senior Executive Service for high ranking officials, selected on merit; and a modernized role for the National Institute for Public Administration (LAN), including provision of leadership development and professionalization activities and evidence-based policy advice.

- **Human resources management changes:** including a new pay grading system based upon level of responsibility/accountability, with open recruitment based on merit and promotion based on performance and qualifications; simplification of the take-home pay components; and mandatory performance evaluation of units and individuals.

The impact of the reforms on public servants themselves was evaluated by a survey conducted by MENPANRB and the World Bank in 2012. The survey questioned 4,000 Jakarta based civil servants from 14 LMAs. The survey found a high level of support for the reforms overall, particularly among LMAs where the BR allowance has already been received. However, staff in ministries where the BR allowance is realistically more than 2 years away were also positive about the reform. Respondents reported that BR agencies were more efficient than non-BR agencies, and staff reported greater effort, less favoritism, and greater focus on public interest in these ministries. However, the causal link between BR and these outcomes is not established. Higher ranked employees were more likely to

TABLE 3.2 **Targets and achievements of bureaucracy reform, 2010–14**

OBJECTIVES	KEY PERFORMANCE INDICATORS		BASE LINE (2009)	TARGET (2014)	ACHIEVEMENT (2014)
Government which is clean and free from corruption, collusion, and nepotism is realized	Corruption perception index (CPI)		2.8	50	34
	BPK's opinion (unqualified opinion)	Central	42.17%	100%	76%
		Regional	2.73%	60%	35%
Quality of public service is improved	Public service integrity	Central	6.64	8	7.22
		Regional	6.46	8	n.a.
	Ease of doing business		122	75	114
	Government effectiveness		-0.29	0.5	-0.04
Capacity and accountability of bureaucracy performance is improved	Accountable government organization	Central	47%	100%	98.80%
		Provincial	3.8	80%	87.90%
		City	5.1	60%	44.90%

Source: Ministry of Administrative and Bureaucracy Reform 2015.
Note: n.a. = not applicable.

support the reform, perhaps reflecting the higher level of allowance for higher ranks of public servant. The survey suggested that substantial morale differences exist between BR and non-BR agencies. If BR is causing lower morale in non-BR agencies, this could impose productivity costs.

Approach to bureaucratic reform and lesson learned

The first wave of BR was initiated by the MoF in response to internal drivers and without many interventions from development partners. By contrast, the second wave was designed as a top-down approach. It was led by the BR Steering Committee and in line with the BR Grand Design and BR Road Map formally issued by the government 4 years after the MoF reform had begun and in light of its positive results. MENPANRB introduced step-by-step guidelines on how to design, implement, monitor and evaluate the progress of the reform at the institutional level, and their approach to the reform was influenced by the experience of the MoF and by best-practice brought in by the World Bank and other development partners.

MoF's focus from 2006 was on reforming organizational structures, HR policies and practices and business processes in order to rationalize and professionalize the Ministry. Central to this was the production of more than 8,000 reformed SOP, which were critical in delivering core business and shaping the image and reputation of the MoF. A new suite of SOPs minimized variability of service level, streamlined processes, improved transparency and accountability. These SOPs significantly contributed to the achievement of MoF's performance on good governance. The powerful Anti-Corruption Commission (KPK) awarded a good governance score of 8.99 to DG Treasury, 8.86 to DG Customs & Excise, 8.38 to DG Budget and 8.18 to DG Taxes in 2010 (2011 Report on Indonesia's Sector Public by Anti-Corruption Commission). In undertaking this task, the MoF drew on experience of the DG Taxes which had revamped its organizational structures 4 years earlier as part of the agreement with the IMF.

By the end of 2009, MoF also managed to deliver and conduct job analysis and job evaluation for more than 23,000 jobs ranging from Echelon I (Director General level) to Staff level. This was later replicated and adopted by remaining LMAs after a Ministerial Decree on job description development was issued by MENPANRB in early 2009.

An international leading HR consulting firm was hired to provide consultancy, advice and technical assistance on HR best practices, such as workload analysis, job descriptions, job evaluation, job grading and finally job pricing. Few LMAs at that time had clear job descriptions for their officials and staff, resulting in poor performance and accountability. Hiring a world-class HR firm was critical for MoF to ensure that HR management in MoF follows international standards and best practice.

Another key element of the reform that MoF introduced was an increase of staff take-home pay through the BR Allowance, which was based on the newly developed job grading. Further, the institution also introduced a new performance management system (PMS) based on the Balanced-Scorecard (BSC) methodology. MoF used a BSC-based PMS to track, monitor and evaluate the progress of strategic objectives and key performance indicators (KPIs) at all levels within the institution. MoF used external experts to help develop the system and a special unit within MoF was established accordingly to monitor, evaluate and report overall institutional performance to the Minister. However, all the legwork was done by internal staff on top of their routine jobs, under the supervision of the experts. Embedding international best practices (sometimes coming with their proprietary rights) to the current MOF work systems—especially to those that are related with HR management concepts and methods—posed some challenges in the beginning. From best practices, MoF learned and adapted contemporary concepts on how to properly construct a job description, how to conduct a job analysis based on the job description, how to conduct job evaluations using international methods, how to construct job grading based on the evaluation of jobs, how to apply concepts of internal and external equity for public sector, how to properly conduct work load analysis, how to set up an assessment center and how to build competency models.

Although there was a lot to learn, strong commitment from the top leaders and management to undertake the reform and the eagerness of the management to learn about new knowledge and skills assisted the process of acquiring new concepts, methods and paradigms. MoF staff who were involved in the reform were also enthusiastic and committed to working long hours, eager to learn about new knowledge and skills, and keen to make sure that all required work was completed in a timely manner. The progress and results of the BR performed by MoF shaped implementation of the second wave. Use of international indicators to track results, such as the EoDB survey and the Corruption Perceptions Index, reflected the embedding of international best practice in the operation of the ministry. Ten books produced to guide LMAs in implementing BR were fully endorsed by the World Bank Team. Concepts, methods and step-by-step processes were mostly inspired and taken from international best practice.

Once the reform was expanded to all LMAs, progress slowed due to several challenges. Civil service laws and regulations were outdated, rigid and inflexible so it was difficult to create the necessary HR policies and practices to move to a merit-based system. LMA staff had limited capacity to promote reform; they had limited technical competence and relevant experience of this kind of reform, even where step by step guidelines were offered. Commitment of top leaders also varied.

The learning curve was steep but started to pay off during the third wave of reform. Particular factors that supported reforms including: availability of a budget for consulting services to assist implementation; better planning with Quick Wins built in to secure support; political pressure from the President, public opinion and civil society, to achieve tangible results especially relating to public service delivery; and shifts in the top leaders' mind-set to support the reforms due to both external and internal pressures (in a hope to receive better BR allowance as a reward). Nevertheless, by 2012, at least 75 percent of the LMAs had submitted their reform proposal to UPRBN for approval. Given the overall progress of the reform that time, MENPANRB as explained in the beginning of this section introduced BR acceleration programs. The substance of the programs was also mostly inspired by international best practice, but this program was difficult to get off the ground because most LMAs were still struggling to implement the existing guidance.

The BR program was originally started in the leading agency in Indonesia—the MoF—and, having evolved over 7 years of implementation at the national level, has demonstrated many positive results despite challenges, difficulties and opposition. There are at least three major areas where the BR program has demonstrated positive results:

- Better results on accountability and integrity, as well as public service delivery as shown on the KPK surveys for the MoF in 2010;
- Laws and regulations related to HR management for civil servants that support a meritocratic and flexible system have been developed and implemented, and are monitored by the KASN, established in 2014, under the terms of the new Civil Service Law;
- Results from the surveys in 2012 that show, among other things, BR agencies were motivated to undertake reforms and able to attract high quality staff; the quality of new applicants had improved significantly; and there was increased confidence and trust, less absenteeism, and more focus on public service.

On the other hand, some challenges remain, particularly with respect to the use of the BR allowance as an incentive. The BR allowances are still mainly rewards for reform intent, and do not measure effective implementation. LMAs which do not perform well, as reflected in the BR score MENPANRB gives every year for example, would not be penalized by allowance reductions. Variations in the level of BR allowance awarded were difficult to understand and this caused some tension initially. Now, LMAs are trying harder to increase their allowance through demonstrating better performance and more positive results, but nevertheless the BR allowance actually awarded is still dependent upon approval by MENPANRB and the availability of the budget (with approval of the MoF).

Some important and valuable lessons learned from the BR design and implementation in Indonesia, include:

- Adopting and applying an international best-practices approach or method to complex reforms such as BR in Indonesia is a good approach, especially when the government has limited experience, knowledge and information on how to design, plan, implement, monitor and evaluate the progress of reforms, and in this regard, to support and provide technical assistance from external parties such as development partners or leading consulting firms. After a period of time and once the reforms show results, then the follow up refining, modifying or even revamping process could be implemented based on review feedback. Reflecting Indonesia's BR experience, local context was applied when redesigning Bureaucracy Reform Implementation Self-Assessment (BRISA) to ensure it was "fit-for-purpose" 2 years after reform implementation. Significant changes were made at this stage, for example in the monitoring and evaluation method.
- Setting KPIs and targets for a national BR program also needs careful and proper assessment. Reflecting on Indonesia's BR experience, there was no clear and strong linkage between the BR Road Map and the BR programs for each institution and the improvement areas that will affect BR indicators such as EoDB and Government Competitiveness Index. Consequently, reforms are not necessarily producing the expected impact on Indonesia's status in these international rankings. To improve Indonesia's ranking in the EoDB survey, for example, requires more than just civil service reform. It also requires close coordination with other relevant institutions such as the State Electricity Agency, for example; as a result, the BR impact areas and indicators, as well as BR scoring, were eventually totally revamped.

- Introducing additional allowances for complex reform such as the BR initiative in Indonesia, which tend to follow a "big bang" approach, also needs a solid and careful assessment, as it is not be easy to cancel or withhold or even reduce an allowance that has been given upfront. Furthermore, increasing pay differentials between agencies and grades could demotivate some groups, and eventually derail the objectives of the reform. Firm monitoring and evaluation is necessary to ensure that all staff are accountable and responsible for meeting their targets.
- In the early years when rules and regulations were still outdated and rigid, it took a long time to implement reform since BR agencies had to "work around the system." This caused delays.
- To the extent possible, staff costs should be part of the operational/program budget so that institutions can keep the surplus when they manage to decrease staff costs. This will act as an incentive for rationalization and meaningful reforms. A right-sizing scheme which would enable redundant staff to exit the civil service in a socially and economically acceptable way should also be introduced.

CONCLUSION

The crisis situation helped to facilitate critical public sector reforms and enabled committed leaders to push through some fundamental transformations in the workings of government. However, challenges faced were often related to a lack of appreciation of the need to build flexibility into reform programs. A commitment to implementing off-the-shelf best practice programs within tight deadlines, in a context of risk aversion due to the excessive power and authority of auditors generated a lack of time for local experimentation, made it hard for new ideas and practices to become embedded in the everyday roles of civil servants.

This review of public sector and PFM reform suggests that there are some key factors to be considered in implementation of international practices, beyond the political will of leaders. First, how much experience do leaders and their subordinates have in implementing programs of similar complexity? Complexity does not just mean more steps in the process; it also means more interdependence between different areas, so that that any missed or delayed step has ripple effects through the whole system. Pilot projects in particular agencies can be useful in developing knowledge and capacity, but can also lead to morale-dampening differences between different agencies in the public service. Second, what issues will have to be "worked around"? This could include rigid rules and regulations or entrenched attitudes to the moral acceptability of particular hiring and firing practices. Third, if flexibility is going to be built into implementation, should it also be built into monitoring and evaluation processes? Flexibility in measuring progress allows room for maneuver without the attachment of blame, but also blurs lines of accountability, while inflexibility can lead to risk avoidance. Fourth, what is the most effective way of rewarding good practice? Financial incentives were central to the momentum of Indonesia's reform, but in a context where downsizing the civil service overall was politically impossible, this is a potentially expensive option.

The difficulties and trade-offs to be considered in answering these questions underline the contention that exercise of judgement based upon knowledge of the context is crucial to effective implementation of projects, even when those projects are considered "international best practice." The most standardized approaches will meet a unique set of constraints and obstacles in each context, and managing the process of implementation thus requires tact, experimentation and flexibility in every case.

BIBLIOGRAPHY

Banuri, S., P. Keefer, and M. Kearney. 2012. *Lessons for Bureaucracy Reform from a Survey of Indonesian Public Officials.* Washington, DC: World Bank.

Hashim, A. 2014. *A Handbook on Financial Management Information System for Government: A Practitioner's Guide for Setting Reform Priorities, System Design, and Implementation.* Washington, DC: World Bank.

Hasnain, Z., S. Synnerstrom, E. Ariadharma, and M. Tambunan. 2013. *Pay Policy in the Indonesian Civil Service: Key Issues and Options for Reform.* Washington, DC: World Bank.

Hughes, Caroline, Sokbunthoeun So, Erwin Ariadharma, and Leah April. 2017. "Change Management that Works: Making Impacts in Challenging Environments." Policy Research Working Paper 8265, World Bank, Washington, DC.

Indonesia Ministry of Finance. 2011. *Bureaucracy Reform in the Ministry of Finance: Presentation to World Bank Mission.*

———. 2016. *SPAN Post-Implementation Review Report.*

Ministry of Administrative and Bureaucracy Reforms. 2010a. *The Bureaucracy Reform Road Map 2010–2014.* Jakarta Indonesia: Ministry of Administrative and Bureaucracy Reforms.

———. 2010b. *The Grand Design of Bureaucracy Reform 2010–2025.* Jakarta Indonesia: Ministry of Administrative and Bureaucracy Reforms.

———. 2015. *Bureaucracy Reform Road Map 2015–19.* Jakarta, Indonesia: Ministry of Administrative and Bureaucracy Reform.

PEMNA (The Public Expenditure Management Network in Asia). 2013. *Treasury Community of Practice (T-COP)—FMIS Study of Selected PEMNA Members: Lessons for Other Countries.* Seoul, Republic of Korea: PEMNA Secretariat.

Prasodjo, E. 2012. *Acceleration Programs for Bureaucratic Reforms.* Presentation to International Business Chambers. Jakarta, Indonesia: Ministry of Administrative and Bureaucracy Reform.

Synnerstrom, S., and E. Ariadharma. 2011. "Restructuring of Institutions as Part of Bureaucracy Reform in Indonesia." *The Indonesia Quarterly* 39 (3): 275–282.

Synnerstrom, S., and I. Sumantoro. 2014. *BBL Presentation: The New Civil Service Law—Aparatur Sipil Negara (ASN) Law 5/2014.* Jakarta, Indonesia: World Bank.

World Bank and Ministry of Administrative and Bureaucracy Reform. 2013. *Bureaucracy Reform in Indonesia: Progress—Challenges—Ways Forward.* Jakarta, Indonesia: World Bank.

World Bank. 2004. *Government Financial Management and Revenue Administration Project—Project Appraisal Document.* Washington DC: World Bank.

———. 2011. *Global Expert Team Mission Report and Aide Memoire: Critical Aspects of Bureaucracy Reform.* Washington DC: World Bank.

———. 2012. *Concept Note 2012–2014 Key Result Areas to Accelerate Rationalization, Increase Impact and Control Costs under Bureaucracy Reform.* Washington DC: World Bank.

———. 2016. *Intensive Learning Implementation Completion and Results (ICR) Report for Government Financial Management and Revenue Administration Project (GFMRAP).* Washington DC: World Bank.

World Bank and Indonesia Ministry of Finance 2014. *Cash Management Reform in Indonesia: Making the State Money Work Harder.* Washington DC: World Bank.

World Bank Office Jakarta. *GFMRAP Implementation Support Mission Aide Memoire.* World Bank.

4 Thailand

BUILDING CAPACITY TO ADJUST TO RAPID
CHANGE IN POST-ASIAN FINANCIAL CRISIS
CONTEXT

THANAPAT REUNGSRI

INTRODUCTION

The Asian Financial Crisis in 1997 had disastrous consequences on Thailand. The country's annual real GDP growth rate went down from over 9 percent between 1986 and 1996 to -1.3 percent in 1997 and -9.4 percent in 1998. The crisis severely restricted the government's ability to manage its economic and financial affairs. Lower revenues together with rising expenditures to meet the social needs of the crisis put the government in a difficult situation, especially with regard to providing decent public services. Significant external financing was needed and led to large fiscal deficits.

The crisis highlighted the huge costs associated with poor economic management, which in turn created new opportunities for identifying efficiency enhancement in the public sector. Thailand's government responded by launching a determined program to reform the public sector, Public Sector Management Reform Plan (PSMRP), which provided the vision for a medium-term institutional transformation to "New Public Management," a vision that focused on enhancing performance and accountability. The government's reform agenda during the post crisis era was large and ambitious. Under the "New Public Management" agenda, there were five areas of reform including: (a) the role, mission, and administration of public sector reform; (b) the budget reform to performance based budgeting; (c) human resource management reform; (d) legal reform; and (e) value changes.

This chapter explores the experiences from three PFM/public sector related reforms in Thailand: Strategic Performance Based Budgeting System; Modernization of budget execution through Government Fiscal Management Information System (GFMIS); and Decentralization. The "Performance Based Budgeting" was the key reform introduced with a sophisticated framework. It introduced a totally new concept to the Thai public sector, including devolution of budget control, medium-term expenditure framework, a focus on outputs and outcomes, and monitoring and evaluation on performance indicators. These terms were not easy to understand and took some time for public sector staff to digest.

The modernization of budget execution was a part of the e-government agenda in Thailand. The public-sector reform momentum continued; the government geared up their reform agenda to cover e-government. The e-government committee was set in 2001 to support e-government projects within a 2-year timeline. The GFMIS project was formed to provide a real-time nationwide budget execution and online financial reporting system. Decentralization reform emerged from the new Constitution drafted in 1997 following political unrest in 1992 (known as "Black May"); it sought to increase citizen participation, enhance transparency and accountability, and provide decentralization with guidelines for decentralizing authority and resources to local administrations. These steps were further advanced following the Asian financial crisis. The government enacted the Decentralization Act of 1999 and created the National Decentralization Committee (NDC) chaired by the Prime Minister. The NDC sought to guide the decentralization process by specifying the functions and resources to be devolved from central government agencies to local authorities, as well as the process and time-frame.

Each of the three reform experiences is discussed in detail in the subsequent sections.

STRATEGIC PERFORMANCE BASED BUDGETING SYSTEM

Issues

Prior to the reform, Thailand's budgeting system was characterized as strongly centralized, input controlled, inflexible, and distorted by government agencies. The system was inefficient on both allocative and operational efficiency grounds. The Bureau of the Budget (BoB), the central agency responsible for national budget allocation, placed a heavy emphasis on budget execution relative to budget preparation, reflecting its focus on input controls rather than the results of spending. Linkages among planning, budgeting and sectoral policy were weak. The fiscal planning process only focused on annual budgeting and lacked a medium-term approach. The BoB did not have adequate information technology to support the budget process; there were also transparency and accountability problems. Thai budget coverage was incomplete as many extra-budgetary activities were excluded such as quasi-fiscal activities conducted by the Bank of Thailand (BoT) and state enterprises.

Reform intervention

To increase allocative and operational efficiency, Thailand decided to adopt *performance-based budgeting* which focuses on the performance or output of the agency rather than controlling input. With technical assistance from the World Bank, performance-based budgeting framework in Thailand was drawn from the best practices in various countries such as New Zealand, the Netherlands, the United Kingdom, the United States, and Australia. Performance budgeting is essentially a systematic method of defining an organization's mission, goals, and objectives, then regularly evaluating its performance as a part of the budget process by linking information on inputs, outputs, and outcomes to policy goals and objectives. It represents a shift from micro management of inputs to a focus on results. The integration of performance via explicit measurable output and outcome targets aimed to improve resource allocation and foster service delivery (KPMG 1999).

In 2000, the BoB setup a steering committee, which consisted of BoB executives as well as assigned junior staff to work closely with the experts from the World Bank. The steering committee worked on seven areas of reform: budget planning, output costing, procurement management, budget and funds control, financial and performance reporting, asset management, and internal audit. The seven areas of reform were also known as the "seven hurdles" because it imposed hurdle standards from best practices on line agencies. The reform effort involved reducing controls over line agencies if they achieved hurdle standards (BoB n.d.; Dixon and Dorotinsky 2002). During 2000–01, the manual on the seven hurdles were developed by the experts, along with capacity building with BoB staff.

Moreover, as a part of the budget planning hurdle, a Medium Term Expenditure Framework (MTEF) was introduced in conjunction with the 4-year ministerial action plans which cascade from the overall Government Administrative Plan.[1] The MTEF is a planning framework for linking annual budgeting decisions to medium term spending strategies. It ensures that the future financial implications of new spending decisions in each budget are consistent with medium term fiscal policy targets (KPMG 1999). The MTEF aimed to facilitate the link between policy, planning, and budgeting, as it allowed BoB to extend its annual budget horizon to be consistent with the 5-year National Plan as required by the 2003 Royal Decree on Good Governance. Hence, the term "strategic" was added to Performance Based Budgeting to incorporate the country strategy into the budget formulation; it became known as "Strategic Performance Based Budgeting," which was implemented from FY2003 onward.

In 2002, to implement the performance based budgeting reform, the BoB used a pilot approach by selecting seven government agencies to implement the initial stages of the performance based budgeting process. The memorandum of understanding (MOU) was signed between the BoB and the pilot agencies to formally express the intention to implement the budget reform. If the piloting agency achieved seven hurdles, the BoB would sign the resource agreement. Under the agreement, the BoB would give more fiscal autonomy to the pilot agency by allowing block grants for the budget allocation at the program level. In exchange, the pilot agency needed to prepare financial and performance reports by comparing actual with the pre-set targets. In addition, the pilot agency and the BoB would collaborate to formulate the pilot agency's medium-term expenditure framework (BoB n.d.; Lorsuwannarat 2002).

Results

The implementation of "Strategic Performance Based Budgeting" through a hurdle approach had a partial success due to a limited understanding of the relevant concepts and a lack of timeframe for pilot agencies to upgrade their standards. Unsatisfied by the slow progress, in 2003 the new government led by Prime Minister Thaksin Shinawatra decided to have every government agency and state enterprise prepare their budget on an output basis and incorporate MTEF as well as activity costing to budget planning. The universal implementation was a year sooner than the BoB's original plan and hence posed numerous difficulties as some ministries and some agencies were not up to the task. Pilot agencies lacked a clear understanding of what was required to achieve hurdle standards. Even among different units within the BoB, the understanding of

"Strategic Performance Based Budgeting" and the seven hurdles varied considerably. Many agencies had problems linking planning and budgeting; some agencies were confused about the fundamental concept of strategic planning and could not distinguish between vision and mission; while others believed they would get more budget by identifying several outputs, and so on. Since there was a sudden reform across all the agencies, around half reported they did not have a committee in charge of the reform, while many of them had never received training in strategic planning and MTEF (Lorsuwannarat 2002).

While Thailand has fully adopted performance and results orientation of the budget since 2003, the Parliament's deliberations generally have focused on inputs, while ministries and agencies often formulate and present input-based budget alongside the performance and results budget (Blöndal and Kim 2006). This was because of the lack of support from BoB to reach out to the whole parliament and inform them about the changes in the budgeting system. Most parliamentarians, especially those with experience in budget scrutiny, kept reviewing the budget request on an input-only base as they felt more familiar and comfortable with it. As a result, the BoB had to work on two budgeting systems in parallel. Therefore, the original intention to move toward block grant has never been reached.

Moreover, the MTEF has been providing a medium-term perspective of budget allocation for Thailand. However, the medium-term expenditure projections were not used as a base for the following fiscal year budget request. Hence, the importance of the MTEF subsided. The current MTEF takes an incremental approach based on a fixed percentage but little rational support, while capital MTEF is a stock of capital projects in the agency's pipeline.

Despite the challenges, the reform process resulted in improved linkage between government strategy/policy to budget; for example, the BoB is now able to provide the total expenditure on each strategy/policy. Another achievement is the implementation of performance indicators: quantity and quality on output. The focus of public service delivery has expanded to not only quantity but also quality.

Lesson learned

The budget formulation reform's momentum was driven by a strong political commitment. It was reinforced and sustained after the Thaksin's government announced its Strategic Plan for Thai Public Sector Development, a package of reforms aimed at streamlining public service delivery and increasing overall government efficiency. One of the strategies was financial and budgeting system reform. The concept of New Public Management (NPM), which focuses on measurable outputs and outcomes, transparency and responsiveness to the needs of the public, has been used to reform the Thai bureaucracy (Chongthammakun and Steven 2012). Thus, the budget process has been linked to a performance measurement system.

The strong political commitment provided the necessary authorizing environment; however, the readiness of civil servants for implementation is key. Reform is a time-consuming process, requiring mutual understanding between stakeholders. It was not the case that Thailand ignored capacity building as the part of the reform: BoB officials received training on relevant issues from the World Bank as a component of the Economic Management Assistance Loan and the Public Sector Reform Loan (KPMG 1999; Sidgwick 2006); BoB also organized several training sessions for line agencies. However, line ministries thought that the trainings were inefficient and ineffective as they were lecture oriented and included no workshop opportunities to practice new skills (Lorsuwannarat 2002). Lastly, there were too many reform initiatives launched during that time (Lorsuwannarat 2002; Scott 2003). As a result, it was hard for agencies to prioritize those changes and mobilize resources.

There were many reasons accounting for the reform challenges in Thailand but the most important one was a combination of a limited institutional capacity among ministries and agencies, overly complicated measures, and a phasing of the reform. From the implementation of the hurdle approach and the strategic performance based budgeting, the measures were too hard to achieve (Blöndal and Kim 2006; Lorsuwannarat 2002) and beyond the capacities of ministries and agencies. Thailand's long history of a highly centralized budget system had undermined agency management competency which reinforced resistance to change. Similarly, Thailand's seven hurdle approach was too complex and too expansive. In fact, easing central control could involve just two hurdles: (a) a computer-based accounting system that meets basic financial control and reporting standards; and (b) identification and costing of agency outputs. Moreover, there should have been a stronger focus on solving immediate needs such as basic financial management system in line agencies rather than later-stage reforms such as introducing accrual budgeting (Dixon and Dorotinsky 2002).

GOVERNMENT FISCAL MANAGEMENT INFORMATION SYSTEM

Issues

Prior to the reform, budget disbursement and accounting were done manually. There was no IT connection between BoB for budget preparation, parliament for budget adoption, and the CGD for budget execution and monitoring (Koeberle et al. 2000). The budget transferring system was complex and time consuming. The process was inefficient, labor intensive, and involved many hierarchies. Every transaction required documents as reference. There was no real-time access to financial data in the public sector, which impeded budget accountability and transparency (KPMG 1999). The accounting system used was a "Cash Basis" classified by program, work, or project and, further, breakdown to type of expenditure according to budget classification from the BoB. Since the accounting system was a cash basis, it was not able to accommodate performance based budgeting, which requires an accrual basis to measure output costs.

Reform intervention

The modernization of budget execution was a part of the e-government agenda in Thailand during Thaksin Shinawatra's government. When he came to power, he announced the policy on June 16, 2001 that: "I wish to see this government as 'e-government'", the government that uses electronics and uses most of internet for faster and convenient service delivery. The e-government committee was set in 2001 to support e-government projects within a 2-year timeline. Examples of e-government projects include smart card, e-auction, and e-passport. The Ministry of Information and Communication Technology was established in 2002 as a mechanism to push e-government, e-industry, e-commerce, e-education, and e-society (Lorsuwannarat 2006). Information Communication Technology Master Plan (2002–06) was formulated in 2003 to support e-government to increase efficiency of the administration and service delivery of the public sector. The GFMIS project was formed by the Cabinet resolution on 22 July 2003.

The GFMIS deployment initiative's objectives were (a) to execute the budget online and real-time across the country; (b) adopt accrual accounting standards and fiscal reserve management according to International Public Sector Accounting Standard (IPSAS); (c) develop electronic payment system; (d) establish computer system, network and data center with disaster recovery center for public financial works, both in central and regional by fiscal year 2005; and (5) develop core public expenditure database which also include personnel expenditure system, civil servant management system, e-procurement system to monitor and evaluate accounting and financial aspects.

The GFMIS is a comprehensive integrated computerized fiscal management system covering all activities related to public finance management. It receives budget allocation data from the e-budgeting system at the BoB to provide a real-time nationwide budget execution and financial reporting, which further reinforced the fiscal transparency by improving quality and timeliness of the data. The operating system of GFMIS supported by SAP R/3 software consists of five components, including fund management, purchasing order, human resource, financial information, and cost accounting (GFMIS n.d.).

The Comptroller General's Department (CGD), the agency responsible for cash management of the government, is the main agency responsible in GFMIS development and carried out the implementation including training for line agency as GFMIS user. The other was the Krung Thai Bank (state enterprise) whose task was outsourcing a private company to design and install the systems (Lorsuwannarat 2006).

In October 2003, six central agencies including BoB, CGD, Public Debt Management Office (PDMO), Office of the Auditor General (OAG), Office of the Civil Service Commission (OCSC), Office of the Public Sector Development Commission (OPDC) and four line ministries including Ministry of ICT, Ministry of Energy, Provincial Authority, and Independent agency were chosen to pilot the GFMIS. In 2005, 1,200 computers and terminals were installed at central and line agencies. The provincial unit of CGD took care of data entry for agencies in the province and facilitating agencies in accrual accounting.

Results

The government officially implemented the GFMIS nationwide in 2005 (World Bank 2012b). For Thailand, the deployment of GFMIS established internal system controls and reduced fiduciary risks. The GFMIS has successfully standardized government financial procedures and centralized the government control of financial management among agencies throughout the country. It has made financial transactions faster and the transactions more transparent, as CGD can monitor agency expenditures at all times (Chongthammakun and Steven 2012).

Lesson learned

In implementing the GFMIS, the government encountered some technical challenges. At that time, Thailand had low readiness in information technology in terms of infrastructure, computer literacy, and accessibility of the internet. The communication network in Thailand was not secured and sometimes not reliable. The preparation of a system and data center was not ready: there were insufficient GFMIS terminals and the system would crash during periods of high traffic. Moreover, there was a problem with limited knowledge and competency of staff in operating GFMIS (Jewseng 2012; Lorsuwannarat 2006; Suksaenrat and Sirichote 2009). These technical challenges have been solved through continuous investment in IT infrastructure, regular training of staff on how to operate GFMIS, and the establishment of GFMIS division under the CGD to drive implementation.

Other challenges were adaptive in nature. There was strong political commitment, which led to a timely implementation. The GFMIS project took less than 2 years to implement country-wide; however, the required adjustment was more challenging. Diamond and Khemani (2006) pointed out that implementing Financial Management Information Systems (FMIS) takes time and requires change management: the steps usually involve preparatory requirements analysis, system design, development and testing; procurement and installation; testing the full system in the user environment; training and conversion. Comprehensive FMIS projects take a minimum of 6–7 years to complete (Dener, Watkins, and Dorotinsky 2011). An overly short time horizon can also adversely impact the project due to poor system design and development. The government had to continuously invest in IT infrastructure, staff capacity building, and the core responsible institutions in order to improve and maintain reform momentum over time.

DECENTRALIZATION

Issues

Prior to the decentralization reforms, Thailand was a highly-centralized country with limited local autonomy in terms of functions, staffing, funding, and decision making (Sidgwick 2006). During the 1990s, Thailand experienced rapid economic growth, which resulted in significant improvements in the living standards of its people. However, the benefits were unevenly shared. Thailand experienced wide regional disparities in income as well as access to education and health care (World Bank 2012a). Thailand's economic development and the spread of democratic ideas throughout the country led its citizen to be more keenly aware of their rights and thus to demand more political participation (Dufhues et al. 2011).

Reform intervention

The 1997 Constitution brought in reforms aimed at decentralizing service delivery responsibility and finances to local authorities. These reforms were intended to make public services more efficient and led to increased public participation in decision making at the local level, and enhanced local economic development (World Bank 2012b). To be specific, chapter V of the 1997 constitution provided the key principle of decentralization and mandated the state to "decentralize powers to localities for the purpose of independence and self- determination of local affairs"; chapter IX (section 282 to 290) also focused on decentralization and local government.

The government embarked its plan by enacting the Decentralization Act of 1999 and creating the NDC chaired by the Prime Minister. The aim of the NDC was to guide the decentralization process by specifying the functions and resources to be devolved from central government agencies to local authorities, as well as the process and time-frame for doing so (World Bank 2012a).

The transfer of services from the central to local level was based on a written agreement between a branch office of the central government and the local authority. The transferred functions consisted of six areas: (a) infrastructure; (b) promotion of quality of life; (c) maintenance of social order and peace; (d) planning and investment promotion, commerce and tourism; (e) management and conservation of natural resources and the environment; and (f) arts, culture, tradition, and local wisdom. In general, the easier services have the earlier target year of completion (Nagai, Tsuruyo, and Kagoya 2008). A total of 245 activities from 50 central departments under 11 ministries were chosen to be devolved within 10 years (ERTC 2008). The transferred functions can be divided into two categories: the optional functions or activities for local authorities, and the mandatory functions that local authorities must perform (Varanyuwatana and Laovakul 2010). Prior to assuming the responsibilities, the local governments needed to meet readiness criterion such as local capacity and performance levels set by the central government. These transferred responsibilities were to be closely linked to expenditure assignments (World Bank 2012a).

On the revenue side, Thailand adopted a revenue sharing approach in reallocating revenue from the central government to lower levels of jurisdiction (Varanyuwatana and Laovakul 2010). The Decentralization Act of 1999 clearly specified that the central government must increase the share of local revenue to at least 35 percent of total government income by 2006, which was an increase from 11 percent in 1999 (ERTC 2008; Nagai, Tsuruyo, and Kagoya 2008; Varanyuwatana and Laovakul 2010; World Bank 2012a). However, in 2009 this target was subsequently revised to 25 percent (World Bank 2012a). The NDC approved the formula for grant allocation (Varanyuwatana and Laovakul 2010). Intergovernmental transfer of human resources was mandated to harmonize with revenue and function transfers, under the condition that transferred personnel's work status and benefits must not be worse off compared to the current employment.

Results

The decentralization initiatives have increased government officials' responsiveness to local demands by expanding access and improving quality of services. A total of 181 services have been transferred to Local Administrative Organizations (LAOs), and those with sufficient capacity have significantly improved their services in response to local needs. For example, garbage collection, water and sewage systems, electricity, and roads services quality within the local community have been improved and maintained. Moreover, many LAOs have developed plans to promote local commerce and tourism which stimulating the local economy. Decentralization also promoted democracy by providing opportunities for political participation, such as elections for head of LAO and council members.

To evaluate the progress of decentralization in Thailand over the past two decades (1997–2013), the Prime Minister's Office, through the Office of National Decentralization Committee (ONDC), contracted researchers from the Faculty of Political Science, Chulalongkorn University, to assess the decentralization's outcomes. The report was in Thai language and very comprehensive, titled "Evaluation Report on Decentralization in Thailand (1997–2013)." Using a sample of 110 local governments from various part of Thailand comprising local governments of all sizes and local contexts, a household survey of 11,430 local residents in the sampled local jurisdictions was conducted, along with several focus group meetings; the study found that decentralization in Thailand has been moderately successful. Local governments are providing more variety of public services that are more readily accessible. These services are also more effectively directed toward indigent, disadvantaged, and low-income people.

Regarding the intergovernmental transfer of functions/services, the study found more limited progress. Out of 245 services, there are 181 services have been transferred, 63 services are still in the hands of the central government, and 1 service under natural resource and environmental protection got cancelled. Most transferred functions are programs on public infrastructure investment and programs on improvement of quality of life. The transfer of functions has encountered several problems, such as the transferred services not corresponding with local contexts or needs, limited capacity of local governments to delivery services, and lack of technical support from the central government. This corresponds to the finding of World Bank (2012a): the local governments are not ready for these extra tasks, especially in health and education; consequently, there has also been a limited transfer of expenditure responsibilities.

The revenue side of the reform has progressed moderately successfully. Most local governments have identical revenue sources: locally levied revenue, centrally shared revenue, and grants or subsidies from the central government. Nonetheless, local governments are heavily relying on shared taxes (50 percent) and subsidies (39 percent) from the central government; only 11 percent that local government can collect these by themselves. Currently, about 25 percent of total central government income is redistributed, still less than the mandatory level of 35 percent. To achieve the mandatory level, the political commitment needs to be strengthened.

The authors also pointed out three main limitations in this area. Firstly, local governments still have limited revenue raising powers, particularly on local tax bases. Secondly, the budgeting and accounting standards of local government need a lot of improvement. For example, there is a weak link between budgeting and outcomes, especially among small localities. The accounting standards are not aligned with the Generally Accepted Accounting Principles (GAAP). Thirdly, there is insufficient monitoring and evaluation from the central government in terms of spending review and fiscal monitoring. Without careful monitoring and evaluation, the financial management of local governments remains inefficient and ineffective.

The findings are aligned with the World Bank's study (2012a). That is, decentralization reforms in Thailand have emphasized increasing the share of net central government revenues, rather than providing greater opportunities and incentives for local self-financing to enhance local government accountability to residents. Additionally, while the Department of Local Administration (DOLA) has implemented an electronic Local Authority Accounting System (e-LAAS) for local authorities to use for budget management since 2005, less than 20 percent of local governments have actually adopted it. Furthermore, the review of local performance conducted by DOLA focuses on process compliance, rather than quality of services and outcomes. As a result, there is not much information on local government finances, fiscal conditions, and service delivery outcomes, which aggravates the accountability problem.

Varanyuwatana and Laovakul (2010) have also pointed out the tradeoff of revenue sharing approaches used by Thailand. The advantage of this approach includes the continuity of revenue received by the local government to finance transferred functions, compared to the discretionary local revenue raising approach. However, since the size of local revenue is arbitrarily determined due to poor accounting/reporting practices of local government, it strains the fiscal capacity of central government to transfer revenue to local governments as required by the law. Moreover, the transferred revenue has displaced the local revenue generating powers, as evidenced by the decline of locally collected revenues, which might worsen the local accountability problem. The formula employed in allocating revenue also fails to capture the differences in economic conditions and fiscal needs of each jurisdiction, which might in turn worsen fiscal inequality among local governments across the country.

The intergovernmental transfer of human resources was not successful. The process consisted of three phases. By the end of phase one (in 2003), only about 4,111 staff have been transferred to local governments; most of them came from the Department of Public Works and the Department of Accelerating Rural Development. By the end of phase two (in 2004), an additional 348 staff from the Department of Social Development and Welfare and the Department of Cooperative Promotion had been transferred. During 2007–08, an additional 89 staff from the Ministry of Public Health had been transferred. It is important to note that these numbers exclude teachers and other education personnel. If that the total number of civil servants in Thailand is around 2 million people, the total number of transferred personnel is thus less than 1 percent, reflecting an imbalance between the transfer of services and the transfer of human resources. The study pointed out that small localities usually received hundreds of service transfers, while on average the transfer of personnel is only about 1–2 personnel. According to World Bank (2012a), there are approximately 7,853 LAOs in Thailand; more than 3,000 LAOs have populations of less than 5,000 people, and many of these have less than 1,000 people. As a result, the small LAOs have limited capacity to provide these services efficiently and effectively. The 40 percent cap on personnel expenditures to total local spending imposes the burden on small Tambon/Sub-district Administrative Organizations (TAO/SAO), which usually already have high workloads. The cap restricts the number of employees it can hire, which negatively impacts the service quality the local people get.

Green (2005) drew a similar conclusion that the problem was driven from both central government and local governments. Central government did not want to let their staff go; poorer local government, especially the TAO, were reluctant to accept more staff because of the tight budget. Moreover, employees hesitated to move as the policies were not clear on comparable pay, benefits (including pension fund provisions), recruitment, dismissal procedures, and career mobility.

Lesson learned

The key lesson learned from Thailand's decentralization reform has also confirmed the importance of understanding the capacity of the stakeholders. The decentralization reform was well planned and detailed in the constitution, which provided sustainability and continuity. The implementation strategy was planned to increase the responsibility and accountability of the local authorities in public services delivery, which expected to be supported with greater human resource reallocation and share of revenue from central to local government. However, there are too many small LAOs to be administratively viable because, after accounting for the fixed cost for administration, very small LAOs will have few resources left to provide services. This, in turn, has fixed the target of revenue sharing at 25 percent instead of at least 35 percent of total government income because the central government still provides most public services.

REFLECTIONS ON THE APPROACHES

Two different approaches were observed in the case of Thailand's Public Sector Reform. Both Performance Based Budgeting and GFMIS reform have adopted "best practices" from other countries and took a "big bang" approach to implementation. On the contrary, the decentralization reforms were implemented through a systematic but gradual approach.

The "best practice" approach was adopted on Performance Based Budgeting and GFMIS reforms. They were new concepts to Thailand during the reform period 20 years ago. Thailand was the pioneer in the region that went through the reforms. Hence, examples from countries with a similar context were not available; drawing on "best practice" was thus the most sensible (perhaps only) option. It is also important to point out that the government was cautious on the distinction between the best practice and current level of public sector capacity. As a result, a "pilot approach" was used prior to the full deployment nationwide, doing so on the basis of a local experiment. This allowed the Thai government to have a better understanding of potential problems when implementing the reforms in Thailand's different contexts, and thus meant they were better prepared to solve those problems. However, a pilot approach takes time to obtain results and to make the necessary adjustments before full implementation. The "big bang" implementations that were used on both reforms to expedite the reform process faced strong adaptive challenges. Readiness to change was important and adequate prior preparation was thus necessary.

On the other hand, decentralization efforts in Thailand reflect a "localized" solution combined with a "systematic but gradual" implementation approach. It can be claimed that the decentralization reforms were demand driven or bottom up; the public was demanding political reform after the 1992 incidents which had brought along the 1997 Constitution that mandated decentralization as a national basic policy. The Decentralization Act of 1999, then, provided the basis for the concrete process of decentralization in Thailand. The setting of NDC to formulate, plan, implement and monitor decentralization processes has maintained the reform momentum. The duties and responsibilities among different types of local government were clearly specified. The sources of revenue for local governments have been arranged.

CONCLUSION

The key achievements of Thailand's Public Sector Reform can be summarized as follow. First, Performance Based Budgeting, in particular the linkage between planning and budgeting, has been improved where budget allocation strategy derived from the national strategy, government policy, and the national economic and social development plan. The focus on results has been emphasized through ministry and agency's measurable performance targets and indicators. A certain level of budget control has been transferred to line agencies. The medium-term perspective has been implanted through MTEF. Second, the GFMIS system has established standardized and centralized government control of financial management among agencies throughout the country. It has also increased financial transactions speed and transparency. Lastly, decentralization has improved public services in response to local needs. The local economy has been enhanced through the promotion of local commerce and tourism. Election of the head of LAO and the council members has also promoted democracy.

The reform implementation process requires patience, i.e., a timeframe which allows sufficient time for the public sector to adjust; but not too lengthy, as this risks losing the momentum. The big bang approach driven by the top of the government put further pressure on the already very ambitious implementation schedule for "performance based budgeting" and GFMIS. Every government agency and state enterprise was required to prepare budgets on an output basis and to incorporate the MTEF in fiscal year 2003, a year sooner than implementing schedule. On the GFMIS, the process from designing the system to implementation throughout the country took only 22 months while similar FMIS projects elsewhere may take a minimum of 6–7 years to complete.

Political commitment facilitates speedy adoption of reform policy and creates the necessary conditions for reform to progress. However, understanding the public-sector context is also important. The combination of a limited institutional capacity among ministries and agencies, overly complicated measures, and overly short time horizon can adversely impact the reform. There was limited bottom-up initiative and ownership to meet the top-down push. In addition, the design of the "hurdles" required for ministries to progress to performance based budgeting with greater autonomy over allocation of funds involved a best practices approach. Consequently, the Performance Based Budgeting system has only been partially utilized and is currently running two budgeting systems in parallel: Performance Based Budgeting as a main with Line-Item as a supplementary. On the GFMIS, during the accelerated implementation, constraints arose due to Thailand's low readiness in information technology in terms of infrastructure, computer literacy, and accessibility of internet. However, these technical challenges have been addressed with continuous investment in IT infrastructure and staff capacity building.

In contrast, decentralization took a systematic and gradual approach to reform. The results of decentralization in Thailand have been relatively successful but also highlighted the importance of understanding the capacity of stakeholders. Both human and financial resources were arranged to facilitate the transfer of functions from central to local authorities. Many LAOs with sufficient capacity have successfully delivering quality services to the local level. However, there are many small LAOs with limited capacity which has caused delays in the reform process and lessened the degree of reform success.

NOTE

1. Government Administrative Plan is the statement of four-year policies including objectives, the agency or entities responsible for each mission and the related estimated income and expenditure estimates, and the proposed results for monitoring and evaluation measures.

BIBLIOGRAPHY

Amornvivat, Sutapa. 2004. *Fiscal Decentralization—The Case of Thailand*. Bangkok: Ministry of Finance. http://www.econ.hit-u.ac.jp/~kokyo/APPPsympo04/FiscDect%20_Thailand.pdf.

Blöndal, Jón R., and Sang-In Kim. 2006. "Budgeting in Thailand." *OECD Journal of Budgeting* 5 (3): 7–36. http://www.oecd.org/countries/thailand/40140263.pdf.

BOB (Bureau of the Budget). n.d. *Budget Modernization.* http://www.bb.go.th/bb/information /reform/his01.htm.

Chongthammakun, Radaphat, and Steven J. Jackson. 2012. *Computerization and Control.* https://www.academia.edu/1134741/Computerization_and_Control_ICTs_and _Managerial_Reform_in_the_Thai_Public_Sector?auto=download.

Chulalongkorn University. 2014. *Evaluation Report on Decentralization in Thailand (1997–2013).* Bangkok, Thailand. http://www.odloc.go.th/web/wp-content/uploads/2014/12 /242.pdf.

Coompanthu, Sawanya. 2007. "The Analysis of Budgeting System Reform in Thailand." Thesis paper submitted to KDI School of Public Policy and Management, Seoul. http://archives .kdischool.ac.kr/bitstream/11125/982/1/COOMPANTHU,%20Sawanya.pdf.

Dener, Cem, Joanna Alexandra Watkins, and William Leslie Dorotinsky. 2011. *Financial Management Information Systems: 25 Years of World Bank Experience on What Works and What Doesn't.* A World Bank Study. Washington, DC: World Bank.

Diamond, Jack, and Pokar Khemani. 2006. "Introducing Financial Management Information Systems in Developing Countries." *OECD Journal on Budgeting* 5 (3): 97. https://www.oecd .org/gov/budgeting/43480378.pdf.

Dixon, Geoffrey, and Bill Dorotinsky. 2002. *Thailand's Hurdle Approach to Budget Reform.* PREM Notes 73. Public Sector. World Bank Group, Washington, DC. http://documents.worldbank .org/curated/en/663331468102887583/Thailands-hurdle-approach-to-budget-reform.

Dufhues, Thomas, Insa Theesfeld, Gertrud Buchenrieder, and Nuchanata Munkung. 2011. "The Political Economy of Decentralization in Thailand—Does Decentralization Allow for Peasant Participation?" Paper presented at the EAAE 2011 Congress, Zurich. http:// ageconsearch.umn.edu/bitstream/114428/2/Dufhues_Thomas_106.pdf.

ERTC (Economic Research and Training Center Faculty of Economics), Thammasat University. 2008. *An Analysis of the Decentralized Budget for Social Services at the Tambon Administrative Organization (TAO) Level.* Bangkok, Thailand: FSPNetwork company limited.

Government Financial Management Information. n.d. *GFMIS: Principles and Scope of Work.* http://www.gfmis.go.th/gfmis_us2.html.

Green, Amanda E. 2005. *Managing Human Resources in a Decentralized Context. East Asia Decentralizes: Making Local Government Work,* 129–53. Washington, DC: World Bank. http://siteresources.worldbank.org/INTEAPDECEN/Resources/Chapter-7.pdf.

Inkakul, Chitra. 2007. *Government Fiscal Management Information System: GFMIS.* Bangkok: Thailand: Faculty of Political Science, Thammasat University.

International Monetary Fund. 2000. *Recovery from the Asian Crisis and the Role of the IMF.* https://www.imf.org/external/np/exr/ib/2000/062300.htm.

——. 2009. *Thailand: Report on Observance of Standards and Codes—Fiscal Transparency Module.* IMF Country Report 9/250. Washington, DC: International Monetary Fund. https://www.imf.org/external/pubs/ft/scr/2009/cr09250.pdf.

Jewseng, Wilailug. 2012. *Problems and Obstacles in the Application of Government Fiscal Management Information System (GFMIS): A Case Study of the Department of Fisheries.* http://www.repository.rmutt.ac.th/bitstream/handle/123456789/2308/145004 .pdf?sequence=1.

Koeberle, Stefan G., Dana Weist, Lars M. Sondergaard, Jamie Vazquez-Caro, and Bill McLeary. 2000. *Thailand—Public Finance in Transition.* Washington, DC: World Bank. http:// documents.worldbank.org/curated/en/240161468312019690/Thailand-Public-Finance-in -Transition.

Kokpol, Orathai. 2011. "Decentralization Process in 1990–2010: In Case of Thailand." Presented at the 1st Meeting of Research Committee of Decentralization in Asian Countries, Tokyo. http://kpi.ac.th/media/pdf/M10_141.pdf.

KPMG Barents Group, LLC. 1999. *Volume 1: Evaluation and Diagnostic of Existing Budget Process.* Public Resource Management Project Component 2—Modernizing. Washington, DC: Budget Management.

Litvack, Jennie, Junaid Ahmad, and Richard Bird. 2002. *Rethinking Decentralization in Developing Countries*. Washington, DC: World Bank. http://www1.worldbank.org /publicsector/decentralization/Rethinking%20Decentralization.pdf.

Lorsuwannarat, Tippawan. 2002. *Budget Reform in Thailand: Case of Budget Preparation in Fiscal Year 2003*. School of Public Administration, National Institute of Development Administration. http://gspa.grade.nida.ac.th/Dr_tippwan/otherarticle/BudgetReform%20 inThailand_case_of_Budget_Preparation_in_Fiscal_Year_2003.pdf.

——. 2006. "E-Government in Thailand: Development or Illusion." *Asian Review of Public Administration* XVIII (1–2): 12–24. https://pdfs.semanticscholar.org/bfd0 /28748f9f815220e2db00318c93155028fa5d.pdf.

Mahakanjana, Chandranuj. 2004. *Municipal Governments, Social Capitals, and Decentralization in Thailand*. Northern Illinois University. http://202.28.199.34/multim/3132425.pdf.

Nagai, Fumio, Funatsu Tsuruyo, and Kazuhiro Kagoya. 2008. "Central-Local Government Relationship in Thailand." In *Local Government in Thailand-Analysis of the Local Administrative Organization Survey*, 1–30. Chiba, Japan: Institute of Developing Economies. http://www.ide.go.jp/library/English/Publish/Download/Jrp/pdf/147_1.pdf.

Nimmanahaeminda, Tarrin. 2000. *Thailand's Reform Program for the Challenges Ahead*. Keynote Speech of the Minister of Finance, Government of Thailand, Washington DC, April 14. http://unpan1.un.org/intradoc/groups/public/documents/apcity/unpan005109.pdf.

Office of the National Economic and Social Development Board. 2017. *National Income of Thailand*. http://www.nesdb.go.th/main.php?filename=ni_page.

Scott, Graham. 2003. "Reform of Budgeting Management in Thailand." In *The Bureau of the Budget Year Book*, 185–88. Bangkok, Thailand.

Sidgwick, Eric. 2006. *Thailand—Country Development Partnership: Governance and Public Sector Reform (CDP-G): Program Assessment and Implementation Completion Report*. Washington, DC: World Bank.

Sujiworapanpong, Warunyoo. 2004. "GFMIS." Proceeding in GFMIS workshop at Royal Irrigation Department, 24 April 2004. http://kromchol.rid.go.th/reform/gfmis.html.

Suksaenrat, Kanokwan, and Poranee Sirichote. 2009. *Problems in the Use of Government Fiscal Management Information System: A Case of Budgeting Account Payable of Khon Kaen Provincial Social Development and Human Security Office*. https://www.tci-thaijo.org/index .php/jiskku/article/view/6681/5775.

Varanyuwatana, Sakon, and Duangmanee Laovakul. 2010. "Progress of Fiscal Decentralization in Thailand: Impacts and Challenges of Decentralization Policy towards Democratization and Development (A Comparative Perspective between Thailand and Indonesia)." Proceeding in International Joint Seminar, Laboratory of Governmental Studies, University of Muhammadiyah, Yogyakarta, Indonesia. https://www.researchgate.net/profile /Duangmanee_Laovakul/publication/305083127_Progress_of_Fiscal_Decentralization_in _Thailand/links/5781474b08ae9485a43bdad5/Progress-of-Fiscal-Decentralization-in -Thailand.pdf.

Weist, Dana. 2001. "Thailand's Decentralization: Progress and Prospects." A paper presented at the KPI Annual Congress III on Decentralization and Local Government in Thailand, November 10–11.

——. 2003. "Reflections on Thailand's Budget Reform." In *The Bureau of the Budget Year Book*, 192–94.

World Bank. 1999. *Thailand: Public Sector Reform Loan Project*. Washington, DC: World Bank.

——. 2009. *Kingdom of Thailand—Public Expenditure and Financial Accountability: Public Financial Management Assessment*. Washington, DC: World Bank.

——. 2012a. *Central-Local Government Relations in Thailand: Improving Service Delivery*. Bangkok: World Bank. License: CC BY 3.0 IGO. https://openknowledge.worldbank.org /handle/10986/17362.

——. 2012b. *Overview*. Public expenditure review (PER). Washington, DC: World Bank. http:// documents.worldbank.org/curated/en/993671468118138134/Overview.

Kostenbaum, Silvana, and Dener, Cem. 2015. "Managing Change in PFM System Reforms : A Guide for Practitioners (English)." Washington, DC World Bank Group. http://documents. worldbank.org/curated/en/993981509959603664/Managing-change-in-PFM-system- reforms-a-guide-for-practitioners.

5 Cambodia

STRENGTHENING PUBLIC FINANCIAL MANAGEMENT FUNCTIONS THROUGH ADAPTATION AND EXPERIMENTATION UNDER PLATFORM APPROACH

SOKBUNTHOEUN SO, LEAH APRIL, PISITH PHLONG, KOK HONG CHEA, PRATHNA MAUN, and CAROLINE HUGHES

INTRODUCTION

Cambodia is a post-conflict state whose current institutions emerged quite recently in a context of high levels of violence and low levels of human development. The current political settlement and state apparatus in Cambodia have their antecedents in the aftermath of the catastrophic levels of death and destruction unleashed upon Cambodia by the Cold War and the Democratic Kampuchea or "Khmer Rouge" regime. The Vietnamese invasion of Cambodia in 1979 ousted the Khmer Rouge, and began the task of rebuilding the state and state services in the context of international isolation and continued internationally backed insurgency throughout the 1980s (Gottesman 2004). The end of the Cold War and the Vietnamese withdrawal from Cambodia in 1989 brought a new era of free market and democratic reforms. A peace deal in 1991 gave rise to a peace-keeping mission which presided over elections in 1993 and the remnants of the insurgency were finally defeated in 1998 (Hughes 2003).

Following the general election of 1993, a comprehensive macroeconomic policy and structural reform program was implemented. This integrated Cambodia into the global economy and facilitated Cambodia's membership of ASEAN and the WTO. The policy was effective in liberalizing and stabilizing the economy, and since the 1990s annual growth has averaged 6 percent–7 percent, while inflation has been contained below 5 percent per year (see various Cambodia Economic Update n.d.; RGC 2004).

Problems of public administration and public financial management (PFM) reform in Cambodia reflected the legacies of civil war and post-conflict state building from the 1980s and 1990s when current state institutions were built.

The context of scarce resources, low human capacities, and continued insurgency and violent political competition entailed that new state structures emerged as steeply hierarchical entities, with strong informal ties of loyalty between lower level functionaries and charismatic leaders, reliance on labor-intensive manual processes comprising numerous simple steps, and limited horizontal interaction. These ways of working are deeply entrenched in the Cambodian public administration.

Since 2013, a new political imperative has emerged to significantly upgrade business processes and improve efficiency in revenue collection, budgeting and service delivery, using new techniques and technologies that require skill and initiative on the part of public servants. The Cambodian government has attempted to drive through these changes through harnessing internationally validated technology systems and working processes, but in doing so has run up against entrenched relationships, attitudes and ways of working in the ministries. An "evolutionary" approach that goes step by step has been crucial to success, and experience shows that permitting middle managers to experiment with new technologies can boost their support. A change management (CM) strategy to promote new working relationships and ways of communicating within ministries was also important to the reform program's success.

An assessment of Cambodia's PFM system in 2002 concluded that PFM was inefficient and that weaknesses created "high levels of fiduciary risk (Taliercio 2009)." Reliance on unpredictable cash payments caused delays, undermined planning and caused backlogs of arrears. At the time the system ranked "well below average" and that it "was plagued by gate-keeping and deficient accounting and reporting systems, thus leading to a weak control environment and increasing opportunities for corruption (Taliercio 2009)."

The Ministry of Economy and Finance (MEF) then launched the Public Finance Management Reform Program (PFMRP) in 2004. The program was characterized by an innovative platform approach, which envisaged four different levels of reform taking place sequentially: (a) enhancing the reliability and predictability of the budget, (b) improving financial accountability, (c) ensuring affordable and prioritized policies linked to the budget, and (d) accountability for results (budget managers become fully accountable for their programs' performance).

Coinciding with increased political stability and high economic growth, the Platform approach has been much more successful, enabling Cambodia to achieve significant progress in reforming public expenditure policy and public finance. Tax revenue administration was strengthened. Budget preparation and management, macro-fiscal discipline, and debt management has improved. Commitments and payment processes were streamlined. The use of cash for government transactions has decreased. Unauthorized bank accounts were closed and the Treasury Single Account was strengthened. As assessed by the External Advisory Panel (EAP) in January 2010, most PFMRP performance indicators under the PFM Platform-one were met. Stage/Platform-two, which began in 2009, focused on providing greater financial authority to line managers while simultaneously ensuring more accountability through the implementation of a Financial Management Information System (FMIS). The FMIS became a system of record for the government in 2017. The government also began to embark on its Stage/platform 3 in 2016.

One of the keys to this success was that platform approach to PFM reform under the PFMRP was well sequenced and considered to be "best fit" for

Cambodia and the general preference for evolution and not revolution in the approach to reform. The platform approach enabled strong government ownership, whole system rather than fragmented/piecemeal effort, and prioritization of what need to be done first in order to support further progress. The approach allows the details of "how to" to emerge and to be adapted as experience is gained, creating room for those most involved in the problem and its consequences to develop and experiment with solutions. It is a mixture of top down and bottom up. The order in which problems are tackled matters as progress of one efforts built the foundation for the next step. Further, the PFMRP followed a sector-wide approach in which all development partners active in PFM are coordinated to avoid duplication of effort and increase synergies in programming and policy dialogue coordination.[1]

This chapter focuses on 3 areas of PFM reform efforts in Cambodia—revenue mobilization, budget execution through implementation of the FMIS, and program budgeting. Each of the three areas is an important element under platform 1, 2, 3 respectively of the PFMRP and represents the order of priority for reform intervention under the program from its inception. They are discussed in detail including specific issues, reform interventions, results, and approaches/lessons learned in the subsequent sections.

REVENUE MOBILIZATION

Issues

In 2004, generating sufficient revenue for public expenditure was a key challenge. The national budget was not credible in large part due to poor revenue collection. Chronic cash shortages resulted in payment arrears which reached a quarter of the domestically financed budget in 2004. This together with poor budget and expenditure planning lead to delays in paying government employee salaries which, in turn, resulted in poor quality services to citizens. Cash rations were introduced to finance priority sectors and activities such as education and health under what was called priority action plan (PAP).

Reform intervention

Strengthening budget credibility and ensuring that sufficient revenues are generated to support public expenditure has been an immediate and ongoing priority under the PFMRP. A series of measures were taken since 2004 to improve revenue including restructuring of MEF with the establishment of non-tax revenue department, establishment of inter-departmental working groups, and procedures for recruitment of qualified and experienced officials, and provision of merit-based remuneration for 250 staff to implement the PFMRP. Simplified procedures, time-saving for tax payers, strict auditing led to some improvement in tax collection from large and medium tax payers (see EIC 2005, 51–53). The effort is further strengthened in 2012 beginning with new management for the main revenue collecting agencies. This began with an appointment of a new leadership in the General Department of Taxation (GDT) in 2012, followed by the introduction of the Revenue Mobilization Strategy 2014–18 (RMS) in late 2013 and appointment of a new director general for the General Department of Customs and Excise (GDCE) in 2014.

The RMS was issued after the national election in 2013 to respond to the development needs of the government of Cambodia. The main target of the RMS was to increase revenue by 0.5 percent of gross domestic product (GDP) per year to finance rising civil service pay and other public expenditures and investments. Improving civil servants' pay was considered as a necessary condition in order to enhance the quality of public service delivery. This was necessary to respond to public demand and to adapt to Cambodia's imminent change of status to a lower middle-income economy (in 2015). As a lower middle-income country, Cambodia's access to grant aid, concessional lending and trade preferential treatments is gradually eroding. The country would need to invest in infrastructure and public services in order to tackle new development issues that reflect the increasingly sophisticated nature of the economy. The introduction of RMS had refocused the main revenue collecting agencies (GDT and GDCE) on revenue administration while keeping revenue policy mostly unchanged. The RMS was therefore designed to: (a) promote a culture of tax payment compliance; (b) improve tax payer services; (c) strengthen tax and non-tax administration. The RMS was based on three pillars: (a) strengthening revenue administration; (b) improving the revenue policy and institutional framework; and (c) strengthening monitoring and evaluation (M&E).

Many of the key initiatives needed to support these reforms focused on improving and streamlining working practices within the MEF creating more flexibility and better integration of different agencies.

First, in response to the need to ensure growth in revenue, MEF developed a credible plan to coordinate and strengthen the work of key tax and revenue collection units, responsible for enforcing tax compliance.

Second, RMS implementation mandated a mixture of training and incentives aimed at improving coordination and data sharing, building the capacity of revenue collecting agencies, and putting in place a new customer service orientation within the key agencies. Prior to the introduction of RMS, access to data and information on revenues was a big challenge. There was no specific data and information sharing mechanism and this made cooperation among departments difficult. Data could be received late or not received at all since there was no legal obligation for concerned departments to share information. To rectify this, RMS monitoring secretariats were appointed in 2015 to oversee coordination, collect all RMS implementation progress reports from tax branches and relevant departments, and communicate with the MEF monitoring and evaluation committee (also created in 2015). This intervention was instrumental to consolidating all implementation reports. However, the reports did not accurately measure performance because outputs were not clearly defined and most measures were qualitative and therefore subjective in nature. To address this issue, in 2016 the RMS Monitoring and Evaluation committee at the MEF conducted two surveys with staff and private sector stakeholders to obtain feedback on the quality of data collection. The result was then presented and co-evaluated with the GDT and GDCE. After that, a ministerial circular on data sharing among the 3 general departments was issued mandating the collection of reliable data to support better data analysis. This helped to further strengthen coordination and collaboration for data sharing since Cambodia is following a civil law tradition.

Third, changes in human resource and staff performance management have been implemented within GDT since 2012. GDT introduced IT systems to monitor and record staff attendance and performance, and installed fingerprint readers in offices. GDT also set up IT systems to facilitate salary payments and incentives to staff by linking record of deliverables of personnel for staff appraisal purpose with their personal bank account. This system also collects and updates personnel information including staff ID, personal information, and total income per year. These mechanisms improved staff attendance, performance and instilled a new work ethos aimed at improving customer service and satisfaction. Together with better incentives and pays, tax officials' mindsets became more focused on achieving the RMS's targets and policy objectives. At the same time, the GDCE leadership took a strong position and tough measures to monitor and crack down on illegal smuggling with rigorous auditing after goods have been cleared. This resulted in the improvement of capacities of post clearance audit teams with import-export companies.

Result

Major achievements have been made in revenue mobilization under the PFMRP. These include improving the legal framework, increasing use of the banking system for government financial transactions, and moving from a situation of chronic cash shortages to cash surplus. Overall domestic revenue to GDP ratio grew from 10.4 percent of GDP in 2005 to 18.5 percent in 2016 and an estimated 19.7 percent in 2017.[2] Rapid improvement began in 2012 and progressed exponentially after the adoption and implementation of the medium team Revenue Mobilization Strategy 2014–18, which aims at improving revenue administration and promoting a tax-paying culture. According to the government's data, tax revenue, which accounts for nearly 87 percent of the total current revenues, also increased by about 4 percent of GDP, jumping from 12.1 percent in 2012 to 16.1 percent in 2016. This improvement in tax revenue puts Cambodia among the leading countries in the region (see figure 5.1)." Data from World Development Indicators, which slightly differ from government data, also put Cambodia in a better position than many other lower middle-income countries (figure 5.2)

Improved revenue mobilization contributed to the total elimination of payment arrears going back to 2007 ensuring the predictability and credibility of the government budget.[3] It also enabled the government of Cambodia to introduce a relatively large fiscal stimulus of 2 percent of GDP during the 2008–09 global financial crisis, to help mitigate the negative impacts of the crisis on vulnerable

FIGURE 5.1

Tax-to-GDP ratio: Cambodia versus peer countries

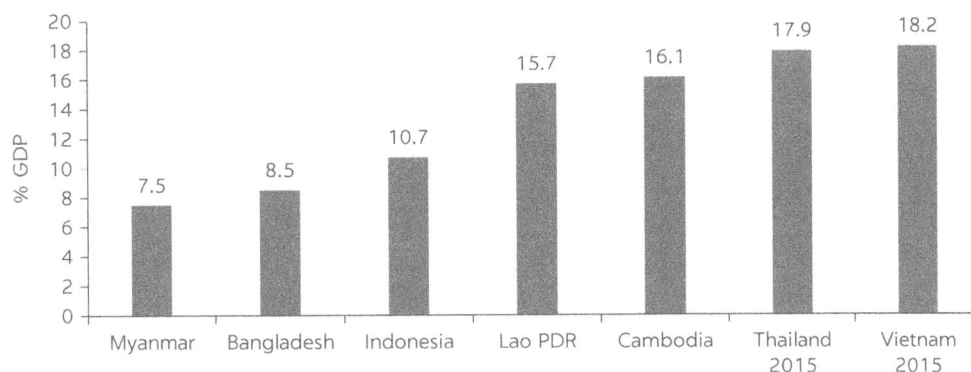

Source: MEF and World Development Indicators.
Note: GDP = gross domestic product.

FIGURE 5.2

Tax revenue to GDP

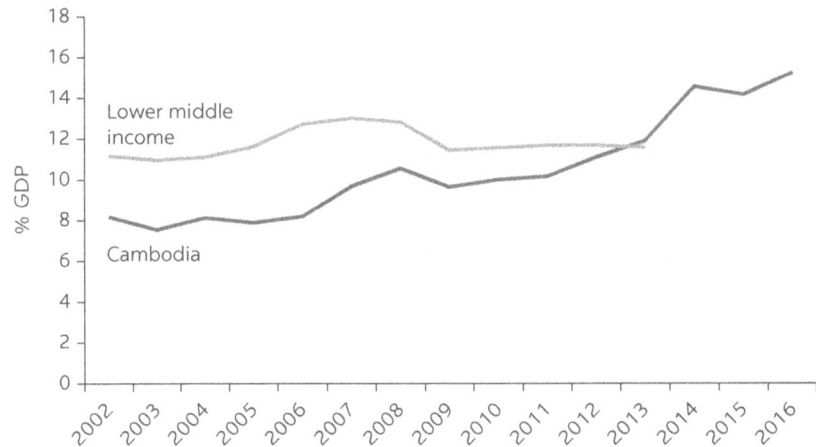

Source: World Development Indicators.
Note: GDP = gross domestic product.

sectors of the Cambodian economy, namely the garment and construction sectors. The increase in revenues also has translated into increased allocations to the education sector with the sectoral budget rising from 1.56 percent of GDP in 2004 to 3.05 percent of GDP in 2017 (and improving), and improved compensation for civil servants.

Per the government's own evaluation, three ingredients combined to make the Revenue Mobilization Strategy a success: the credibility of the strategy, its effective implementation, and appropriate monitoring to ensure that the plan was followed properly. This required particular emphasis on transforming working practices.

The human resource management reforms enacted by the leadership of GDT, including the introduction of the new IT system and associated incentive system, have improved performance among tax collectors and officials. There is now greater emphasis on punctuality, discipline, accountability for fulfilling roles and responsibilities in the workplace and improvement of services to taxpayers. The total number of enterprise audits carried out has increased from 1,305 in 2013, to 1,464 in 2014, and 2,143 in 2015. Stronger performance and better service by GDT officials in collecting tax from taxpayers is also a factor that can improve the level of voluntary compliance among taxpayers.

The decision to select General Department of Policy to monitor and evaluate the RMS progress was an astute decision to improve capacity and strengthen institutions within MEF. To respond to the task of implementing the RMS, General Department of Policy leadership began to build a capable team. A group of young officials, who are tasked to set up action plans relevant to the Cambodia's context, were sent for overseas trainings (Vietnam, France, and Thailand). The training enabled the young officials both to consolidate data for RMS progress report and formulate policy for macroeconomics, public finance and fiscal frameworks. The team is currently playing a role as the secretariat for the Policy and Strategy committee and prepare regular statistical reports including annual GDP, GDP by sectors, total domestic revenue, current revenue, inflation and exchange rate, country's macro-economy and Government Financial Statistics. The team is currently developing the Tax System Reform Framework (2019–23) which will look beyond tax administration to include tax policy to ensure healthy revenue mobilization in the long term.

Approach to reform and lessons learned

The increase in revenue collection can be attributed to four factors: strong political commitment and support for the RMS; strong ownership and leadership among revenue collecting agencies to implement priority actions and drive institutional reform including staff capacity building; improved coordination in data and information sharing among relevant departments; and proactive performance and support by M&E team (RMS's Monitoring Secretariat) to follow up progress of RMS implementation. Achieving this required tackling an entrenched working culture within the MEF which had emerged in a different era in Cambodia in response to a different set of economic, social, political and policy problems.

Several key challenges arose. First, the complexity of revenue collection strategies, and the poor quality of the document produced to describe them, meant that these were not fully understood by ministry officials and taxpayers. In response, the revenue mobilization strategy was amended into a list of simple and practical priority actions that could be easily understood and achieved by collection agencies. Another challenge was the lack of communication, coordination and information and data sharing for M&E purposes among implementing agencies. The reform benefited from putting in place an independent monitoring team to evaluate performance and provide relevant and useful feedback for improvement. This team created a data-sharing protocol in 2015 to formalize the mechanism for coordinating and collecting reports on the progress of implementation across all the revenue collecting agencies. This allowed reports to be consolidated for evaluation purposes.

The actions taken to resolve these challenges reflected the adaptive/experimental approach adopted for implementing the reform, which fostered an environment for policy makers and implementers to test, evaluate and recalibrate the plan as required. This environment was supported in particular by innovations and incentives introduced to encourage a shift in the culture and mindset of employees. Performance evaluation was introduced, for example among GDT officials, which contributed greatly to improved service and revenue mobilization.

IMPROVING BUDGET EXECUTION THROUGH IMPLEMENTATION OF THE FINANCIAL MANAGEMENT INFORMATION SYSTEM

Issues

Cambodia's PFM was highly centralized before the PFMRP took place. The administrative procedure for budget execution was channeled vertically with limited interaction between units and departments. Each work unit was highly specialized in one specific area and engaged in only that specific area of work as part of a long process before budget expenditure could be processed and approved. For example, the process from procurement of goods and services to payment involves approximately 280 steps between the relevant departments within MEF (Unpublished consultant report 2014). Such a long process required a high level of coordination that did not exist and thus failed to provide high quality and timely services to ministries which submitted expenditure requests to MEF. Much of the budget execution process was prepared manually. The in-house system Khmer Information Technology (KIT) was used by the central Treasury and a handful of provincial treasuries (PTs) but lacked the ability to link data electronically.

As a result, program managers had little responsibility for how their budgets were managed and implemented throughout the year. In addition, financial accountability at the sectoral ministries and agencies was problematic given the fact that the PFM system was highly centralized. Even within the centralized PFM system itself, the lack of accurate and timely financial data caused by the manual accounting and booking practices, created a burden for public officials to meet reporting requirements. For example, PTs must submit monthly financial reports to the center, but because data had to be gathered manually using financial data generated by the KIT and spreadsheets, reports were not produced in a timely manner and the data often was incomplete. Producing financial reports was a long process that could take up to a few days or weeks and involved intensive staff labor.

An assessment of budget system in the 2015 report of Public Expenditure and Financial Accountability (PEFA) suggested that although the government of Cambodia had an orderly process for making budgets and releasing money to different state agencies, there were serious weaknesses in monitoring expenditure, as well as large deviations between the allocations of resources in the budget approved by the legislature and the actual allocation of resources between other ministries and MEF (RCC 2015).

Reform intervention

The FMIS was envisioned as the backbone of the reforms under Platform 2 aiming to devolve greater budget responsibility to program managers through enhancement of internal controls and accountability mechanisms. It is an automated financial system implemented to help improve the efficiency, transparency and accountability of PFM. By radically simplifying procedures and facilitating immediate access to real-time information across a wide range of agencies in different locations, the FMIS offered an opportunity to radically restructure the hierarchical arrangement within the MEF.

The FMIS was to be introduced in 2006 in preparation for Platform 2, which was officially launched in 2009. FMIS enables governments to control aggregate spending and deficits and prioritize expenditure across policies, programs and projects for allocative efficiency and equity. To improve financial accountability at the center of stage 2/platform 2 of PFMRP, a step towards de-concentration of the financial management (while maintain centralized cash management) has been introduced with a policy for establishing budget entities (a key concept for developing budget authority) below ministerial level. To ensure accountability while deconcentrating, internal audit was introduced and subsequently strengthened and internal audit departments across ministries were established. A new integrated uniform account code structure was developed to unify budget and accounting functions into a single structure—backbone of the FMIS (World Bank 2011).

Initially the FMIS was to be installed in MEF and across all ministries in a single implementation stage or phase; however, the scope was too ambitious and after a failed procurement, a new two–phase plan emerged. The first phase included the core treasury and budget execution functions (Budget Allocation, Purchase Order, Account Payable, Account receivable, Cash Management and General Ledger) for MEF and all PTs. The second phase involves expansion of these basic functions to all line ministries and remaining functional modules—budget preparation, purchasing, and asset management by 2020.

The initial smaller scope was deemed to be more appropriately sequenced to reflect the government's capacity at the time, although this meant the devolution of greater budget and financial accountability and responsibility to other ministries would be delayed until a future (second) phase—line ministry rollout phase. This made the project simpler to implement. However, the project was initially referred to as a "Treasury-Centric System," which had the adverse and unintended effect of a lack of ownership of the system by some key departments outside the Treasury.

Results

The FMIS has been implemented successfully and is currently operational in general departments of MEF and 25 PTs. The system began to be rolled out across the central offices of MEF and PTs in mid-2015. Starting from January 2017, FMIS is the only system used by PTs and central offices of MEF to process financial transactions.[4] As of July 2017, over 500 users from these general departments and PTs are using the system.

Spending ministries at the center and spending departments in the provinces submit their transactions to the central treasury or the corresponding PTs for processing. The web-based portal provides easier access to financial information to the spending ministries and departments. As a result, the government is able to speedily capture all payment transactions enabling greater fiscal control and more timely financial information. The 2 day or longer financial report production is replaced by a standard report produced within a few minutes from the FMIS. In addition, the reports contain a wealth of information about government financial resources across various programs, projects and various ministries and can provide important information for management and policy making purposes.

In addition, approximately, 25 percent of existing payment processes within MEF were initially streamlined to facilitate more timely payment processing at GDNT. Standard operating procedures (SOPs) was also put in place to help guide system users.

Approach to reform and lessons learned

The FMIS implementation represented both a technical and adaptive challenge. Technical challenges included developing the capacity to implement and support the IT solution and manage the technical roll out of the system. However, more difficult were the adaptive (non-technical) challenges including the inadequate coordination among the FMIS Project Management Working Group (FMWG) and the resistance to change at various levels within MEF. These arose because the reform directly challenged hierarchical lines of control within the MEF that combined both entrenched formal reporting lines and equally longstanding informal links of loyalty. The belated but ultimately effective addition of a CM strategy, incorporating stakeholder engagement and strategic communication plans, focused specifically on changing the attitudes of staff to the reform, assisted in overcoming these adaptive challenges.

Because of the challenge FMIS posed to hierarchical lines of control, middle management proved the greatest impediment to change. At several points during the implementation, the FMIS was nearly compromised by demands from several departments that demanded the software be customized to incorporate existing hierarchical processes rather than transforming and improving the processes within MEF. However, after the system went live, enthusiasm significantly increased at all levels of the MEF once many realized the workload savings from automation introduced. MEF leaders' adoption of an "evolution not revolution" approach helped to build confidence in the reform but this also slowed delivery.

A further issue related to difficulties in coordination among members of the Financial Management Working Group (FMWG). The group comprised many managers representing different departments that were not used to working together or negotiating decisions among themselves. Coordination issues also emerged among key implementing departments. The lesser status of the lead department (the IT department) within the structure of MEF vis-à-vis the key implementing general departments (Treasury and Budget) made it difficult to secure cooperation. Commitment and intervention from MEF top leadership helped to break barriers to discussion among all of these stakeholders.

Sequencing was useful to reform implementation. Ambitious reforms proved challenging and unsuccessful. Focusing on basic system first allows the reforms to progress more credibly albeit slowly. The ambitious approach originally envisioned under Platform 2 was amended and recalibrated to better suit the capacity and implementation realities at that time. The first procurement which was failed proved to be a lesson learnt for adjusting the reform strategy by introducing a "basics first" solution and then introducing more complex automation over time.

An important aspect of the success of the project was the ability to adapt good practice in the FMIS to the local context. The technical support on CM was significant in transforming the "authorizing environment." The CM team began by undertaking detailed research to analyze the situation, particularly regarding attitudes towards and understanding of FMIS, and this was crucial to informing the CM strategy. Different CM techniques were tried, with varying success, as the team experimented with different approaches. The CM team focused on attempting to bring together middle managers to discuss the reform with senior leaders in power lunches and other kinds of networking events, but found this difficult in the context of the hierarchical structure. To break the ice for improved coordination, the CM team worked to ensure that there were sufficient incentives for FMWG members. They also organized study tours and events that improved the personal relations between working group members, so that their ability to collaborate in decision-making on the project improved. Provincial treasuries were relatively more positive about the implications of the reform, although they were initially concerned about their technical capacity to implement it. Once FMIS was rolled out, and PTs got their hands on the software, enthusiasm at provincial level proved to be strong.

To support the CM work in Cambodia, Indonesian experts were brought in to share CM expertise and they quickly found that CM strategies needed to be significantly adapted to fit a very different context of Cambodia. Close cooperation between Cambodian and Indonesian CM teams and the openness of key stakeholders in the government facilitated by strategic communication was eventually successful in significantly promoting understanding and acceptance of the reform, particularly at the provincial treasury level. CM team organized change readiness assessment survey and then incorporated findings into effective channels of communication with messages tailored to the constituencies targeted. Change managers attempted to identify different reasons for resistance, and to tackle these with bespoke messages intended to reassure and persuade. At the same time, the morale of pro-reform constituencies was boosted by good news stories about progress and achievements. Once FMIS in Cambodia went live, and PTs began using the system, some became its most enthusiastic advocates. Organizing interactions between provincial treasurers to share their experience leveraged this effect, as could organizing opportunities for senior management to engage directly with the provincial treasurers, thus placing pressure on middle managers in the central ministry to come into line.

FMIS was an international best practice solution, and intentionally so. It was intended to radically reform an area of Cambodian governance that has long imposed a significant constraint on the government's aspiration to promote financial accountability and transparency and the quality of service delivery. However, it encountered significant resistance from within the civil service. This prompted experimentation jointly between international and national change managers to elaborate a CM strategy tailored to the local context. This can be considered an aspect of experimenting approach, and the lessons of this have been learned through reflection on the process of collaboration between Indonesian and Cambodian change managers. The lessons learned include: (a) the importance of CM in complex IT projects; (b) the importance of initiating CM plans early; and (c) the context-specific nature of CM approaches and the need to calibrate and introduce strategies as appropriate.

PROGRAM BUDGETING

Issues

Prior to the introduction of program budgeting under the PFMRP in 2008, the Cambodia's budgeting system followed a line item approach. This was a centralized and input-based budget management system in which new fiscal year budgets are decided by the MEF based on the previous fiscal year's budget growth. The increase of new fiscal year budgets does not have any clear purpose of expenditure, or linkage between the government's strategic development plan and ministries' policy. Budget execution focused on input controls rather than the results and outcomes of spending. The linkages among planning, budgeting and sectoral policy were weak.

Reform intervention

It is important to note that successful implementation of the FMIS with its uniform account code system has enabled proper establishment of program-based budgeting. Following the global trend, Cambodia committed to PFM reform toward international standards, involving gradual change from an input-based and centralized system toward a result or performance oriented, decentralized budgeting system as articulated in the concept note on Strategic Direction of Budget System Reform 2013–20. A new strategy for budget system reform 2017–25 was introduced to further clarify the direction of and provide a road map for Cambodia's budget system reform. The strategic goal is that by 2025 Cambodia budget system will be based on programs that are linked to policy and incorporate mechanisms for performance accountability. "Performance Informed Budgeting" in which allocated "resources are indirectly related to proposed future performance or past performance" is the adopted model for budget reform.

Challenges posed by the reform also focus on the change in working practices that are entailed. For one thing, the reform implies a shift in decision-making power away from the MEF and towards line ministry budget managers. It also implies better monitoring of the performance of different agencies and programs. Improving human resources and management information systems is planned to take place to support the change. Successful implementation of the strategy is expected to contribute to a more open and transparent budget process with timely reporting in line with international standards.

This budget reform vision is being implemented under the PFMRP (Platform 3's objective). Program budgeting was piloted in 8 ministries beginning in 2008 when budget strategic plan was introduced. This had the aim of improving the four stages of the budget cycle: budget preparation, budget appropriation, budget execution, and result and performance M&E (p. 5). MEF prepared guidelines for the implementation of budget entities in 2013 to support and prepare different ministries for the decentralization of the budget to spending entities in the future. The MEF implemented program budgeting beginning with 10 ministries in 2015, and expanding to additional 11 ministries in 2016, and 15 more in 2017. As of 2017, 36 ministries are implementing program budgeting and an additional 3 ministries will begin implementing program budgeting in 2018. It was also introduced to sub-national governments in 2016.

Results

The decision to implement program budgeting by MEF produced several incremental results that contributed to gradual improvement in Cambodian budget system. These results, while being further refined, include improved capacity to support the implementation of program budgeting in the General Department of Budget (GDB); improved discipline in budget expenditure among line ministries, improved discretion by budget managers with the creation of budget entities, and more importantly better linkages between policy and budget. Through the reform effort, MEF improved budget monitoring by requiring all ministries to set up an internal audit department. As of 2017, 27 ministries and 11 public enterprises have set up internal audit departments and developed internal guidance to monitor and evaluate budget execution. Furthermore, ministries can execute certain types of spending without requesting spending permission from MEF for some regular expenditures such as their utility costs and wage bills. MEF has delegated greater power to ministries by out-posting financial controllers to different ministries to monitor and approve expenditures below a certain threshold. More budget entities with full authority to execute their budget have been created with support from MEF. Two forms of budget entities were established (a) fully authorized budget entities that have full discretion to execute budget under their control and (b) budget entities with less authority to spend (mainly at the central levels of ministry).

A recent review of program budget implementation (Beazley 2016) suggested that Cambodia has made good progress in developing program budgeting although the quality of programs and its effectiveness need further improvement. The year 2015 was the first year that 10 ministries began to implement program budgeting for 100 percent of their budget.

The challenges for budget system reforms were twofold. Within the GDB itself, although program budgeting was implemented from 2008, 8 years later (in 2015) many implementation issues remained, while staff lacked the capacity to address. Organizationally, ministries were not prepared and many lacked the appropriate organization structures to commence implementation. Prior to full program budgeting implementation in 2015, the General Department of Finance of different ministries had full authority over decisions about budget, but this was changed once budget entities were empowered to manage their own budgets. However, because these budget entities had limited understanding of the new procedures, spending performance during Q2 and Q3 of 2015 was low (30.4 percent in Q2 and 56.2 percent in Q3 of 2015) (PFM Reform Program 2015 Annual report, p. 9). In light of these experiences, MEF supported ministries and improved the implementation of program budgeting by a series of guidelines, and increased training to budget entities by the Economy and Finance Institute (EFI), a training institute under the MEF.

Approach to reform and lessons learned

Initial achievements in relation to budget reform to date have been incremental and the budget reform strategy foresees additional 8 years toward its envisioned budget system (2025). Implementation of program budget with the aim to promote budget and policy linkage is complex and difficult. Complexity of PFMRP increases as reformers advance to the next platform.

Through a phased implementation between 2008 and 2015, the government of Cambodia has allowed a realistic amount of time for program budgeting to be rolled out and for learning to take place along the way. In addition, MEF, with support from development partners, has provided a substantial amount of training, technical support and guidance to line ministries. The MEF has followed international good practice, by limiting the number of policy goals, programs and indicators. This has helped to keep the process more or less manageable.

Through the discussion with MEF, the process of preparing budget strategic plans has already helped some ministries to plan their expenditure better and with a clearer focus on results. Although it has not been advertised as performance budgeting, the government has already introduced performance and results into the budget process by including performance indicators into budget strategic plans. However, performance oriented budgeting requires that performance based systems be put in place including among other things result measurement, M&E, performance management of budget managers, and incentive for good performance. This requires the complementarity of other critical reforms and thus focusing on getting the basics right and appropriately sequenced budget reform in line with other two critical reforms, decentralization and public administration reform, are critical. Based on recommendations from the 2016 review and experiences from OECD countries, the MEF has made informed decision by choosing to move to "performance-informed budgeting" instead of "performance based budgeting" as initially envisioned. Arguably, because program budgeting was introduced prior to other enabling reforms as sequenced under the platform approach, the complexity and confusion of reform and the subsequent implementation challenges were exacerbated. Nevertheless, after much careful internal reflection and successive consultation, the budget reform approach was adjusted to better sensitize the organization and to stay in-step with the other two critical reform agendas essential for achievement of the envisioned objectives of budget reform.

CONCLUSION

Cambodia has travelled far in its PFM reform journey, albeit from a very low base in 2004. At the time, Cambodia was beset by poorly designed PFM systems inherited from several legacy (hybrid) systems. Budget formulation and execution was an inefficient cash-based PFM system. Chronic cash shortage led to payment arrears reaching a quarter of the domestically financed budget in 2004. To fund public spending, Cambodia was heavily dependent on external finances which accounted for almost a third of total outlays.

Today, the Cambodia PFM systems have been substantially strengthened particularly at the central level. Cambodia is committed to pursuing international public sector accounting systems (IPSAS). Key achievements under the PFMRP include: (a) revenue collection going from 10.3 percent of GDP in 2004 to about 19.7 percent in 2017; (b) the total elimination of payment arrears going back to 2007; (c) an improved policy-informed budgetary process with smooth implementation of the budget; and (d) the implementation of an FMIS—which is now fully operational at central offices of MEF and all PTs. The FMIS has greatly helped with the timeliness of payments and the accuracy of financial reports.

While more remains to be done, there is good reason to celebrate. The key to success was Cambodia's approach to reform: experimenting with best fit approaches. This approach involves a combination of standardized "best practice" and customized "best fit" solutions. The platform approach and its inherent flexibility to recalibrate an identified set of core activities to achieve best fit, allowed for experimentation and intervention to advance the reforms. The three described interventions illustrate well this approach. Empowering the tax department to tryout and introduce new incentive schemes accelerated a cultural shift to a more customer-oriented tax administration; introducing a comprehensive CM approach (albeit somewhat late) for the FMIS implementation helped build buy-in for the system (at all levels of the organization) and changed the way staff conduct their daily work; and recalibrating an overly ambitious budget reform strategy to better reflect the pace of other key reforms needed to achieve the intended budget reform objectives assisted the government in keeping the reforms on track over the years.

Furthermore, certain practices were introduced e.g., data sharing arrangement for M&E of revenue mobilization was created before formally institutionalized; the process of business process streamlining was tried and negotiated before an SOP was adopted; performance indicators have now been introduced in ministries' reform strategy; and internal budget negotiations are now based on program performance for a growing number of ministries. This represents a radical shift in the working cultures and practices of Cambodian ministries, and a pronounced change in the way that public servants are expected to relate to their work. The approach involved creating both instruments and a "culture" for doing adaptive, experimental, iterative work.

The "best fit" platform approach to PFM reform adopted has helped the government of Cambodia achieved its progress slowly but surely over the last 13 years. Having the flexibility to build consensus i.e. to agree on how the reform is progressing and when to move on to the next phase is important. Although this has been contested at times, and the reform drive stalled during transition from Phase 1 to Phase 2, designing a catalyst strategy to accelerate key reforms to ensure implementation of the FMIS under Phase 2 represents an inventive and flexible approach—one that desperately was needed to avoid collapse and maintain the reform momentum. The sequenced platform approach is in-step with the government's mantra for the reform "evolution not revolution" by building incrementally on previous and demonstrative success of the previous platform set of reforms. In addition to the right approach and reform design, consistent commitment by government leadership with changes in leadership in many key posts by design to spur and push the reform on many fronts, together with appropriate and adequate attention to CM has helped and will continue to help the government stay the course in the future.

NOTES

1. The World Bank supported the PFMRP in two successive projects. The first was the Public Financial Management and Accountability Project (PFMAP), which ran from 2006 to 2013. The project was co-financed by a Multi Donor Trust Fund (MDTF) with contributions from the European Union, the United Kingdom, Australia and Sweden and an IDA grant. PFMAP's objective was to strengthen public financial management by strengthening: (a) mobilization of public resources; (b) management of public resources (c) management of human resources; and (d) external audit. The second was the Public Financial Management Modernization Project (PFMMP), which ran from November 2013 to May 2017. The project was financed from a further MDTF with contributions from the European Union (EU), Australia, and Sweden totaling USD18.8 million. The PFMMP aims to enhance public financial management by strengthening (a) revenue mobilization and (b) budget execution processes through the implementation of the FMIS. In addition to the two projects, the PFMRP also received direct technical and financial support from several other donors including the Asian Development Bank (ADB), Japan International Cooperation Agency (JICA), the US Treasury, and the International Monetary Fund (IMF).
2. See regular Cambodia Economic Update by the World Bank
3. Expenditure arrears is defined as delay in payment beyond 60 days (90 days before 2015) counting from payment request summited to GDNT till payment date.
4. The central offices of MEF using FMIS are: General Budget Department (GBD), General Department of the National Treasury (GDNT), General Department of Public Procurement (GDPP), General Department of Sub-National Administration Finance (GDSNAF), General Department of International Cooperation and Debt Management (GDICDM), General Department of Internal Audit (GDIA), General Inspection Directorate (GID) and Information Technology Department (ITD).

BIBLIOGRAPHY

Beazley, Ivor. 2016. *Cambodia Program Budget Review*. Unpublished Report.

EIC (Economic Institute of Cambodia). 2005. *Cambodia Economic Watch*. Phnom Penh: EIC.

Gottesman, Evan. 2004. *Cambodia After the Khmer Rouge: Inside the Politics of Nation-Building.* New Haven, CT: Yale University Press.

Hughes, Caroline. 2003. *The Political Economy of Cambodia's Transition 1991–2001.* London: Routledge.

Ministry of Economy and Finance. 2015. *Annual Progress Report.* Phnom Penh: Ministry of Economy and Finance.

PDP Australia. 2010. *External Advisory Panel(EAP) Report 2009 on Cambodia Public Financial Management Reform Program.* Phnom Penh: Cambodia.

RGC (Royal Government of Cambodia). 2004. *Public Financial Management Reform Program.* Ministry of Economy and Finance. Phnom Penh, Cambodia.

———. 2015. Report of the Evaluation on the Public Financial Management System of Cambodia Based on Public Expenditure and Financial Accountability (PEFA). https://pefa.org/sites /default/files/assements/comments/KH-Dec15-PFMPR-Public.pdf

Taliercio, Robert. 2009. "Unlocking Capacity and Revisiting Political Will: A Review of Cambodia's Public Financial Management Reforms, 2002–2007." *International Public Management Review* 10 (1): 90–118.

World Bank. 2011. *Integrated Fiduciary Assessment and Public Expenditure Review (IFAPER).* Washington, DC: World Bank.

———. n.d. *Cambodia Economic Update Selected Issues 2014–2017.* Phnom Penh, Cambodia: World Bank.

6 Vietnam

GRADUALIST APPROACH TO ADDRESSING PFM REFORM CHALLENGES

PHUONG ANH NGUYEN and KAI KAISER

INTRODUCTION

Prior to the economic reform under the Doi Moi in 1986, Vietnam faced various difficult development challenges due to economic problems. Price controls on goods and services did not stop inflation from rising, reaching 700 percent annually; high military expenditures and subsidies to state-owned enterprise created pressure for budgetary resources for other key development expenditures that are critical to addressing poverty alleviation (see ANU E Press 2003; Mallon 1999). In response, the Vietnamese government embarked on a major innovation (Doi Moi) to its economy, leading to impressive development outcomes and transitions to market-driven development and economic liberalization. The reforms successfully transformed the country from one of the poorest in the world to lower middle-income status. Since 1986, Vietnam's GDP has expanded more than fivefold, per capita income has quadrupled, and the poverty rate declined markedly from 49 percent in 1993 to just 2.9 percent in 2014.[1]

Despite Vietnam's progress, ensuring efficiency of public sector performance to address the changing needs of citizens remains a key challenge. As the country becomes more modern, new challenges and complexity has emerged and the Public Financial Management (PFM) system needs to keep pace with that development. The government of Vietnam was in the driver's seat to implement the PFM reforms, with technical and financial support from the World Bank and other development partners. Modernizing the PFM system to support the government's development agenda is one of the key areas Vietnam has tried to address in the last 20 years. This chapter focuses on three public sector reform experiences in Vietnam: (a) the implementation of the integrated Treasury and Budget Management Information System (TABMIS); (b) fiscal decentralization; and (c) public investment management. It analyzes the transformation of the PFM system in these three areas since 1996, and how Vietnam is aspiring to become by 2035 a government that is capable of producing resilient fiscal policy function, reliable regulatory function, and transparent and trustworthy public finance system.

The rest of the chapter is organized as follows. Following this introduction, the three PFM reform experiences are discussed in detail, including specific issues, reform interventions, and the results they have generated. We then discuss specific approach to the three reforms. The chapter concludes with some reflections and key lessons learned from the three cases.

FISCAL DECENTRALIZATION

Issues

Vietnam has evolved from a centrally planned economy to one increasingly characterized by social and economic decentralization, and hence revenue and expenditure decentralization. The process of preparing subnational budgets is lengthy and that has made the budgetary process less transparent. Vietnam is one of the few countries that still operates on the "nested" budgeting system, in which the budget preparation process is done at each level of government from the lowest level of communes (See figure 6.1). The budget needs to be approved both horizontally by the People's council at the same level and vertically by the upper level. This lengthy process shortens the time for the People's council at the central level to adequately review the budget. There is also lack of formal requirement to seek the council's approval before the executive makes change to the budget appropriation. Lack of budget scrutiny of in-year adjustments by the legislative body could lead to fraudulent and intentionally misuse of the budget at the local level. There is not a clear expenditure assignment between each level of government; some items are spent by both the central and provincial levels

FIGURE 6.1

Budgeting system in Vietnam

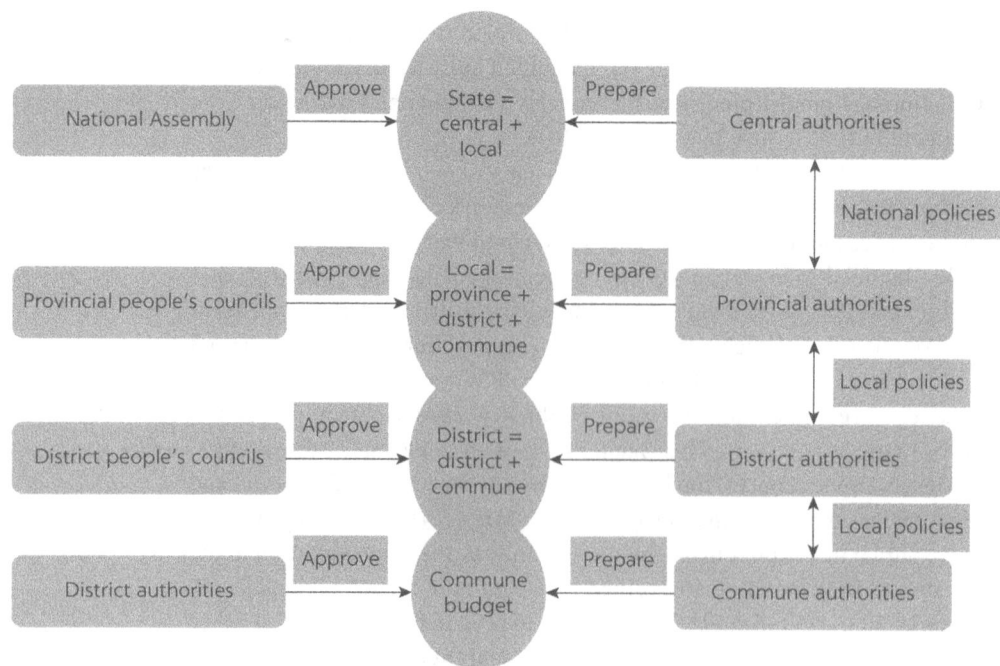

Source: Rab et al. 2015.

such as spending for security and police. This leads to duplication in spending for the same intended service delivery and at the same time there is no clear responsibility and accountability of each level of government.

Reform intervention

The Ministry of Finance (MoF) studied international practices to inform its design of a formula-based transfer system, including indicator-based allocation norms. Separate formulae were developed to determine recurrent and capital spending needs of provinces from the central to provincial level. The formula was developed based on several indicators such as the population, poverty rate weighted proportionately to determine the transfers to each province. Each province will then have discretion to design their own criteria for transfers down to the district and commune levels.

As specified in its Constitution, Vietnam is a unitary state consisting of four tiers of government with their own executive and legislative authorities.[2] At the central level, the head of the executive branch is the Prime Minister, supported by 26 ministries; the National Assembly holds the legislative authority. At each tier of the local government, the People's Committee exercises executive authority and is scrutinized by the People's council. Effectively, this means that each Committee is accountable to a number of different government bodies—horizontally to its council, and vertically to the authorities above it in the hierarchy (see figure 6.2).

There was a pilot in the past to remove some of the district levels in selected provinces. During the pilot, the communes would report up directly to the provincial level. However, this has proved to be not successful since the administrative agency of the provincial level does not have capacity to manage many communes and ward under their territories.

The State Budget Law (SBL) 1996 set a clear budget preparation process and for the first-time regulated decentralization of expenditure to the lower level. In 2002, the SBL was revised to allow greater decentralization of expenditure

FIGURE 6.2
Vietnam's state administrative structure

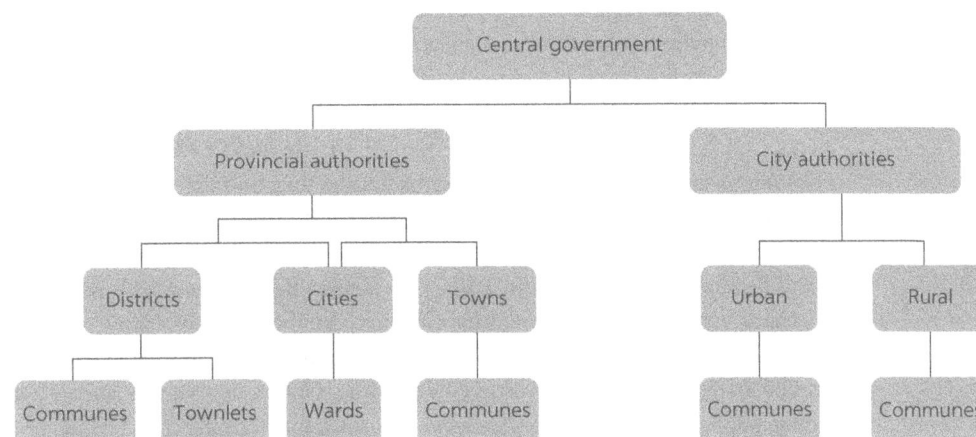

Source: Rab et al. 2015.

assignment and fiscal autonomy to the provinces. More than half of the total expenditure was executed at the subnational level. The subnational share of total capital spending accounted for more than 70 percent. This is also evidenced in 80 percent and 85 percent of expenditure executed at the subnational level in the health and education sector respectively. MOF received in-depth technical assistance from the World Bank and other development partners to revise the SBL in 2015. The latest SBL has clear authority of each level of government in preparing, executing, and reporting their budgets including the medium-term budget plans. This helps to make the budget preparation process clearer and more transparent. In-year adjustment to the budget needs to be approved by the people's councils before they are executed. This new policy helps to strengthen the cross-check function of the legislative branch in making sure that the budget is spent for the right purpose.

Result/Implementation progress

Overall result of decentralization reform can be described as mixed. The SBL 2002 has enabled decentralization of important fiscal responsibilities to local authorities over the past 10 years. However, as pointed out earlier, greater fiscal decentralization was not undertaken in tandem with accountability and transparency. The revision of SBL 2015 drew on analyses of expenditure decentralization, and adopted amendments to provide more time for the people's councils to scrutinize the budget, greater autonomy of people's councils over budget approval, clearer provisions on budget appropriations, and inclusion of off-budget financing in local budgets.

Vietnam could sustain fiscal equity through the fiscal transfer arrangement but it does not necessarily promote efficiency. The country has developed a relatively transparent, rules-based system of intergovernmental fiscal transfers. This has helped develop a highly predictable system of balancing (or unconditional) transfers to provinces and districts. However, the formula was fixed for the stability period of 5 years and did not take account of inflation. This was addressed in the revised fiscal transfer formula for the period 2016–20 as promulgated in the resolution for budget allocation norm. A further challenge that has yet to be addressed is that the fiscal formula does not compensate for negative externalities created by non-residents or temporary migrants using local services in richer city provinces such as Ho Chi Minh and Hanoi.

Targeted transfers continue to play an important role in local spending even though its relative share has fallen over time. The lack of predictability in targeted transfers poses serious challenges for both provincial and district authorities. For example, it impedes on planning, budgeting, and delivery of national targeted program targets. Vietnam has made a big step to consolidate 16 national targeted programs into two programs, namely poverty reduction and a new rural development program in 2016. The former helps to reduce poverty in Vietnam, especially in the provinces with high numbers of poor ethnic minorities. The new rural development national targeted program helps to increase the welfare of people living in rural areas by building roads, schools and hospitals for better public service delivery. The level of resourcing of target transfers generally, however, is not closely aligned with the targets and objectives, which are quite ambitious. Complex, input-based guidance on national targeted program implementation reduces flexibility and increases the burden of reporting.

Fiscal decentralization policies have helped to channel more spending to the poorest parts of the country. However, institutions of fiscal transparency and accountability have not kept pace with greater spending responsibility (World Bank 2014). There is a need to have more clarity of spending responsibilities and local level accountability, including for national priorities and objectives, for the spending performance of local authorities. At the same time, local government has little autonomy over revenue policy to meet their spending needs. This remains an important ongoing reform effort.

INTEGRATED TREASURY AND BUDGET MANAGEMENT INFORMATION SYSTEM

Issues

Implementing high levels of decentralization requires a good management information system to underpin budget execution and control. Vietnam established and maintained a system of aggregate and detailed fiscal controls, which are similar to those which many other countries use to maintain basic fiscal discipline. The lack of a fully consolidated budget made it difficult to monitor total revenues and expenditures, as well as the true fiscal position of the government. Extra-budgetary funds, on-lent official development assistance, and much of commune-level spending were not consolidated into the budget. The manual consolidation of budget data from multiple satellite databases proved to be laborious and inefficient. These deficiencies contributed to the poor flow of budgetary information between government ministries, between the government and the oversight agencies, and between the government and the citizen.

The environment for the operations of the various financial systems of government had different departments, under the administration of the Minister of Finance, as the core owners of these systems. Two general ("independent") departments within the Minister's portfolio responsibility (the General Taxation Department and the State Treasury Department) are the owners, respectively, of the Taxation and Treasury systems, while the State Budget and the Public Expenditure Management Departments of the MoF were the owners of the budget preparation and monitoring systems. None of these systems interfaced with each other. Prior to TABMIS, the State Treasury System was a cash only system, built in-house. The system had a number of shortcomings that effectively restricted its usefulness as a long-term solution for Vietnam. Some remaining and potentially serious shortcomings of the system include the lack of recording of commitments and accruals; and lack of subsidiary ledgers for tracking debtors, creditors and other balance sheet items. The system did not have conventional concepts of journals or a logical link between, for example, purchase orders, accounts payable, expenditure, assets or inventory nor automate bank reconciliations. In addition, because it was a bespoke (custom built) system, there were difficulties in attempting any significant upgrading toward becoming a full accounting system.

In terms of cash management, cash was kept at more than 700 Treasury offices across the country. There was no central Treasury single account so the Vietnam State Treasury (VST) did not have adequate information on the daily cash balance in the system. The State Treasury had to borrow short-term cash from the market while there was some cash sitting idly in the Treasury accounts somewhere. Cash was managed inefficiently and fragmented, causing high borrowing cost as a result.

In terms of reporting, the system lacked any analytical capability (mainly caused by the lack of useable data extraction tools such as report writers). There was a great need to make access to the data easier for designing and building more reports, and empowering users to access data for themselves through the use of any of the standard database report writing tools (e.g., Cognos, Brio, CorVu, Crystal Reports etc.).

Reform intervention/implementation processes

To address the above challenges, an integrated TABMIS was implemented as one of the main components of the government's Public Financial Management Reform Project, approved in 2003. The design of the project was realistic from a technical perspective and in terms of sequencing. The design of TABMIS was focused on the core functions of budget preparation, budget execution and accounting. This was mainstream work in information and communications technology (ICT) terms, with well-established solutions and internationally recognized software packages readily available to facilitate it.

At the time of project preparation, it was realistic to estimate that the implementation of TABMIS could be completed within about 6 years. It was mainly because of the increase in the number of users from the originally estimated 5,000 to more than 15,000 and the resulting expansion of the scope of TABMIS that the project needed 10 years for completion. Although the project took a long time to complete, as do many financial management information systems projects, it delivered a highly successful outcome for Vietnam.

Many strong and innovative features of the design played a prominent role in shaping the project's success. The turn key contract structure, careful oversight of procurement and independent verification and validation of delivery meant that the government could deliver a strong design and had the necessary support to manage this complex procurement contract.

Result/Implementation progress

TABMIS was successful in achieving its objectives. It has helped to establish an orderly and transparent budget execution process with strict control throughout four levels of government. TABMIS has realized commendable benefits for the government during challenging budget times due to improved accuracy, timeliness, and transparency in budget execution and reporting at each level of government.

Some specific policy, procedure and process reforms which have been introduced through TABMIS implementation include: unification of budget procedures and processes; clear definition of budget revenue and spending coverage at all levels of government; reduction of budget adjustment period (from 5 months to 1 month); clear definition of functions, duties and roles of different agencies in budget allocation and execution (through TABMIS workflows); a clearer way of calculating budget deficits in accordance with international practices; introduction of commitment accounting; centralization of real-time and integrated budget revenue and expenditure information enabling timely, consistent and accurate reporting for better serving management needs.

In the past 2 years, the government has begun introducing a treasury single account which replaced approximately 700 bank accounts and reduced the cost of borrowing for the government. At the end of the day, the cash balance in each Treasury office is swept to the central Treasury account. The State Treasury can now manage cash more proactively and does not have to incur any borrowing cost for fund shortage. This reform was supported by a series of development policy lending operations as well as technical assistance from the World Bank.

TABMIS was well established and operational and the MOF had successfully assumed full responsibility for the system and its environment, with IBM withdrawing completely in September 2013. The MOF administered the system database and security with support from an outsourced contractor for system administration and user support. GOV has allocated funding in the budget for maintenance costs to cover licensing and other costs to ensure that MOF will be able to administer the system, especially at the database level.

There are many positive outcomes that were not anticipated at the design of the project. The MOF team devoted considerable time and effort to improving their capabilities in relevant areas to better manage the TABMIS contract and overall change management process. TABMIS is a single centralized system, albeit with users at all levels of government. This has made it possible to recruit a team of qualified IT staff at State Treasury headquarters to support the system.

At the same time, the project has also created some negative responses from the government, largely concerning the increased workload for Treasury staff. As TABMIS includes the database of the provinces, districts and communes, and because the number of users has increased almost three times from 5,300 to 15,000, workload of the staff in the MOF and the Treasury for managing more data has significantly increased.

In addition, the vastly improved flow of fiscal data arising from TABMIS should enable decision makers, and a wider set of legislative and civil society stakeholders, to scrutinize the use of public resources. However, to date, the reporting facilities around TABMIS are structured around routine procedural reporting requirements, rather than the basis for more dynamic and data-driven analysis.

PUBLIC INVESTMENT MANAGEMENT

Issues

Responsibility for PFM in Vietnam is split predominantly between the MoF and Ministry of Planning and Investment (MPI). The MOF is responsible for revenues, recurrent expenditures, financing, accounting, debt, reporting and the overall fiscal position. The MPI is responsible for the 5-year Socio-Economic Development Plan, procurement, economic forecasting and capital projects and expenditures. Because of dual budgeting system, capital budget is done separately from recurrent budget. New projects were approved without consideration of operation cost to maintain the assets.

Capital investments were highly fragmented and not strategically aligned with the Socio-Economic Development Plan. Vietnam sustained high rates of capital investment with a significant role played by the SOEs. The country devolved from the central planning state to more decentralized implementation of investment projects at the subnational levels. The allocation of capital investment lacked strategic prioritization and was spread too thinly in many areas. The completion rate of projects managed by central government was only 20 percent in 2000–14.

Plans tend to be over-ambitious, particularly in relation to the financial resources available for their implementation. SEDP 2016–20 acknowledges the slow progress on certain reform priorities in the previous planning period and emphasizes the need to accelerate reforms over the current planning period in order to achieve targets. Some of the slow progress may indeed have arisen from implementation delays, but over-ambitious targets, set with insufficient attention to financial resource constraints, are very likely to have been part of the problem. This is a function of a planning system with teleological origins (as opposed to a more demand-driven, indicative system).

Responsibilities for different components of first-level screening are fragmented. This can be illustrated by the roles assigned to different agencies for reviewing Group A projects. While the MPI and MOF are jointly responsible for assessing affordability, "technical" line ministries are involved in assessing the cost estimates and preliminary design aspects of projects. The lead central agency or local authority has responsibility for confirming the "necessity" for the project. Fragmentation can be managed if there is good coordination, but this is not always the case: for example, the assessment of cost estimates may not always precede the MPI/MOF assessment of affordability, as would be logical. Even within the MPI there is some fragmentation of responsibilities, with the Department of External Economics being responsible for assessing ODA-funded projects (Group B and below), which it does largely independently of the Appraisal and Monitoring Department.

There was regular reporting on project implementation. Reporting requirements—contents, frequency and timeliness—were established in the Construction Law. Reports indicate variances from plans and analyze causes. The flow of information to the planning agencies (MPI and DPIs) has been less frequent (twice yearly), less reliable and in cumbersome formats, making it difficult for them to assemble a comprehensive picture of portfolio performance and identify projects at risk of delivery failure.

Vietnam had a well-regulated process for project acceptance and handover of newly created fixed assets;[3] However, after the handover to the managing and operating entity, the newly created asset is not adequately recorded in its asset register. The asset registry was incomplete. It did not record all types of public assets and only limited to public administrative assets such as buildings, vehicles that are utilized by government agencies. Asset registers were not dynamic instruments with regular revaluations and assessments of the condition of the assets therein. Some efforts in this direction have been and are being pursued, notably in the roads sector, but this was not the general practice.

Reform intervention

The government, through the MPI, has made efforts to curb the fragmentation of public investment by providing stricter provision in the public investment law (Law #49/2014/QH13), which requires all projects to be screened and included in the medium-term investment plan. The law has introduced good international practice by moving from an annual capital investment plan to a medium-term horizon. However, the law is not aligned with the rolling medium-term budget plan, an issue that only emerged after the issuance of the SBL. After the first trial, the MPI is seeking to revise the public investment law to synchronize with the SBL by moving from the fixed MTIP to a rolling one. The law also aimed to achieve better discipline in capital management whereby all agencies that allowed capital arrears in the past had to prioritize their budget to pay off the arrears first before starting new projects. In addition, any arrears that were incurred after 2014 will not be paid by the central budget.

The MPI undertook in-house development of an information system for capital budget allocation and monitoring, including projects funded by official development assistance. The system is home grown and web-based, using in-house server. Even though it has been rolled out nationally to all spending units, not all projects are recorded and reported through the system. The MPI realizes the system weakness and is seeking to improve the usability and functionality of the capital information system, especially with linkage to the TABMIS.

The GoV has also increasingly sought to strengthen public asset management. The 2017 Amendment to the Law on the Management and Use of State Assets offers a strong engagement framework relevant to physical infrastructure and land at the national and sub-national levels. The new PAML will be effective from January 1, 2018, and is an amendment to the original 2008 Law. The 2017 law expands coverage of assets beyond land, property, motor vehicles and other assets valued at more than VND 500 million (currently about USD 20,000). Transport sector coverage will now include all road assets, as well as rail, inland waterways, and seaports. The 2017 Law also provides for a full-fledged national database, and some provisions for disclosure.

Results/Implementation progress

Effort at PIM reform have generated mixed results. The Ministry of Finance's Division for Public Asset Management, working with line agencies and provinces, is responsible for implementing and maintaining the associated information system. The office is staffed with about 60 people, almost exclusively in Hanoi. The Center for the National Database accounts for about 20 of these staff. While a system has been established, and partially populated, the procedures with respective entities for regular updates are still being refined. At present, the system does not include geospatial referencing for physical assets. Managing this reform requires setting effective incentives, including penalties and rewards (in cases where there are gaps), in addition to providing requisite IT-related resources and recurrent management budgets.

Processes for prioritizing expenditures remained ineffective due to the absence of a credible multi-year fiscal framework. While the public investment law 2014 meant to put a hard budget constraint through the development of the fixed medium-term investment plan, expenditure planning was conducted without reference to medium-term resource constraints. Prioritization was carried out separately for capital spending (by the MPI) and for recurrent spending (by the MoF), with significant imbalances between the two. The level of capital arrears remained continue to persist although the government put a strong emphasis to clear off the arrears. Some provinces still had a high number arrears from the past that they could not afford to pay off with the current budget.

The World Bank has recently completed the public investment diagnostic in 2017, which benchmarks the PIM system in Vietnam against the international public investment management framework of the World Bank. The framework assesses the management of public investment across the planning, budgeting, procurement, implementation and evaluation phases. The diagnostic assesses the allocative, productive efficiency and the efficient use of assets. In doing so, the diagnostic has pointed out that Vietnam's PIM system have a number of deficiencies, ranging from the gap between the legal framework, regulations, and practice on the ground to misallocation of resources and loopholes in the appraisal, budgeting, implementation, and evaluation of public investments.

Evidence showed that resources were allocated to weak, low priority and unaffordable projects. Once the resources are allocated, the government failed to optimize the use of resources, leading to cost overruns, delays and departures from specifications. The cumulative effects of earlier inefficiencies led to blockages, such as over-extended investment programs and arrears, which undermine well-intentioned reforms, even if these make sense in isolation.

A major factor behind the slow progress in addressing inefficiencies and restructuring public investment is the lack of a well-designed reform program with clear specific objectives and priorities. While the decision to overhaul the PIM system was already made 6 years ago, no specific reform program has been developed. Effective implementation of the newly promulgated legal documents also requires considerable work such as the issuance of detailed guidelines to guide their application, especially in a highly decentralized setting. Public investment is governed by a complex regulatory framework, which includes many laws, and remains fragmented.

As mentioned above, Vietnam has a dual budgeting practice in which investment planning is led by the planning and investment section of the responsible organizations, which oversees preparation of the strategic documents (SEDS and SEDP) and investment plans. Planning departments of line ministries and provinces formulate their investment plans which includes a list of on-going and new investment projects and their costing. In the planning process, the planning departments of spending agencies coordinate the prioritization and selection of projects between and within sectors/sub-sectors. Investment plans of spending agencies are reviewed by the MPI and the MOF to make sure that demand for funding from the central government is compatible with the national capital budget. The planning sector also assumes the leading role in the monitoring and evaluation of public investment projects.

As a result of decentralization, provinces have overwhelming authority over all investment projects, except nationally important projects. Central government has limited tools to influence allocations or monitor results of local investments beyond the approval of plans, master plans or appraisal of financial availability. Poor selection in combination with soft budget constraints has been one of the drivers of the multiplication of projects and demand for resources, which are often beyond the capacity of the state budget to fund.

With the PIL 2014, Vietnam introduced a positive paradigm shift in PIM, moving from the traditional annual capital budgeting approach to medium-term financial frameworks to integrate better capital and recurrent expenditures. The shift also aims to strengthen the strategic efficacy of public investment which has been downplayed because of growing decentralization. Medium-term planning and budgeting were introduced to tackle the issues of time inconsistencies between the long-term nature of investment and annual budget processes, and to improve the predictability of resources available for investment. On the other hand, the empowerment of MOF, MPI and technical ministries, such as MOT and MOC, regarding appraisal, aims to deal with widespread negative consequences of an increasing decentralized PIM, in particular the proliferation of provincial expenditure arrears and growing concern about the technical deficiencies of on-going projects.

APPROACHES TO REFORMS

The current generation of PFM reforms successfully aligned to Vietnam's context, challenges, and capabilities. The reforms were selected, designed and implemented by the government, while selectively drawing in external support and outreach. The 10-year financial strategy and 5-year financial plans were the successive foundations for PFM reform actions. Reform design and implementation navigated a context of a unitary but highly decentralized budgeting systems, dual budgeting practices, transition economy legacies, and a political system that required brokering internal consensus among key bureaucratic and party stakeholder for major reform drives.

Many technical issues could be tackled with reference to international standard and good practice, but required due customization to the evolving Vietnam context. Vietnam was able to leverage development partners and ICT to advance its core reform trajectory. The government used international diagnostics to measure and benchmark their performance with other countries such as the Public Expenditure and Financial Accountability (PEFA), the tax administration diagnostic assessment tool (TADAT), the debt management performance assessment tool (DEMPA), and the public investment diagnostic. Once endorsed, these have been typically associated with a commitment from both the leadership and technical staff to improve the performance and the scoring of these indicators, but fundamentally responding to inherent concerns and ownership with government.

Vietnam has been taken a gradualist—and arguably quite incremental—approach to policy reform. At one level this has been about opting to get certain basics right before venturing into new policies. Incrementalism and a lack of critical challenge to both new and existing activities could be seen as comparatively true to Vietnam. In practice, most policy change, as with most budgetary change, has been incremental and phased. The challenge has therefore been to pave the way for more transformation changes, for example by employing a combination of pilots, successive legal reviews, and time. The successful PFM reform tracks identified in this chapter progressed gradually, but ultimately substantively. Part of this gradualism stemmed from a need to align key interests and stakeholders in government, and to ensure that reforms in systems and practices could be aligned to requisite legal revisions.

Out of the three reform experiences, TABMIS was considered as successful while the other two (fiscal decentralization and PIM) were considered as mixed. Fiscal decentralization and PIM's reforms were guided by formal laws without much support to facilitate the transition to the new practice. Adoption of specific law was useful but did not translate into automatic compliance by concerned stakeholders. Legislations need to be implemented, enforced, and communicated well all the way to the grassroot level. In the case of public investment management reform, the public investment law by itself cannot change the system and improve PIM. Concerned stakeholders needs to be guided and trained how to implement in practice. Some legislations might also create conflicting ways of doing business as witnessed between the public investment law and the SBL. But it will need to be reviewed and revised to make sure they align as they are implemented.

Some pilots had proven to be unsuccessful and was not followed through. In the case of fiscal decentralization, the government once tried to remove district levels in piloted provinces but it was considered premature in the end due to many unanticipated capacity constraints to accommodate the change. While Vietnam's budget system is unitary in design, it its quite decentralized in practice. Through decentralization, a growing number of transactions were occurring at the provincial level and below. Reform in fiscal decentralization is limited by contextual constraints that need to be looked at more broadly.

Gradualism together with appropriate plan and adequate support was important to the success of TABMIS. The TABMIS implementation in Vietnam illustrates how project implementation for similar systems needs to be phased to achieve significant outcomes such as good budgetary control and cash management early in the project. It is necessary to first implement modules to cater to core budget execution processes and processing of payments and receipts transactions, across government, before going on to other noncore elements, such as fixed assets/inventory management, human resource or fleet management.

Leadership support has also played a strong role in facilitating change. The implementation and operation of TABMIS would not have been successful without the strong support of the MOF Vice Minister who acted as the chairman of the inter-ministerial steering committee, and the group of highly skilled technical staff who oversaw the daily operation of the project. VST engaged an additional 17 staff, four of whom worked on the TABMIS implementation project, as part of IBM's subcontract team. These skills and experiences enhanced the sustainability of the MOF in operating TABMIS. The government allocated funding in the budget for maintenance costs to cover licensing and other costs to ensure that the MOF would be able to administer the system, especially at the database level. There was stability on both the government and World Bank side, with key members of the team that designed the project remaining engaged in its implementation for the first few years ensuring an effective transfer of knowhow to field-based and other staff.

In addition, capacity development was one of the important facilitating factors to carry out successful reforms. Training staff in the Treasury offices to comply with new legislation or use of the new system emerged as crucial, especially for staff at the grassroots levels. It was also necessary to incentivize the staff to stay at the job after the training through promotions and recognition from the leadership. Training workshops were done in batches and avoided the time when the staff are busy with the budget process.

CONCLUSION AND LESSON LEARNED

The two decades of PFM reform reviewed in this paper have paralleled a period of rapid growth and significant social and economic transformation. Vietnam's PFM reform successes have centered on a number of major laws, as well as process and systems developments although the laws do not represent a magic bullet and setbacks can be still be observed. The 2002 and 2015 SBLs, in particular, represent two major milestones framing the recent history of PFM reforms in Vietnam, and some of the key successes in strengthened systems such as new integrated budget and accounting system (TABMIS). While taking almost a decade to fully complete after the 2002 SBL, the TABMIS reflects a significant modernization of PFM in Vietnam. Public investment and asset management laws have also been added to the overarching development of the legal framework although the laws have yet to translate into attitude change and substantive improvement in PIM.

The gradualist PFM reforms in Vietnam have not had to contend with major crises, but rather have sought to adapt to emerging pressures. Going forward, the pressures for fiscal consolidation, greater transparency and accountability, and public-sector performance are likely to shape the PFM reform agenda. Lessons from the legal and TABMIS reforms to-date include the importance of: (a) sequencing reforms to avoid conflicting legal documents; (b) integrating management and institutional reforms with ICT investments; (c) ensuring government commitment and management support for the overall reform through extensive and deep dialogue with the authorities in all aspects of project design and implementation and through workshops in different provinces of the country; (d) the importance of inter-agency coordination; (e) the importance of developing organizational capacity and technical skills; (f) the need for formal project planning and systematic processes for management of change; and (g) the need to develop user requirements, functional and technical specifications and procurement documentation in advance of the main procurement of an ICT solution.

Result on public investment management has been mixed. While the country has moved towards the right direction by tightening capital spending through the public investment law. Implementation has not been effective since the law was issued in 2014. Coordination between MoF and MPI had been always the bottleneck in Vietnam. Institutional arrangement needs to be structured such a way that enables the state functions in capital investment management.

Three features remain important to the context of PFM reforms in Vietnam. First, while the budget system is unitary, public expenditure management is quite decentralized. Second, dual recurrent-capital budgeting, stemming in part from a legacy of state planning, remains a pronounced feature of prevailing institutional arrangements, particularly around finance and planning. Finally, the demand for and disclosure of fiscal information continues to evolve in Vietnam, particularly as legislative actors and the public engage more actively in decision making. The continued existence of a large state-owned enterprise sector means that wider issues of public corporate sector governance and accounting will remain prominent.

As Vietnam moves towards the middle-income country status, there are new challenges that the country faces, for which it needs to be prepared as the country sets its sights on the next generation's growth and reform objectives. The first of these is to maintain fiscal discipline in the face of increasing demands on the public expenditure, as the complexity and size of the public sector increases at least in absolute and most likely in relative terms. Secondly, the government will need to further transition away from having a central bureaucracy that is focused on maintaining compliance and processing transactions towards a central government that drives policy across the public sector. Finally, as Vietnam further opens up and integrates into the world economy, the government will need to deepen its engagement with outside actors as a way to gain the trust of the citizens and external investors.

Going forward, Vietnam's adaptive changes will center on balancing reform objectives around PFM institutional design and implementation. The reform trajectory of Vietnam, as illustrated by the evolution of the three budget laws, very much illustrates the interplay between overall structural context (and challenges) and tactical approaches to moving reforms forward. Vietnam's gradual but sustained PFM reforms over the past generation have crystalized both achievements, as well as presenting a new generation of challenges. The challenges of working across levels of government, greater integration of planning, budgeting, and execution, and bridging information silos across the bureaucracy will present a new generation of adaptive challenges.

NOTES

1. Under the poverty line of USD 1.90 a day, 2011 PPP.
2. The central government, 63 provinces, 680 districts and 11,000 communes.
3. Pre-acceptance tests are performed to ensure that assets are fit for purpose. Acceptance committees are created to formally accept the assets and transfer them to the users. Acceptance and handover are documented by the acceptance committee at a formal meeting and the minutes serve as the legal confirmation. The handovers can occur concurrently or with some delay. If there is a delay, the project owner temporarily becomes responsible operating and managing the asset.

BIBLIOGRAPHY

Eckardt, S., G. Demombynes, and D. Chandrasekharan Behr. 2016. *Vietnam: Systematic Country Diagnostic*. Washington, DC: World Bank. http://documents.worldbank.org/curated/en/334491474293198764/Vietnam-Systematic-Country-Diagnostic.

IEG. 2016. *Vietnam: Evaluation of Public Financial Management Reform (Project Performance Assessment Report)*. Washington, DC: World Bank.

Krause, Philipp, and Sierd Hadley. 2016. *A Capable Public Finance System for Vietnam in 2035*. Oxford: ODI.

Lienert, Ian; Habib Rab, Minh Van Nguyen, Quyen Hoang Vu, Sandeep Mahajan, Sudhir Shetty, Victoria Kwakwa, Gert Van Der Linde. 2014. "Revising Vietnam's state budget law (2002) : Proposals drawing on international experience (English)." Washington, DC: World Bank Group. http://documents.worldbank.org/curated/en/236951468176957875/Revising-Vietnams-state-budget-law-2002-Proposals-drawing-on-international-experience.

Mallon, R. 1999. 'Experiences in the region and private sector incentives in Vietnam', in S. Leung (ed.), *Vietnam and the East Asian Crisis*, Edward Elgar, London:165–92.

Rab, Habib Nasser, Jorge Martinez-Vasques, Anwar M. Shah, Quyen Hoang Vu, Minh Van Nguyen, Nara Francoise Kamo Monkam, Abha Prasad, Quang Hong Doan, Indira Iyer. 2015. "Fiscal Decentralization Review in Vietnam: Making the Whole Greater than the Sum of the Parts : Summary report (English)." Washington, DC : World Bank Group. http://documents.worldbank.org/curated/en/389051468187138185/Summary-report.

Van Arkadie, Brian, and Raymond Mallon. "The Introduction of Doi Moi." In *Viet Nam — a Transition Tiger?*, 65-78. ANU Press, 2004. http://www.jstor.org/stable/j.ctt2jbjk6.14.

World Bank. 2012. *Fiscal Transparency in Vietnam*. Washington, DC: World Bank.

———. 2013. *Vietnam PEFA Assessment*. Washington, DC: World Bank.

———. 2015. *Making the Whole Greater than the Sum of the Parts: A Review of Fiscal Decentralization in Vietnam (Summary Report)*. Washington, DC: World Bank.

———. 2017. *Vietnam: Public Expenditure Review 2016—Spending for Results*. Washington, DC: World Bank.

———. n.d. *PFM Reform Program in Vietnam: Achievements, Challenges, and Lessons for Other Transition Countries (Presentation)*.

World Bank and MPI. 2016. *Vietnam 2035: Toward Prosperity, Creativity, Equity and Democracy*. World Bank Group and Vietnam Ministry of Planning and Investment.

7 Myanmar
LATECOMER'S LEARNING AND ADAPTING FROM INTERNATIONAL EXPERIENCES

ATUL B. DESHPANDE and PIKE PIKE AYE

INTRODUCTION

Myanmar, also known previously as Burma, is one of the largest countries in South East Asia, with a population of about 52 million people comprising multiple ethnicities. Myanmar is also one of the least developed countries in the region, and has been characterized by a complex combination of challenges including vulnerability to natural disasters, food and nutrition insecurity, armed conflict, inter-communal tensions, and recently, displacement of significant numbers of people. Myanmar has also had economic problems including inflationary pressures, a slowdown in new investments and low socio-economic development indicators. Nevertheless, Myanmar has witnessed a remarkable process of change since 2011, when the country took initial steps to open to the world. Myanmar's first free national elections were held in November 2015 and a peaceful transfer of power to a civilian government took place in March 2016.

Since opening in 2011, the country has been undergoing a slow transition from a closed authoritarian system to a more open democratic system; from a centralized government to a level of measured decentralization; and from long-standing conflicts towards peace. These transitions are complex and interlocking, and since then the country has embarked on a series of political and economic reforms. The political reforms include the release of political prisoners, negotiations and signing of ceasefire agreements with armed ethnic groups, relaxation of media controls and censorship, and the creation of a Parliament, while the economic reforms include liberalizing the foreign exchange market, relaxing controls on foreign ownership of companies, separation of the Central Bank from the Ministry of Finance, and the planned reform of State Economic Enterprises (SEEs). All these reforms have enormous potential to improve development outcomes in the country and the standards of living of its people; they have also brought about higher levels of economic growth and foreign investment.

Performance of public sector and public financial management (PFM) represents one of the key development challenges in Myanmar. In 2011, Myanmar's PFM system was quite basic when compared with that of other

Southeast Asian countries, with manual and relatively outmoded systems and a lack of awareness about international developments in various areas of PFM reform, due to its long isolation. The PFM system in Myanmar operated without the umbrella framework of foundational laws such as a PFM Law, a Procurement Law or even updated financial and administrative regulations. Processes and systems for basic financial management and procurement functions were outdated and required revision, while the capacity within the public sector was very weak. The availability of information and its authenticity was a challenge and information on the same subject from different sources could vary. The various departments and ministries within the government have operated in silos and communication between them has been inadequate. Internal decision-making processes were complex and there was a very low level of administrative and financial delegation to various levels within the administration.

In 2012 the government developed a PFM strategy that recognized the need for PFM reform "to be able to support political, economic and social objectives of the Republic of the Union of Myanmar, to sustain macroeconomic stability of the nation and to ensure economic development." In addition, the strategy recommended adoption of a policy-based budgeting system for effective implementation of the government's policies. The strategy also recognized the linkages between PFM and sectoral reforms and the development of public service functions, in accordance with the current situation and consistent with international standards. At the same time, multilateral and bilateral partners also began their engagement with Myanmar. With the support of the World Bank, the government conducted its first comprehensive diagnostic work on its PFM system using the Public Expenditure and Financial Accountability (PEFA) Performance Measurement Framework. This informed the development of a three-phased reform program that covered a 10–15 years' period coordinated by a PFM Executive Reform Team (ERT) led by the Deputy Minister for Finance. Phase 1 (3–5 years) aimed to improve the control and stability in expenditure and revenue management processes while building internal capacities. Phase 2 (5–8 years) strives to develop the ability to produce, analyze and interpret more sophisticated financial management data as a basis for holding all levels of management accountable for results in their collection and use of public finances. The final phase 3 (8–12 years) aims to develop more sophisticated budget and expenditure management systems to improve the quality of expenditures in relation to achieving policy objectives.

The Modernization of Public Finance Management (MPFM) project was put in place to support the government of Myanmar in modernizing and strengthening the public finance systems in the country in line with its strategy and modern international practices. The project is informed by priorities as set out in the government's PFM reform strategy and provides support for improvements across the whole cycle of Public Finance Management (PFM). The government's PFM reform strategy and the MPFM project are anchored in the Union Ministry of Planning and Finance (MOPF) and are led by Deputy Minister MOPF supported by the PFM ERT. As such, there is a very high level of engagement and ownership of PFM reform in the country. There are eight implementing agencies (IA) in the MPFM project, of which six are under the MOPF, while the other two are the Joint Public Accounts Committee (JPAC) of the legislature and the Office of the Auditor

General (OAG). A high-level reform team (ERT) led by the Deputy Minister was put in place to lead the PFM reform agenda. Each component is managed by the relevant implementing agency, led by their respective Directors General. The PFM reform units within the implementing agency are responsible for coordination of the reform efforts and for providing timely support and technical inputs as required. By design, the MPFM project is anchored in the MOPF, and directly connects to the IA.

Since October 2014, the MPFM project has been supporting reform in key areas across the PFM cycle including revenue administration; budget formulation and execution; planning and public investment management; treasury systems and banking modernization; financial management and procurement reforms and strengthening accountability through external oversight. This chapter examines experiences of two of these reform areas, specifically strengthening tax administration and supporting budget formulation. Each of the area is detailed in the subsequent sections.

STRENGTHENING TAX ADMINISTRATION

Issues

The tax administration system in Myanmar suffered from legacy issues and had not been modernized and changed over the years. There was an absence of a tax paying culture in the country and, given the weak level of bookkeeping and limited availability of data and information, and tax settlements were often a "negotiated" affair between the officers and the tax payers. The tax administration system had outdated rules and procedures, which hampered the task of tax collection, and did not provide for a constructive relationship between the state and the taxpayers. Multiple departments, agencies and state enterprises were involved in revenue collection, with minimal coordination; as such, the big picture on revenue was not easily available to decision makers.

The Official Assessment System (OAS) for tax assessments depended entirely on taxpayer accounts and records. Taxpayer registration was manual and cumbersome, and prevented authorities from assessing the size of or managing the taxpayer population. The tax administration was based on the tax type rather than function and this required creating different client files for different tax types. This further complicated the management of the taxpayer population and increased the administrative and compliance burden on them. The existing taxation system also employed a commercial tax regime, which was affected by issues like tax cascading, input tax credits, and tax evasion activities. Finally, the level of automation in the Internal Revenue Department (IRD) was minimal, as was the IT capacity of the staff. These weaknesses led to low tax collections and inefficiencies, which in turn affected public investment, growth and progress at a critical time for Myanmar. The framework for Myanmar's tax system therefore required a fundamental revision and a move towards a simpler, less distorting, and more efficient taxation system.

Reform interventions and design strategy

A two-phase strategy was adopted to tax administration reforms. The first phase (2012–16), focused on organizational reforms, setting up of the Large Taxpayer

Office and introduction of the self-assessment system (SAS) and intensive tax audits to enhance the tax base and compliance. The second phase (2017–22) will further strengthen the policy and legislative framework and the automation requirements of the IRD, including the Integrated Tax Administration System (ITAS). Specific interventions include the following:

(a) Strategic and policy advice to IRD to support modernization and reform across the entire gamut of tax operations. Examining options for the reform of the organizational structure of the IRD, including introducing a functional (rather than tax type) organizational structure and suggest appropriate restructuring.

(b) Setting up of a Large Taxpayer's Office (LTO) and three Medium Taxpayer Offices (MTO 1,2,3) in Yangon to streamline tax collections from the highest capacity taxpayers in Myanmar and help with the move towards a SAS.

(c) Reorganizing the IRD Headquarters to strengthen efficiency and transparency of tax operations, update the rules and regulations, and modernize the operational procedures and administrative processes. It also entailed supporting preparation of the Tax Administration Procedures Law (TAPL) and the new Income Tax Act and facilitating its approval.

(d) Providing technical assistance to IRD in identifying their IT and automation requirements and suggesting the most appropriate sequencing for implementation, along with technical support through the planning, procurement and implementation of IT solutions covering all processes connected with tax administration.

(e) Training and technical assistance for business process reengineering and capacity building to manage the change process.

Results

To date the IRD has established a Directorate in Headquarters designed to improve taxpayer services and enforcement activity. Other organizational reforms in IRD underway are the review and update of current rules and operational procedures and the legal framework, including the proposed TAPL and the new Income Tax (IT) Act.

Large Taxpayer Office (LTO) was established to support direct tax collection efforts by focusing in areas where returns were expected be the highest. The LTO initiated a program of auditing large taxpayers and reviewing their books to check taxpayer compliance and assess arrears. This resulted in a nearly 95 percent on-time filing rate during 2016/17 and the collection of some outstanding "large taxpayer" debt, following the first round of tax audits. In addition, the tax self-assessment process and functions in the LTO have been streamlined, which has resulted in expansion of the tax payer data base. As a result, over 500 tax payers filed returns at the LTO during the financial year 2016–17 and the revenue collected increased from about MMK 1,105 billion to about MMK 2,390 billion within a year. Furthermore, as the self- assessment system was introduced at the Medium Taxpayer Office from 1 July 2017, the LTO has been providing guidance and technical support to ensure a successful transition to the new method of taxation. An additional development at the LTO has been the provision of guidance to large taxpayers on the implementation of the new specific goods tax.

IT and automation requirements for the IRD have been identified and a sequenced implementation approach has been taken to reflect capacity and technology challenges. To date, data centers and hardware have been procured for the tax offices in Yangon and Nay Pyi Taw. The functional and technical specifications for the procurement of an integrated tax assessment system (ITAS) solution for the tax administration system have been prepared. The ITAS is expected to integrate the various components of the tax management cycle such as taxpayer registration, compliance, returns processing, payments, arrears management and risk analysis while making organizational improvements through effective IT based automation efficiencies in all major areas of tax administration and key tax functions.

These improvements have helped the IRD to exceed its revenue collection targets during FY 16–17 and achieve a 20 percent increase in tax revenues from the private sector. However, the revenue collections from the SEEs have declined, leading to the overall revenue collections falling short of target. In addition, the tax-to-GDP ratio is expected to remain steady in the current year or only rise marginally and concerted efforts are required to increase revenues (See figure 7.1 and figure 7.2 for revenue collection performance in Myanmar).

FIGURE 7.1

Tax revenue and GDP in Myanmar

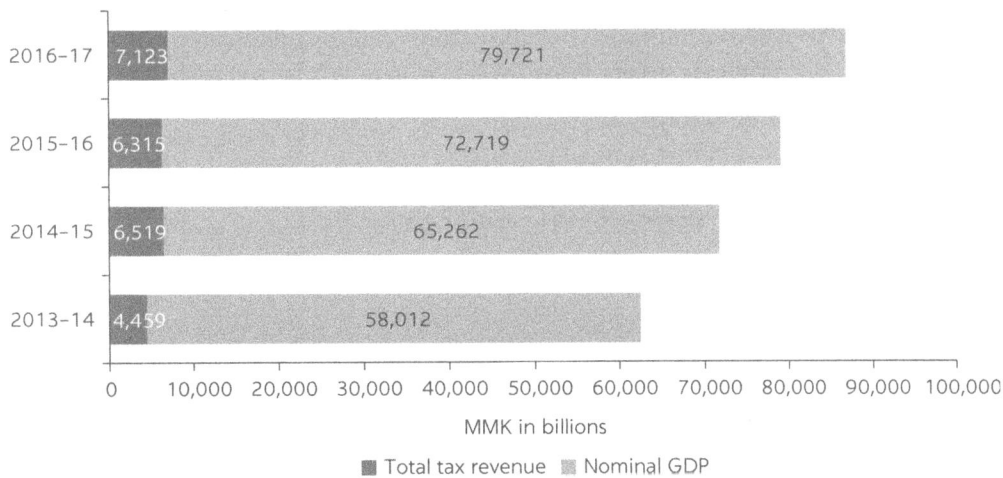

Source: World Bank, Fiscal Master, August 2017.
Note: GDP = gross domestic product.

FIGURE 7.2

Tax revenue to GDP ratio in Myanmar

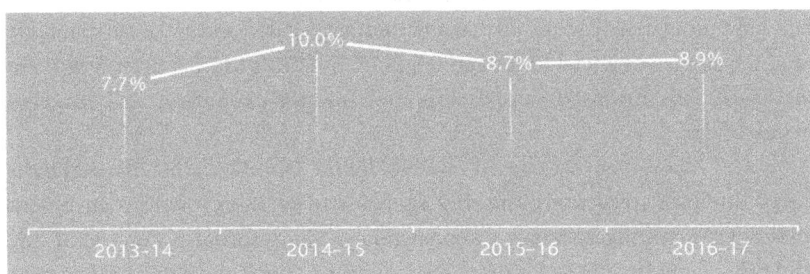

Source: World Bank, Fiscal Master, August 2017.
Note: Figures for 2016–17 are estimates. GDP = gross domestic product.

The key challenge in enhancing revenue collections in Myanmar is the mindset of not paying tax and a culture of negotiated settlements that was being followed until recently. Intensive and ongoing efforts are required to change this mindset and culture and to demonstrate the individual and collective benefits of paying taxes. This also requires transformation at all levels within IRD, both technical and non- technical, to help accelerate the nascent process of reform.

The revenue collection systems in Myanmar are quite fragmented, with the IRD being responsible for collecting tax revenues (Income Tax, Specific Goods Tax, Commercial Tax, Stamp Duty and State Lotteries) but not non-tax and other revenues of the government. IRD currently has no role in other revenues, especially from the oil and gas sector as well as from the SEEs, as these are the responsibility of the concerned ministry/department/SEE. The government is considering the benefits of bringing all tax and non-tax revenue collection under one organization, the IRD, so that better coordination and efficiencies could result.

The incentives and tax exemptions provided by the government for attracting foreign investment in Myanmar are thought to be partly responsible for the lower tax collections, and they are also believed to be resulting in the erosion of the tax base. Also, related companies who are both under the jurisdiction of the LTO and the MTO (essentially subsidiaries of the companies under the jurisdiction of the LTO) are thought to have been pushing much of the profit-making activity to the MTO firms that were not under self-assessment until recently, and thereby avoiding taxes. This affects the overall tax collections and the transparency of the tax system. Phase 2 will support estimation and analysis of tax incentives and exemptions.

BUDGET FORMULATION PROCESS

Issues

Prior to the recent reforms, budget processes were manual, outdated and not an effective tool for management information and decision making. The credibility of the budget was low because of significant variations of budget out-turns compared to original budget, and the regular use of supplementary budgets. Weak revenue forecasting, limitations in public investment planning, and the lack of information on donor funded projects were some of the other key issues. The compilation of financial and budget execution reports was almost entirely manual, significantly delaying reports and impeding timely receipt and analysis of information and data. The use of ICT in budget preparation was largely limited to data entry, and given the constraints in connectivity, all information was initially submitted in hard-copy format and then aggregated and re-keyed manually into IT systems. Financial Rules and Regulations (FRRs) dating from 1986 were not revised or updated, which affected budget execution and internal processes.

Public procurement was based on Presidential Directives that allowed individual line ministries and spending agencies to set their own procurement guidelines, resulting in a lack of consistency. The internal processes of line ministries, including those for processing appropriations and expending money, were onerous and caused delays in service delivery. In addition, the delays in availability of timely financial information (from about 5,400 individual spending units submitting monthly detailed financial statements) and the difficulty in analyzing the amounts reaching the frontline service delivery units made it difficult for management to respond to emerging challenges in expenditure management. The combination of factors such as outdated PFM systems, manual planning and budgeting processes, limited use of ICT, and FRRs that had not been revised since 1986 posed significant challenges to the overall public finance administration in the country and there was an urgent need for reform.

Reform interventions

Budget reform efforts aim to strengthen the budget formulation processes and develop budgetary and planning capacities that link policies with budget appropriations. The key reform interventions under the MPFM project are:

Preparation of a realistic Medium Term Fiscal Framework (MTFF) as a framework for assessing policy objectives with a medium-term constraint and with macroeconomic fundamentals, anchored within a sustainable debt management strategy.

(a) Better integration of the planning and budgeting processes, both on the recurrent and the capital side, to ensure policy linkage with budget appropriations.
(b) Strengthening budget performance analysis and monitoring to better budget credibility and reduce the need for significant variations at the supplementary budget stage.
(c) Development of a simple tool that strengthens revenue projections and formula-based calculation of intergovernmental transfers.
(d) Review and updating of the 1986 FRRs and the 2013 presidential procurement directives to suit current requirements.
(e) Working towards improving the quality and timeliness of information available through basic automation of current manual compilation process for the current and investment budgets; this will help inform decision making on budgetary allocations.
(f) Acquisition of computing equipment and connectivity, software and training to the personnel of the budget department.
(g) Automation and improved connectivity among the Budget and Treasury departments, line ministries, the Myanmar Economic Bank (MEB) and the Central Bank of Myanmar (CBM) to improve more timely and efficient flow of information (planned).

Results

Development of medium-term fiscal framework

The Budget Department, with the support of the World Bank, has prepared a MTFF. This has involved compiling a consolidated set of fiscal accounts in an analytical framework, establishing an inter-departmental team to periodically meet and update the framework; moving towards good practice in fiscal classification (e.g., analytical method for budget balance) and now using the framework to inform policy (e.g., spending ceilings, spending cuts, revenue targets, intergovernmental fiscal transfers).

The MTFF is transforming the way that the Union Budget is prepared in Myanmar. To date, the MTFF has been applied in two budget cycles

(2015/16 and 2016/17) and was updated to account for new reduced ministries structure after the formation of the new government. It has enabled MOPF to review links between government policies and budget allocations. It has also helped to inform budget adjustments at a time of fiscal constraints emanating from slowing growth, declining commodity prices and exchange rate depreciation. The MTFF provided the basis for setting ministry-level expenditure ceilings for the budget submission phase. The instrument is constantly evolving as new data becomes available and interdepartmental coordination increases. It has been a center piece of policy-based budgeting reforms of MOPF. Going from a largely incremental budgeting process only 5–6 years ago, the MOPF now has a consolidated fiscal frame that enables them to allocate resources to policy priorities within overall macroeconomic constraints. The results have been clear in terms of strategic reallocations of the budget, improved budget credibility (lower variance between budget plan and outturn), and significantly enhanced budget transparency.

Notwithstanding this progress, Myanmar faces ongoing challenges to further improve the MTFF. As the MOPF now has a good framework and team in place, the next stage will be to deepen further the analytical and forecasting capacities within each of the individual components of the MTFF. On revenue, there has been a tendency to underestimate government receipts in the budget plans, requiring more in-depth understanding of gas revenues and how fluctuations there (due to worldwide commodity trends) could affect the fiscal position.

On expenditure, there has been the opposite problem of overestimating spending in budget plans. Part of this has been due to overestimation of interest payments, but also other areas such as capital investments. For capital investment, there may be merit in linking together the medium-term expenditure estimates for large projects, which could also provide the basis for developing a medium-term commitment framework for critical capital expenditure. The Debt Management Office is working to prepare more accurate projections of interest payments and principal repayments on existing and new debt.

Budget performance analysis and monitoring

The MPFM project continues to provide technical support to the Budget Department on budget performance analysis. Budget analysis in five key line ministries has been completed covering expenditures, budget variances, and key bottlenecks to budget implementation. Templates for reporting budget performance, the introduction of a comprehensive and timely budget circular, and ongoing training on budget formulation have strengthened the annual budget formulation process and reduced the variations during the supplementary budget. The MTFF and the budget analysis exercise are closely interlinked, as the latter helps inform spending projections in the MTFF. Ministerial Budget Briefs providing background information of the ministry with the analysis of their spending as well as the bottlenecks of budget execution in each ministry have been introduced. The Budget Brief is used during budget preparation process as a guideline to negotiate the ministry's budget allocation and improve communication with line ministries. A number of new reports have been designed, including: (a) Summary of Technical Assistance to Budget Department on Budget Data Analysis; (b) Ministerial Budget Brief; and (c) Analysis of causes of variance and recommendations for more efficient budget execution.

More remains to be done:

The Budget Department plans to extend the Budget Analysis training to another five ministries. A train-the-trainers program to build the analytical and training capacity of budget officers to support more ministries and agencies aims to further strengthen budget allocation decisions. The Budget Briefs are expected to support improved communication both internally in MOPF and also between MOPF budget analysts and line ministries on budget performance and future allocations. In addition, the Budget Department is planning to explore the possibility of introducing "Performance Indicators" in the ministries and line agencies. The indicators will aim to link budget performance to government policy.

The envisioned Budget Integration Manual will help strengthen linkages between recurrent and capital budgeting. Electronic budget forms (that resemble the current budget request forms issued by the Budget and Planning Department) will be developed to support easier data entry with greater accuracy. By using existing forms rather than developing new forms that meet a specific international standard, this incremental yet transformational step towards automation has a greater chance of acceptance and will be less likely to create extra burden on the line agencies or confuse them with new forms. Once the Budget Integration Manual is finalized and the new budget classification and chart of accounts have been approved, the e-forms will be revised to be in-line with the new budget classification and chart of accounts.

CHALLENGES, APPROACHES TO REFORM, AND KEY LESSONS LEARNED

Over the course of the reform process a number of key and context-specific challenges have been identified that temper both the speed and trajectory of reform and what is possible at any point in time.

While a democratically elected civilian government has taken over after decades of military rule, much of the bureaucracy are still appointments from the earlier dispensation while the political leadership have limited experience of administration. As such, sustained efforts at trust building are required between the new political dispensation and the bureaucracy or other appointees from the earlier regime, as this perceived trust deficit could influence the decision making and reform process. The military continues to control three key ministries (Home Affairs, Defense, and Border Affairs), and one-third of the seats in the Parliament, and so there is a precarious balance of power between the earlier regime and the current democratic set up, in an evolving political environment.

Complex approval processes and a lack of adequate delegation to lower levels are also key issues affecting the decision-making process and the project implementation and disbursement. There is a need for appropriate delegation of administrative and financial powers to functionaries at all levels, so that the decision making can be faster and result in greater efficiencies. The MOPF is well placed to provide overall guidance to the agencies to streamline the approval process and make it more efficient.

There is also a reluctance to spend project funds for expenditures like workshops and study tours. The government is expected to finalize a policy on training and other capacity building activities so that staff from the agencies of the MPFM project can benefit from these trainings and exposure visits, and these can be important tools for building much needed human capital.

The policy on engagement of national and international consultants needs clarity so that the agencies can plan and take forward the consultant recruitment process in a timely manner, given the very lengthy and time-consuming internal approval processes.

The two specific examples were following the "best fit" approach to PFM reform rather than the best practice internationally. In budgeting, Myanmar has stayed away from program budgeting for now, because this would mean a change in how the government classifies and accounts for spending. In a low capacity environment, this would have been very difficult and there was a risk that the reform may have slowed down considerably. The MPFM project rather went for incrementally strengthening key aspects of the existing budgeting process and ensuring significant transparency. In the course of time, the possibility of going in for program budgeting and/or outcome based budgeting will be explored, based on the progress achieved in the existing reforms.

In financial management and accounting, the international best practices in PFM reform is to go for modern Integrated Financial Management Information Systems (IFMIS) systems that are expected to cover not just all aspects of the core PFM system (Planning, Budgeting, Expenditure Management and Control, Accounting and Reporting, Internal controls, Audit), but also have linked modules for Tax administration, HR and payroll, procurement and asset management. The aim is an eventual move towards a full cycle end-to-end integrated approach. However, the Myanmar MPFM project focuses on modernizing the PFM system by strengthening the current planning and budgetary processes, the payment, accounting and reporting systems, and the internal controls. Simultaneously stand-alone automation of some functions of the MOPF is being carried out (Tax Administration, CORE Banking systems for MEB), while also addressing the issues related to the administrative, legal and regulatory framework related to the PFM system in Myanmar. The next planed step is to go for a basic automation of the core PFM functions within the MOPF and of stabilizing the system. Finally, the plan would be to move to an integrated FMIS with either a modular approach or an end-to-end integrated approach. This re-engineering approach will promote transparency, accountability and responsiveness of public financial resources. Other benefits expected will be curtailing wasteful spending and corruption, enhancing controls and audit procedures as well as strengthening fiscal planning and reporting. And all of this is being done in a proper sequence and by simultaneously building the necessary human skills and capacities.

Myanmar's reform approach to introducing PFM reforms was to be flexible and to draw from international experience and lessons, and adapt these to the Myanmar context and situation, rather than seeking to import and superimpose international best practices. The approach sought to employ international experience to not only improve individual processes but to link them together as part of the whole PFM cycle. The thinking at the time was that wholesale reform of existing systems and process with outside solutions would not have suited Myanmar given its unique system, shaped in part by its isolation. Furthermore, the system that existed had many positive aspects that were working well—largely around oversight and internal control processes and systems. As a result, the incremental, iterative approach to reforming certain processes building on what already existed and learning from international experience has helped and continues to build a relationship of trust between the government and development partners; it promotes confidence in government officials at many levels to undertake reforms; and enables reforms to be undertaken and take root at a pace appropriate to the Myanmar context. The aim was to guide Myanmar away from certain approaches that are excessively complex, as well as to leapfrog or advance certain reforms more quickly by taking advantages of key lessons learned by other others in the region (and more broadly) implementing PFM reforms. PFM reforms are on-going; it has been just 2 years since the activities have commenced, and the lessons from implementation are still being learned. Nonetheless, the lessons learned to date have been used to effect mid-course changes and corrections along the way.

Myanmar has taken an incremental and stepped approach to ICT through introduction of basic tools and systems while simultaneously building capacity, with an aim to scale- up over time. By drawing on international experiences rather than international best practices, Myanmar was able to avoid certain approaches that may have been excessively complex. For example, by defining key concepts and objectives for achieving fiscal *discipline* and *supporting key policy priorities*, the government could build appropriate tools (for example, the MTFF, inter-government fiscal transfer formula) to enable them to address these objectives within a policy based budgeting framework. Also, the government was able to take advantage of the growing body of evaluation work drawing from extensive international experience of both successes and failures in PFM reform to inform the design of the government's PFM strategy and the supporting project. Lessons drawn from these experiences have been reflected in the project design and adapted as the reforms proceed.

There is international consensus that reform design and implementation need to be tailored to the appropriate institutional and capacity context. Reform design has therefore been informed by considerable diagnostic work including a PEFA Assessment to better understand the Myanmar context given a long period of non-engagement with the country. Also, in developing the PFM Reform Strategy, the government of Myanmar had has also studied reform experiences of other countries in the region.

As is reflected in all the case studies in this volume, the Myanmar case underscores that PFM reform delivers results only where high-level political ownership exists. The government has clearly demonstrated high-level political commitment to the reform and the PFM modernization agenda. PFM is the first item on the Economic Reform policy of the new government in Myanmar. The Deputy Minister of MOPF continues to be the Project Director for the MPFM project even after his elevation to the ministerial position. Also, this case underscores the importance of proper coordination among donors to achieve synergies and provide consistent advice to the government. The established PFM sector working group for the Development partners has proven to be an effective mechanism to facilitate communication not only among development partners but in sustaining a dialogue with the government as well.

International reform experience has also shown that PFM operates in a systemic way, with its strengths deriving both from the quality of individual process areas (such as planning, budget preparation) but also the links between those processes. This was the approach adopted in Myanmar in that reforms were not undertaken as individual processes in isolation but linking them within the context of the whole PFM cycle—in such an approach, "form" follows "function" rather than being driven primarily by institutional imperatives or existing structures. Sector ministries were consulted to better understand the constraints faced under the PFM system, so that the PFM modernization process could address these concerns and support front line service delivery.

Also, the enabling environment for accountability and dialogue has been conducive in Myanmar, helping to -build the trust necessary with stakeholders and to make sure policies are being designed and delivered effectively to ensure a voice from citizens, civil society, business, development partners and other actors in PFM reform program.

CONCLUSION

The government's PFM transformation strategy has been under implementation for a little over 2 years. A key conclusion that can be drawn from the progress to date is that the reform approach and strategy adopted by the government is relevant, particularly in the new and post-election environment in Myanmar. There is a continued commitment to the project by all the stakeholders and it is on course to achieve the expected results and the development outcomes as planned. There are countries in the region where the PFM reform process has been underway for more than a decade and they have had time to make midcourse corrections or changes in approach on more than one occasion. Myanmar has tried to learn from these experiences and is also learning from the path taken by such countries, thereby hoping to leap frog in the reform process. The encouraging results of some activities in the first stage of reforms are just becoming apparent and so Myanmar does not (yet) have experiences across many areas of the PFM cycle. As the reforms progress and results are achieved, or not achieved, it is hoped that the PFM reform journey will have more experiences to share with the region and with the rest of the world.

The Myanmar case demonstrates that the best international practice is not necessarily the best option in a country like Myanmar, which is emerging from decades of isolation, has outdated administrative and financial systems, and very low local capacity. We are adopting an incremental stepwise approach that first addresses the weaknesses in the existing system and ensures that it delivers the outputs and results that it was intended to deliver. We are simultaneously examining the possible best fit options that will be relevant to the needs and environment of Myanmar, based on international experience.

BIBLIOGRAPHY

World Bank. 2013. *Republic of the Union of Myanmar: Public Financial Management Performance Report*. Washington, DC: World Bank.

——. 2014. *Project Appraisal Document for a Modernization of Public Finance Management Project*. Washington, DC: World Bank.

——. 2017a. *Myanmar Modernization of PFM Project MTR Mission 2017—Internal Aide Memoire*. Yangon, Myanmar: World Bank.

——. 2017b. *Performance and Learning Review of the Country Partnership Framework for Republic of the Union of Myanmar for the period FY15-FY 17*. Washington, DC: World Bank.

——. 2017c. *Implementation Status and Results Report (ISR) for the MPFMP*. Internal Report. Yangon, Myanmar: World Bank.

——. 2017d. *Fiscal Master*. Yangon, Myanmar: World Bank.

8 The Lao People's Democratic Republic

BUILDING PFM FOUNDATIONS UNDER FIRST-GENERATION REFORM

FANNY WEINER and SAYSANITH VONGVIENGKHAM

INTRODUCTION

After independence in 1975, the Lao People's Democratic Republic introduced a centrally planned economic system, but over the coming decade the weak performance of the country's economy was not able to stimulate the expected growth and development. In 1986, the transition from a centrally planned to a market oriented economy was initiated ("New Economic Mechanism") and reached considerable achievements. However, the Asian Financial Crisis in the late 1990s caused severe macroeconomic turbulences, including triple-digit inflation.

In 2000, GDP/capita was just slightly above USD300, and social indicators were lagging behind regional peers. While a large part of Lao PDR population was initially shielded from the effects of the Asian Crisis due to prevailing subsistence agriculture practices, the stalled progress in improving social conditions was a concern (see table 8.1). The country was still on the path of transitioning to a market economy, setting up conditions for private sector development, and starting to exploit its natural resource potential while struggling with macroeconomic instability and high dependency on foreign aid flows.

The Asian Crisis also exposed the weaknesses of the country's public economic and financial management framework, which was characterized by an underdeveloped human capital base, weak institutions and slow implementation of policy reforms. Monetary and fiscal policy was ad-hoc and ineffective; budget processes were inefficient with little transparency, accountability and controls within the public financial management (PFM) framework. Budget plans and execution reports were not published in a timely manner and the budget nomenclature did not allow for a comprehensive view of budget execution, tracking and control of spending, while most processes were done manually. This meant that while the budget system was able to allocate across sectors it was difficult to determine exactly what was spent over the course of the

TABLE 8.1 **The Lao People's Democratic Republic development indicators, 1999**

	LAO PDR	EAST ASIA & PACIFIC	SUB-SAHARAN AFRICA
Life expectancy at birth (years)	53	69	52
Infant mortality rate (per 1,000 live births)	101	39	91
Under 5 mortality rate (per 1,000 live births)	140	47	147
Maternal mortality rate per 100,000 live births)	650	—	—
Adult literacy rate (%)	43	17	41
-Of which for females (%)	56	24	53
Net primary enrollment ratio (%)	77	99	—
-Of which girls	66	98	—
Access to safe water (% population)	39	84	45
Physicians (per 1,000 people)	0.2	1.4	—
Hospital beds (per 1,000 people)	2.6	2.1	1.2
Paved roads (%)	13.8	—	17

Source: World Bank Country Assistance Strategy 1999, quoted from World Development Indicators.
Note: — = not available.

budget year. Commitment controls were not in place, resulting in inconsistencies between planned and actual expenditures and causing significant arrears. The financial management and reporting responsibilities of the central ministries, provinces and districts were insufficiently specified in the legal framework, which in light of the government's rapid decentralization reform contributed to inefficiency and insufficient transparency and accountability in budget preparation and execution. At the time, there were also hundreds of bank accounts linked to government departments on all administrative levels. Furthermore, oversight bodies such as the State Audit Organization (SAO) did not operate independently and public accounting standards throughout the public sector were not aligned with international standards. These deficiencies resulted in a lack of transparency and consistency in tracking and accounting for expenditures and revenues at both the national and sub- national levels, leading to delays in compiling and producing in-year and annual comprehensive financial reports and impeding the submission of year-end financial statements to the SAO for their review and audit. The lack of capacity of civil servants across government agencies further compounded the problem, as they lacked the understanding and skills to improve the status quo and to implement reforms.

The weak status and performance of the central government to efficiently manage public finance and to use them appropriately formed a major bottleneck to economic and social development of Lao PDR.

REFORM INTERVENTION

PFM reforms in Lao PDR can be viewed as falling into the following periods:

1. First generation: 2000–13
2. Pace of reforms decelerated compounded by lack of formal dialogue between the government and development partners: 2013–16
3. Second generation preparation and implementation: 2016 onwards

The first generation of reforms is the focus of this chapter in terms of the reform intervention and results of reforms, as these constitute the main reform experience to date. The processes involved in the first generation, and in the subsequent phases in the reform journey, are then discussed in section on the approaches to reform.

The first generation of PFM reforms were developed to support the implementation of the government's national development strategies as Lao PDR moved towards a market-oriented economy. These included the 2004 National Growth and Poverty Eradication Strategy (NGPES), and the sixth National Socio-Economic Development Program 2006–10 (NSEDP). The early PFM reforms sought to tackle structural problems in budget formulation and execution with the goal of increasing efficiency of public spending and reducing fiscal imbalances. This first-generation PFM reform focused on putting in place regulations, processes and procedures required for a basic PFM framework, and on enhancing transparency and accountability through increased public disclosure.

The high-level objective of the reforms was to enhance public sector effectiveness to contribute to the socio-economic development of Lao PDR people. Specifically, PFM reforms were aimed to increase accountability, transparency, and reliability of public financial processes and information, which in turn would better inform policy and decision making regarding public spending. The reforms were captured in the Public Financial Management Strengthening Program (PFMSP), officially adopted in November 2005 as a medium-to-long-term program. The strengthening of the legal and institutional framework and capacity building were the starting point of the reforms. The cornerstone of the reforms was the revision of the State Budget Law, followed by the strengthening of the Ministry of Finance's information management system and pilot roll out of the system to the provincial and sector levels. These were accompanied by intensive capacity building to strengthen the human capital for the implementation of reforms.

Together these sought to provide the foundations for strengthening three core functional areas of PFM, namely: budget preparation, budget execution and public accounting and auditing. Budget preparation and budget execution together constitute the core institutions and processes which determine how public funds are spent, while public accounting and auditing is central to transparency of public spending.

The content of these reforms was as follows:

(a) Budget preparation: Reform activities initially concentrated on the revision and implementation of regulations and procedures to facilitate a proper budget planning process, and to achieve appropriate balance between recurrent and capital spending. The budget planning changes included adoption and adherence to a budget calendar, introduction of budget ceilings, use of functional classification, and disclosure of budget documents to the public.

(b) Budget execution: The government sought to strengthen and streamline budget execution and controls by improving basic cash management, reporting, and control systems through the revision and implementation of the respective regulations and procedures. The aim was to establish a single network of treasury accounts, internal audit and control systems. To support the government's decentralization process, it was also envisaged to enhance budget controls and reporting systems at the district level. The treasury function was intended to be centralized and strengthened, specifically through the introduction of a Treasury Single Account (TSA) through consolidation of bank account balances in the Bank of Lao PDR (BOL) and commercial banks to a single account in the BOL HQ using zero balance account method. Further emphasis was given to cash management, through establishing a cash management unit which would project and monitor cash inflow and outflow, and the improvement of payment processes.

(c) Public Accounting and Auditing: The blueprint for the accounting and auditing reforms foresaw a long-term approach to amend the Public Accounting Decree, adopt international public accounting and auditing standards and to increase transparency by publishing audit reports. Establishing the autonomy of the SAO and strengthening the capacity of the external audit function were another cornerstone of the reforms. These activities were to be accompanied and continued through training and capacity building and ultimately a roll-out of the new accounting standards to the provincial and district level. As a measure for long-term sustainability, the accounting profession and the Lao Association of Accountants would be strengthened to act as a professional body for training, accreditation and registration of accountants.

The key institution driving the reforms was the Ministry of Finance (MoF) and its key technical departments. Those included the Fiscal Policy, Budget, Tax and Information and Communications Technology (ICT) Departments and the National Treasury within the MoF. The SAO was also involved.

The government's reform efforts had extensive support from the wider donor community.[1] During 2003–11, PFM reform design was supported by several donors through bilateral support and bundled support in multi-donor TF. The World Bank implemented several multi-donor initiatives of the GoL through the Financial Management Capacity Building Project (FMCBP), and from 2009 to 2013 through the PFMSP financed through a multi-donor[2] trust fund. From 2005, there was a series of Poverty Reduction Support Operations (PRSO), which had the objective to ensure efficient management of public sector resources and increase the poverty reduction impact of public spending.

The NT2 Hydropower Project[3] played a significant role in the design of the PFM reforms. The NT2 Hydropower Project commenced in 2005. It included a Revenue Management Program (RMP) component which specified arrangements for budget preparation, execution and reporting of the NT2 revenues received by the government arising from the NT2 Hydropower operation. At the time, it was envisaged that as part of the broader PFM reforms, the RMP framework would be rolled out to the broader budget process. The results were mixed and resulted in misconceptions on what constituted success and demonstrable reform, and strained relations between the government and the institutions financing the project.

The first-generation reform took about 12 years (2000–13) and received direct World Bank and multi-donor funding of USD21.3 million. In addition, the PRSO[4] series, which among other sectors also supported PFM reforms, provided a total of USD118 million to Lao PDR government, and through the preparation of the NT2 Hydropower Project technical assistance was provided.

RESULTS OF FIRST GENERATION PFM REFORMS

While progress has advanced on some key reforms, various aspects remain a work in progress. As the pace continues, most of the reforms remain incomplete signaling the need for continuous internal dialogue and negotiations to reach consensus and a way forward.

Budget preparation: After initial slow progress, considerable groundwork was laid and budget preparation was improved. This included the approval of a new Budget Law in 2006 and its implementing legislation in 2008, and the adoption of new budget nomenclatures and a chart of accounts. However, these have not been adopted fully by all ministries. Similarly, adherence to the new budget calendar remained weak, and ceilings were not introduced. On the other hand, pilots were undertaken in rolling out processes to line ministries and the subnational level and steps toward institutionalizing reforms were undertaken. The Budget Law was revised in 2015, but has not yet been fully implemented.

Budget Execution: The first-generation reforms brought significant progress for the country's treasury function by centralizing the National Treasury, and the introduction of the TSA. Zero-balance account arrangements were implemented in BOL and some commercial banks; however, a final agreement with one remaining commercial bank had not been reached. Payment processes have improved, specifically in the payments of the central government's payroll, which was moved from cash transactions to direct deposits on bank accounts. The most important achievement was arguably the roll-out of a locally developed Government Financial Information System (GFIS) in 2006, and its expansion to provinces in 2008. The implementation of the GFIS connected the whole country and Financial Statements were generated for the first time, while reporting, the timeliness and disclosure of the state budget was improved. However, the upgrade of the National Treasury's business processes and the envisaged enhancements to the system's functionality—initially agreed to be replaced by a commercial-off-the shelf (COTS) system—was never implemented, and at present the government is still considering options for its future development.

Public accounting and audit: During the same years, improvements to public accounting and audit functions also progressed. Implementing legislation for the Accounting Law and a new Audit law was approved by the National Assembly, granting autonomy to the SAO. While the use of IPSAS was foreseen in the Accounting Law, it has not been adopted by the ministries. So far there has been no progress on setting up internal control functions within the ministries, resulting in a continued weak control environment. SAO had initially made progress in establishing its mandated role, gradually being recognized by the public, and had made some early contributions to the government objective of transparency and public accountability in the management of public resources (it published a summary of audit findings for the FY2008/09 in the public media). However, SAO continues to suffer from low capacity (both financially and on human resources), and in recent years, no audits have been disclosed. Plans to strengthen the auditing profession have been slow, resulting to a continued shortage of qualified accountants in the country.

THE PFM REFORM PROCESS AND APPROACH

Despite starting with strong government commitment, PFM reforms in Lao PDR suffered periods of slowdowns over the past 15 years. Throughout most of the first-generation reforms, Lao PDR government demonstrated strong commitment to PFM reforms and to strengthening public sector capacity. This was reflected in the government's program and supported through a donor-funded capacity and technical assistance program (FMCBP), a series of PRSOs, and the

FIGURE 8.1

Reform timeline in Lao PDR

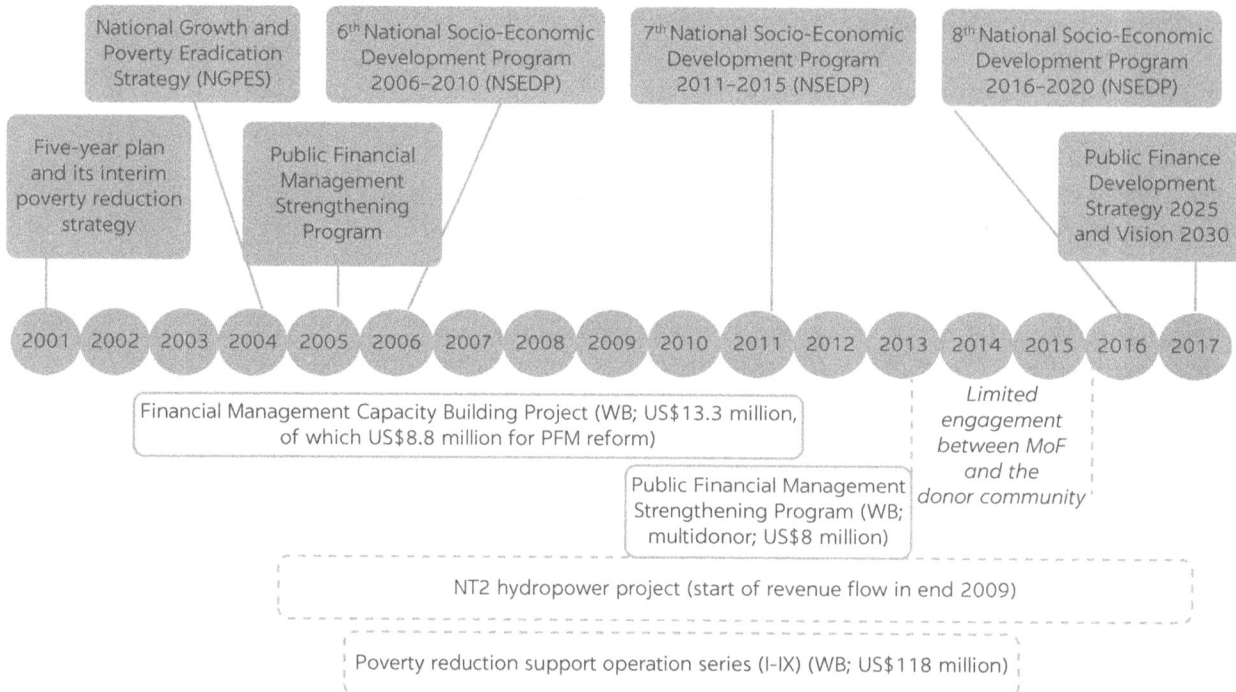

NT2 Hydropower Project (see figure 8.1 for a timeline of the reforms). At the onset of the reform, the Financial Management Strengthening Unit (PFMSU) under the External Financial Department (EFD) in MoF was established in 2003. Its main purpose was to lead the primarily donor-financed PFM reforms and to build up the required institutional capacity for reform implementation.

As other reforms were initially prioritized, PFM reforms experienced a slow start and only picked up in 2006. At the inception of the first-generation reforms in the early 2000s, the GoL initially focused its capacity on reforms in the financial sector and State-owned enterprises (SOE) during 2003–06, leading to a delayed start of PFM reforms. Insufficient capacity as well as a lack of understanding or exposure to new concepts within MoF to implement the ambitious overall government reform program across several areas was also a prevailing constraint. However, as reforms picked up in 2006, significant progress was achieved in several reform areas such as the centralization of the National Treasury, customs and tax functions, the introduction and partial implementation of a TSA and the upgrade and roll-out of GFIS to the provincial level.

In 2009, the initiation of the second multi-donor program (PFMSP-MDTF) provided additional momentum and support to the reforms. The oversight unit was strengthened and led by an Implementation Committee (IC) and assisted by a Secretariat. In addition, four task forces were established for several PFM reform areas (coinciding with project components). The then-Vice Minister heading the Steering Committee championed the reforms, supported by a strong team of technocrats.

Three years later, in 2012, changes in MOF's senior management and implementing arrangement resulted in substantive changes in the administrative and institutional arrangements for the reform implementation, leading to deceleration of the reform momentum. The promotion of a key reform champion to a higher level resulted in a leadership vacuum. From then, until closure of the donor supported project, there was no Chair for the Steering Committee. At the same time, key technical staff working on the oversight reform implementation were promoted and rotated to technical departments. While this strengthened the technical leadership of the individual departments, the overall reform oversight and momentum for the government reform agenda supported by the donor project rapidly evaporated.

At the same time, inadequate coordination led to confusion and further contributed to the deceleration of reform effort. The creation of a PFMSP Management Unit (PFMSP-MU) under the Fiscal Policy Department (FDP) was intended to support the government's broader reform agenda; however, there were some difficulties in coordinating a large number of ministerial departments and implementing agencies to identify, prioritize and plan for their own TA activities. Another source of confusion was that many ministries and implementing agencies did not understand that a donor-funded project (PFMSP) was in place to support the government's reform strategy (and not the reverse!); many did not see or understand the link between the two, which resulted in confusion and lack of ownership for both the government's strategy and the donor funded project.

Around the same time, additional development partners pledged their support through bilateral arrangements, which changed the dynamics of the existing donor coordination. Ultimately, in April 2013, MoF senior management appointed a national private firm to design and implement an integrated treasury system for the Ministry, even though the donor-funded program had supported the preparation of the system and a follow-up program for its implementation had been prepared in partnership with MOF technical and high-level staff. The decision of the MoF to turn to other funding sources and implementation arrangements including procurement, ultimately halted the program, leaving many first-generation reform initiatives incomplete.

In the absence of a broader reform agenda, coordinated donor support and a formal platform for dialogue, progress on the PFM reform agenda slowed down significantly. Dialogue between MoF and the wider donor community was continued but on a limited scale, mainly through the other development partner supported projects and ongoing activities including the PRSO series and the NT2 Hydropower project. Donor coordination and support were provided in an ad-hoc manner. A change in the management of the MoF in 2014 and the rotation of some key technical staff revived some of the reform initiatives, leading to revisions of the Budget, Tax and VAT laws. Also, MOF laid the groundwork for the introduction of a new tax collection IT system. Irrespective of the operating atmosphere, dialogue between a handful of development partner representatives and key technocrats within MOF continued, paving the way for future engagement when the enabling environment improved. During this period, MoF technocrats drafted a Long-term Fiscal Strategy as a guiding framework to address the aftermath of the economic and financial crisis, and to initiate second generation PFM reforms.

A turning point came in 2016 with the appointment of a new government that ushered in new MoF management and re-invigorated the commitment for PFM reforms and initiated the preparation of the "second-generation reforms." The 10th Party Congress of the People's Revolutionary Party took place in January 2016 with notable changes in the Politburo, followed by the appointment of a new government under a reform-oriented Prime Minister. With the top leadership and commitment, including the new Minister of Finance, who is also Deputy Prime Minister, and his management team, the dialogue with the donor community was revitalized. The approval of the Public Finance Development Strategy 2025 and Vision 2030 by the Prime Minister in July 2017 placed PFM reforms as the government's priority and initiated the preparation of second-generation PFM reforms. The wider donor community renewed its commitment to support those reforms through funding and technical assistance.

The Strategy provides the framework for the medium and long-term reform envisaged by the government. The main objective of the Public Finance Development Strategy for 2025 is to strengthen public finances to contribute to sustaining dynamic and stable economic growth and a graduation from least developed country (LDC) status by 2020. Emphasis is on regional and international integration of Lao PDR, while at the same time focusing on protecting the environment, creating prosperity, and enhancing the livelihoods of all ethnic groups.

The PFM agenda has benefited greatly from the government's emphasis on openness and regional integration, allowing for Lao PDR finance officials to engage more fully in regional PFM events and networks, including the Public Expenditure Management Network in Asia (PEMNA).[5] Lao PDR has already taken the opportunity to learn from other countries, especially its peers in the region by drawing on their experiences and challenges including good practices and lessons-learned in their reform process. The enabling environment also has created the space for the country to embark on a new era of PFM reforms. The envisaged "second generation" reforms have been formulated in a strategy and have high level political support, including from the Prime Minister, Minister of Finance/Deputy PM and the Vice ministers. Reform champions at various crucial technical and functional levels are in place who can play a crucial role in its implementation. At the same time, the donor community is willing to provide funding and technical assistance. Finally, the dynamic development of enhanced ICT tools is envisioned to support Lao PDR PFM reforms by providing the foundation on which advanced planning, budgeting and resource management reforms can be anchored and progressed.

The initial design of the reform was aligned with good international practice. As the first-generation reform aimed at laying the groundwork and setting up a legal framework and consequently processes for PFM, well-established and proven international approaches were embedded in the reform: attempting to implement international accounting and auditing standards; introducing a budget calendar, and establishing the TSA. This did not provide, nor did it require, much room for innovation or experimentation; in fact, the country had the advantage of being able to draw on existing international practices, which facilitated the reform design process for Lao PDR. At the same time, the national context was considered, as for example through the development of a locally developed GFIS system. However, in retrospect allowing more flexibility to adapt these practices and anchor them more firmly within the country context may have resulted in a "good enough" approach for addressing system issues and challenges.

Several factors contributed to the bumpy first-generation reform process. A key factor underpinning incomplete reforms was arguably the changing authorizing environment. PFM reforms experienced remarkable progress in the times of a favorable authorizing environment and plentiful technical and financial support from development partners. This trajectory stalled when the government's direction changed, resulting in an uneven, often suspended, agenda. Broader government commitment and change agents or the lack thereof are possibly among the main factors for reform success or failure.

Insufficient availability of skilled human resources emerged as another key obstacle. While there is no evidence of significant resistance from middle management or civil servants to reform initiates, inadequate human capital at the technical level also prevented a more rapid implementation of the reforms. Often, officials and staff had little exposure to new ideas or were unable to establish a reference point for reform processes and concepts being introduced that they could understand, adapt and make their own. On the other hand, progress was made and led by small groups of government staff with some level of introduction and exposure to new, often outside ideas and concepts, who as a result had some technical skills and had the access and ability to navigate the political economy structure of MoF. However, this scarce capacity was either concentrated on specific reform areas or spread thin over a range of activities. This also significantly contributed to the (habitually perceived by development partners) slow and often partial implementation of reforms.

The lack of enforcement of the existing legal framework constitutes another obstacle to formalizing the progress achieved. While a solid legal framework was established in several areas, in many cases laws implementing policies and procedures were not put in place, leading to non-compliance and often to continuation of the pre-reform status quo. Similarly, even with the existence of secondary legislation, these were not adapted and enforced to ensure the institutionalization of new processes and rules.

Development partner engagement has played an important role in driving the reforms. Donor commitment and continued engagement, paired with the provision of funding resources and technical assistance, was an important enabling factor. While the government's restricted financial situation did not allow for major investments, technical assistance and guidance in the reform process was probably the most important contribution from the donor community. Long-term engagements such as the PRSO series and the NT2 Hydropower Project also provided a platform for not only continuous dialogue, but also facilitated transitions towards international practice on reporting standards. Furthermore, the reporting requirements under the NT2 Hydropower Project's RMP constituted a donor-driven reform push for public expenditure reforms.

CONCLUSION AND LESSONS LEARNED

Lao PDR PFM reforms can be characterized as establishing the basic PFM framework, while adopting international best practice without full consideration of local context. The design of the first-generation reforms was focused on establishing a basic PFM framework using international experience as examples and did not provide sufficient space for significant experimentation or country adaptation. For example, the revenue management requirements under the NT2 Hydropower project, which guided initial PFM reforms, reflected international best practice on revenue management, resource allocation and financial and program reporting. However, at the time of the reform design, aiming for international standards might have been too ambitious for the country. The building of solid foundations on PFM concepts were yet to be laid and the awareness and knowledge on PFM principles within the government had not been developed sufficiently. The centrally controlled and planned environment with little exposure to international practices and ideas was often at odds with the reform agenda they were undertaking, one that embraced greater transparency, accountability and internal controls. Such transformative endeavors require time and a substantive adaptation period for the government staff involved to enable the proper environment for implementation. Lao PDR first generation reforms might have benefited from a more experimental and innovative and nuanced approach grounded in greater realism and adapted to the country context.

Initially the scope of the reforms was focused largely on the expenditure side and somewhat missed a more holistic approach. The first-generation reforms focused on expenditure management, and revenue management was only marginally included or treated as separate reforms (i.e., customs reforms). There might be several reasons for this approach: (a) as previously mentioned, the government did not have the capacity to concentrate on several reforms efforts at the same time; (b) fiscal space was not a major concern, as revenues through natural resources increased during the time of the first generation reforms, and significant donor funding continued to be available; and finally (c) donor interest was focused on improvement of the expenditure side—i.e., by supporting the building of a framework to comply with the NT2 revenue management requirements. Again, the expenditure management initiatives and reforms were often out of step with the realities on the ground and what realistically could be achieved.

Independent of the reform approach used, sufficient human capital with the right skill set is needed to implement the selected approach. The selected reform approach should take into consideration the existing level of capacity and integrate capacity building as a prerequisite for reform implementation. It is necessary to accurately assess the government's capacity within and among the existing institutional environments when designing reforms. While capacity building was an integral part of Lao PDR reform program, its effectiveness could have been enhanced through the integration of some adaptive and—given the country circumstances—innovative approaches.

Institutional implementation set-ups should facilitate an effective oversight and coordination mechanism. The strong government team overseeing the reform initiative was key in Lao PDR PFM reforms. High-level leadership and technical skills often compensated for low national capacity to deliver timely outputs. While such a team could focus on certain critical areas where strong capacity is needed to bring about timely results, realism on what can be achieved and within what timeframe is necessary.

Government commitment and proactive implementation driven by a champion/change agent also is an essential ingredient. For most of the reform years, Lao PDR reforms benefitted from high commitment and the presence of champions on several levels. However, changes in this enabling environment had immediate consequences for the pace of the reform. The departure and nonreplacement of the Steering Committee's Chair resulted in loss of leadership and led to delays and uncertainties, which in turn affected project reform implementation and results.

Reform champions familiar with the government's internal processes and hierarchies, and the ability and clout to navigate through them at all government levels, appears to be a crucial feature of reform success. They are typically well-connected, participate and understand intragovernmental coalitions and partnerships, and are capable of transmitting information and messages up and down internal hierarchies and externally with the donor community. They often have benefitted from international experience and exposure to new ideas. These players and small group of actors were essential for bridging the gap between the rest of the government and development partners by fostering greater alignment, communication, clarity and understanding while negotiating what was possible in the immediate and longer term. Reform champions can act as an official or informal voice of the government towards bigger or smaller groups of donor representatives, which is often preceded by a period of trust building. At the times when those individuals were in place in Lao PDR and supported by higher management, reforms were progressing. During the period when formal communications stalled, these individuals were able to keep the lines of communications open, and quietly progress technical reforms in partnership with development partners to pave the way for broader engagement when the enabling environment on both sides improved.

Cutting red-tape and working across bureaucratic silos in government facilitates internal processes, communication and decision making that contribute to a timelier reform process. One of the leading causes of delays during the reform process remained the numerous and overlapping internal reviews and approval procedures in the government. A reform oversight team that is empowered to facilitate cross-agency coordination and streamlining institutional procedures can help to reduce bureaucratic procedures and pave the way for future reforms.

Lastly, donor engagement can act as a platform in transition towards international good practice. Besides the benefits of donor-provided funding and technical assistance, long-term engagements between the government of Lao PDR and the donor community facilitated the country's transition towards international good practice in several ways. The support through international experts and access to regional and international practitioner networks and experience paved the way to a gradual adaptation of international good practice. While the reforms remain underway the foundations for a solid PFM legal framework, a single treasury account, an autonomous state audit institution, and more transparent practices has been put in place, along with the necessary space for advancing existing and future reforms.

NOTES

1. WB, ADB, AusAid (DFAT), IMF, GTZ, EU, JICA, French government, SIDA, SDC.
2. Australia, EU, SIDA, SDC.
3. Nam Theun 2 Hydropower plant has received financing support from the World Bank, Agence Française de Développement, the Asian Development Bank, and the European Investment Bank.
4. The PRSO series was a series of budget support operations linked to the implementation of Lao PDR's Poverty Reduction Strategy.
5. Although Lao officials participated in PEMNA since its creation, in the past several years efforts on the part of the Laotian officials to rotate and expand the number of finance officials attending and participating in PEMNA events has increased, culminating in hosting an event for PEMNA budget officials.

BIBLIOGRAPHY

Ministry of Finance. 2017. *Public Finance Development Strategy 2025 and Vision to 2030.* Vientiane, Lao PDR: Ministry of Finance.

Phimphanthavong, H. 2012. "Economic Reform and Regional Development of Laos." *Modern Economy* 3 (2): 179–86. doi: 10.4236/me.2012.32025.

World Bank. 1999. *Laos—Country Assistance Strategy*. Washington, DC: World Bank. http://documents.worldbank.org/curated/en/437961468753022405/Laos-Country-Assistance-Strategy.

———. 2002. *Laos—Financial Management Capacity Building Credit Project. Project Appraisal Document*. Washington, DC: World Bank. https://hubs.worldbank.org/docs/imagebank/pages/docprofile.aspx?nodeid=2030334.

———. 2011. *Lao PDR—Financial Management Capacity Building Project (FMCBP)*. Implementation Completion and Results Report. Washington, DC: World Bank. https://hubs.worldbank.org/docs/imagebank/pages/docprofile.aspx?nodeid=15650451v.

———. 2013. *Lao PDR—Public Financial Management Project*. Project Appraisal Document. Washington, DC: World Bank.

———. 2014. *Lao PDR—Public Financial Management Strengthening Program*. Implementation Completion and Results Report. Washington, DC: World Bank. http://documents.worldbank.org/curated/en/839321468091770842/pdf/ICR28880P108780IC0disclosed03040140.pdf.

———. 2017. *Lao PDR—Systematic Country Diagnostic*. Washington, DC: World Bank. http://documents.worldbank.org/curated/en/983001490107755004/Lao-PDR-Systematic-Country-Diagnostic-Priorities-for-Ending-Poverty-and-Boosting-Shared-Prosperity.

9 Papua New Guinea
OVERCOMING DIVERSITY, DISTANCE, FRAGMENTATION, AND RESOURCE DEPENDENCE

DAVID CRAIG

INTRODUCTION

This case study considers two significant current (2014–17) reforms in Papua New Guinea, and their potential combined significance in strengthening "Public Financial Management for Service Delivery": (a) Public Financial Management (PFM)/Budget execution (including an Integrated Financial Information System (IFMS), in reforms driven principally by the Department of Finance (DoF)); and (b) Public Sector and Institutional (PSI) reform, including decentralization and local service delivery, in reforms driven by the Department of Provincial and Local Government Affairs (DPLGA).

The study presents them in their early, current forms, as examples respectfully of translation of "best practice" (the PFM reforms) and "best fit" (the PSI decentralization and service delivery: see Andrews, Pritchett, and Woolcock 2013, 2017) approaches. But it also proposes that for either reform to succeed, both will need to find ways to bring Papua New Guinea capabilities and international experience together. This is because of the scale of challenges the country faces as a highly diverse, heavily resource-dependent economy and society. The ways this resource dependency is shaping PFM and PSI creates distinctive challenges, choices and opportunities that these important reforms cannot ignore.

PUBLIC FINANCIAL MANAGEMENT

Issues

Quality PFM requires strong central agency leadership; and there has been considerable investment over the years by the government of Papua New Guinea and donor partners in central agency capability building. Positive outcomes were reflected in the country's 2015 PEFA scores around credibility of fiscal strategy and budget, policy based planning and budgeting, and comprehensiveness and transparency (table 9.1). On the other hand, scores for budget execution, accountability and reporting, and management of public assets reflected significant challenges to Papua New Guinea's PFM capabilities.

TABLE 9.1 **Papua New Guinea PEFA scores, 2015**

PFM PILLARS	PERFORMANCE INDICATOR (PIS) SCORES[a]			
	A	B	C	D
Credibility of fiscal strategy (PI:1–3)	1	1	n.a.	1
Comprehensiveness and transparency (PI: 4–9)	n.a.	2	1	3
Asset & liability management (PI: 10–13)	n.a.	n.a.	n.a.	4
Policy-based planning & budgeting (PI: 14–18)	n.a.	1	2	2
Predictability and control in budget execution (PI: 19–25)	n.a.	n.a.	1	6
Accounting, recording and reporting (PI: 26–28)	n.a.	n.a.	n.a.	3
External scrutiny and audit (PI: 29–30)	n.a.	n.a.	n.a.	2
Total scores	1	4	4	21

Source: Government of Papua New Guinea and Ministry of Finance 2015.
Note: n.a. = not applicable.
a. Each column includes "+" scores, so "D"; includes D and D+.

Certainly, the PEFA scores reflected difficulties in the historical development of PFM capability in Papua New Guinea. Overarching problems with data integrity and regulatory reach created systemic weakness in budget execution. Regulatory frameworks dating from post- independence failed to grasp the scope of contemporary public finance, leaving considerable resources managed outside public expenditure frameworks, in trust accounts and quasi-state entities not subject to core PFM legislation. Financial management systems dating from the 1980s were installed in only Finance, Treasury and Planning ministries.

Meanwhile, the Papua New Guinea Accounting System (PGAS system) has had limited connectivity, in part a legacy of previous technological limitations, but also the result of autonomy over four decades, as from early post-independence onwards, each province developed its own systems. Currently, ahead of IFMS rollout to subnational levels, each subnational "site" (province, district, statutory authority, agency) is disparate, and independent of all other users. There is no consistency in Chart of Accounts, meaning budgets or expenditure are not comparable between sites. Nor do local budgets align with National Program Budget Structures. Each subnational unit's reporting requires substantial manipulation for reporting, making it very difficult to track funds from national budget (functional grants, PSI/DSIP, etc.) to subnational level. Upload of sub-national data into IFMS is usually months after it occurs, and statutory reports—bank reconciliations, annual financial statements—are months, and in many cases years, overdue. The PGAS system can be manipulated at the local level; particularly the creation of unauthorized warrants that allow payments/cheques to be created. Personal emoluments can be paid (illegally) through PGAS; cheques are issued are without further accountability for producing outcomes.

Thus, despite that grants to subnational government are now based on transparent formulae related to population, geography and other variables, there remain serious challenges providing both predictability and accountability around intergovernmental flows and subnational investments. Fragmentation of the capital budget, very limited links with recurrent expenditure and problems in its execution, inhibited public investment management. Cashflow issues (linked in part to resource dependence volatilities) have compounded difficulties, embedding a range of informal practices at various levels, by which officials have tried to deal with the recurrent problem of funds arriving too late to be expended by regular means. As outlined below, accountability for MP expenditure of significant grants for local services has been very limited indeed.

These issues were well recognized ahead of Papua New Guinea's 2014 PEFA review process: and the process served to highlight the deficiencies once again. There was nonetheless hope within the government that the PEFA "should provide confidence to development partners to gradually rely on government systems" (Government of Papua New Guinea 2016, 46)—hopes commentators described as "optimistic to say the least."[1] But, as narrated below, with strong and focused leadership the PEFA report did indeed prove itself to be a first important step in what has become a highly significant reform process in Papua New Guinea PFM and beyond.

Reform intervention

The country's budget execution reforms emerged from a combination of political and executive leadership, benchmarked against international standards via a robust PEFA review process. The Department of Finance has a clear and focused mandate in financial administration.[2] Appointment of a new Permanent Secretary (PS) in 2012 opened the way for substantial reform. The PS had a particularly strong background as associate professor of accounting at the University of Papua New Guinea, national president of the Papua New Guinea CPA, and through a long involvement with development financing. Crucially, he has enjoyed strong and sustained backing from Prime Ministerial and Ministerial/National Executive Council levels, underpinned by a wider government policy commitment framed in the 2012 Alotau Accord.

In early 2014, the Ministry of Finance drew together and led a team of government officials for the PEFA review. Multiple agencies were involved over the next 10 months: Finance, Treasury, Planning and Monitoring, Personnel Management, Internal Revenue, Customs, Auditor General, Education, Health Central Supplies and Tenders, National Economic and Fiscal Commission (NEFC), Provincial and Local Government Affairs, Prime Minister and Cabinet, National Executive Council (i.e., cabinet). The process included a self-assessment, the results of which lined up strongly with the external PEFA reviewers' conclusions. The results, as above, were mixed, and damning in several areas. Nonetheless, the PEFA with its subsequent road map has provided a clear and overarching framework for PFM reforms, and created a rationale for legislative reform and investment in IFMS systems and wider training. All of this has been able to be supported by international donor partners with a range of government-coordinated inputs.

As an early step in the road map, Ministry of Finance initiated a Financial Framework Review in February 2016. By August 2016, new legislation greatly extending the regulatory reach of the Ministry of Finance had been passed through parliament. Crucial implementation frameworks were also developed and passed in early 2017; actual implementation will depend on commitment from the government elected in mid-2017.

The new Public Finance Management Act clarifies mandates and functions which had been blurred in the recent separation of Treasury and Finance, making financial administration the preserve of Finance, and precisely spelling out the PFM obligations of both ministries. At the same time, it simplifies and broadens

PFM jurisdiction by recognizing only two types of bodies: public and statutory. Both receive public funding; both are subject to all the Act's provisions. Non-compliance with PFMA, the Finance Manual or Finance Instructions is now a criminal offence. The Act clears the way for important reforms including the regulation and dismantling of an informal trust account system elaborated over time by government agencies struggling themselves with expenditure management.

The roadmap placed considerable emphasis on the wider benefits that could accrue from better data, and from expanding the coverage of the IFMS to cover all government and regulatory authorities, including the subnational. As noted above, in 2014 Papua New Guinea's IFMS was only operational within Finance, Treasury and Planning ministries, with the wider public sector depending on PGAS, an accounting system dating from the 1980s. Expansion to all parts of government including authorities and subnational government promised benefits in terms of "improved information quality, information consistency, more disciplined commitment and expenditure controls, and more timely reporting" (Government of Papua New Guinea and Ministry of Finance 2015, 7). Momentum for the wider rollout of the IFMS grew during 2015, with implementation in 22 agencies. By mid-2017, despite wider budget challenges associated with the rollout, 46 national agencies, one statutory authority, and one province (and all its districts) were operating IFMS for core budgeting and expenditure processes.

Expanding IFMS reach across government will be a core focus. High-level central agency coordination will help this: the Central Agencies Coordinating Committee (CACC) have been asked to establish an Interdepartmental Committee to oversee all government finance systems (including payroll). This in time is envisaged as enabling a whole-of-government approach to procurement, licenses, and will make it illegal for public and statutory bodies to procure without DoF approval.

IFMS subnational strategy involves developing an interface and alignment with the government payroll system (Alesco). The reform aim is to remove payment of salaries through PGAS and have single source of payroll through Alesco to enforce 1PPP (1 position, 1 person, 1 payroll). This could reduce the likelihood of people being paid through multiple agencies and ghost employees. At the same time, Papua New Guinea's public sector rules heavily restrict ability to redeploy or refresh human resource capability. The Finance secretary's response was setting up a range of professional development opportunities, including an Association of Government Accountants and Public Finance Managers, dedicated courses in Public Accounting for public servants at the country's national university, and mandatory IFMS training for all Finance staff.

Other reforms underway include restructuring of procurement arrangements across government, including at sub-national level. This innovation, along with the monitoring opportunities associated with the IFMS, face serious challenges, and implementation is not easily assured. But together, these arrangements could for the first time create a platform for greater scrutiny and compliance around the SIP funds, which are currently subject only to unenforced acquittal. Cashflow issues, which continue to debilitate subnational government in a range of ways, should also become clearer through the lens of IFMS: these are due to be subject to a review of the government's cash management system, cashflow forecasting, and banking framework. Monitoring of subnational government trust accounts and improved timeliness of reporting have the potential to increase PFM visibility and accountability across subnational government.

Result/Status of reform

Papua New Guinea's PFM reforms' success to date has come as a result of high-level support and trusted leadership for a broad reform including extensive and open review, legislation, implementation of IFMS, changes to procurement, and human resource management innovation. This leadership has enabled establishment of a strong platform for reforms, onto which international supporters and functions have been invited and organized. In this, Papua New Guinea's reforms in some ways mirror more successful cases, including Tanzania and Indonesia, where IFMS projects began with significant political and management commitment, maintained throughout the entire reform process (Cherotich and Bichanga 2016; Hughes et al. 2017; Rodin-Brown 2008).

Within a fairly short timeframe, and as a result of being adequately resourced by local and international funding, reformers have been able to review existing practice, frame a PEFA road map, and to both legislate and to have subsequent implementation frameworks passed by parliament. Linking reforms, and especially IFMS, to procurement are significant remaining issues; as will be the effective rollout of IFMS down into provinces and districts. Expanding the reach of IFMS has rendered extensive areas of government expenditure visible, and enabled internal control on expenditure to be implemented simply and quickly. This has been especially important during the buildup to the 2017 election period, where in the past significant diversion of project funds into electioneering has occurred, with limited remedy. Notwithstanding the care and attention being paid to IFMS rollout, and the level of leadership and political support, seeing its capabilities realized on the ground, and applied to improving service delivery remain detailed, expensive and extensive challenges.

Beyond crucial initial success, realizing the potential of the reforms for overall accountability remains a significant challenge. Papua New Guinea's 22 provinces and 89 districts still require roll-out support, especially training; but the goal of a transition from PGAS by late 2018 still seems possible. It will require a considerable effort to get infrastructure in place, and have a core of DoF staff (PFO/DFO) "competent" using IFMS so they will be able to support provincial staff and regional approaches to provinces and LLGs. Based on the rollout, the PFM subnational strategy will also explore rationalizing bank accounts to achieve better control of money and improve the likelihood of reconciliations being done. It will also involve a user focus, simplifying IFMS workflows for budget execution and procurement/payments processes, to get buy-in and reduce potential operational/support problems, while still maintaining internal controls and separation of roles. The major obstacles to achieving all of this are funding and reliable system connectivity (and not least, the cost of this connectivity).

Within central government agencies and provincial government, bringing trust accounts into IFMS visibility and internal control will be a significant development.[3] Seen as having potential to bring many millions of Kinas back into current budgets, it will also considerably curtail agency flexibility about expenditure and procurement, in an environment where cashflow issues mean money often arrives too late to be spent effectively within budget cycles. Standardized, automated reporting would enable comparisons and identification of outliers, and feed information directly into budget allocation mechanisms in ways that will disadvantage some actors. Thus, in a number of ways, IFMS and PFM reforms enable enhanced central control; and constrain local practices, if not autonomy.

This does not mean local actors are powerless. Sub-nationally, challenges will include creating sufficient buy-in from local officials and others aware that IFMS will increase visibility and demand processes that will reduce existing autonomy and secretion over resource use. As Cambodia's case demonstrates, middle managers as well as local officials will have well-established, perhaps idiosyncratic existing procedures, and will be tempted to try to customize IFMS procedures to fit existing practices, rather than vice-versa (Hughes et al. 2017). The Papua New Guinea IFMS configuration is managed centrally, and cannot be changed "locally"; system enhancements have been implemented that strengthen internal control, by, for example, removing the ability to use inappropriate or illegal accounts. Nonetheless local practices will inevitably impact on IFMS-related visibility and accountability.

Certainly, in Papua New Guinea there have been levels of resistance in a number of agencies where IFMS has been implemented; and training and credentialing of local users remains an issue. Understanding the patterns of this resistance and moving to reduce their impact will be an important part of realizing IFMS potential. No reform process involving this scope of reform will be without its implementation issues. At district level, existing high levels of autonomy and low reporting and compliance obligations for the country's powerful Open MPs dispensing DSIP funds (as above, only simple acquittal is currently required) are an important potential source of potential resistance to effective implementation. Open MPs will need to adjust practices in line with the new visibilities: a range of desirable and undesirable local practice seems likely to emerge, and will need to be firmly dealt with by supervisory agencies supported in this by top level central leadership. Only with attention to these issues will IFMS potential for improving local service delivery be substantially realized.

More directly, current challenges to IFMS rollout in Papua New Guinea have come from the wider fiscal situation; meaning considerable resources for subnational IFMS rollout will need to be found beyond current restricted budgets, and then need to be made available at District level to pay for staff time. Kenya's experience shows that local government's ability to allocate resources to operationalizing IFMS is crucial to success (Cherotich and Bichanga 2016). These areas hold potentially crucial "pain" or "inflection" points in the reform process: that is, critical junctures at which point reforms will either progress, and draw more actors and resources in, or at which reform will be resisted, isolated, minimalized, and draw in the commitment and day-to-day practice of fewer actors at all levels.

Thus, the impact of these legislative and administrative reforms will depend on leadership persisting with reform within the constraints of the wider institutional environment. In particular, it will depend on the ways IFMS, PFMA and procurement reforms are and aren't used to create wider structures of accountability across subnational government. The opportunities for finding ways to increase accountability will emerge over time, and in dialogue with other agencies, including Departments of Planning, Provincial and Local Government, and Implementation and Rural Development. It will depend on central leadership in wider regulatory reform, especially in implementing the review of the 1995 Organic Law on Provincial Governments and Local-level Governments. Other agencies will need to come to see the IFMS as more than a bookkeeping innovation, and as something which can provide more clarity and clearer expectations about where the money goes, and when.

DECENTRALIZATION AND SUBNATIONAL GOVERNANCE REFORM

Issues

Providing services to Papua New Guinea's diverse and dispersed population would stretch the capabilities and resources of any government, no matter how well resourced and efficiently run. But the country's three level government system (central, provincial, local level government) has struggled to function effectively, with high levels of centralization in executive arrangements, and both province and local level government (LLGs) thrown from the outset into competition for resources with District-level elected MPs. Political accountability at province and lower government levels is restricted; and there are strong incentives for governors, MPs and others to act unilaterally, as patrons choosing to allocate resources as they will. All levels of subnational government have needed to be reformed and adapted, over time—so far with highly variable success, and subject to much local and personal leadership variation.

Subject to irregular, inadequate resourcing and limited political and executive accountability, provincial government has never been able to achieve the levels of functionality hoped for. Initial attempts at reform of subnational government—especially the 1995 Organic Law on Provincial Government and Local Level Government (OLPGLLG)—deepened the problems. Reforms 2000–10 driven by the NEFC succeeded in establishing equitable function grants for provinces, considering, for example, the inequalities that resource revenues bring to provincial income. Ongoing fragmentation of expenditure and the predominance of SIP vertical grants means the share of the national budget that provinces get is now just 3 percent. The proportions of budget to be spent at District, urban authority and other levels now makes extending the "funding follows function" principles down into those domains imperative.

Subsequent recent reforms (2012 onwards) have formally left the difficult (but constitutionally protected) three-tier governance arrangements (central, provincial, local-level) in place. But at the same time, they place significant new emphasis on improving the delivery services at the level of the District, through new District Development Authorities (DDAs). Over the 40 years since independence considerable amounts of money have been made available for constituency MPs to implement projects via various grants, initially with Electorate Development Funds, and more recently with District Services Improvement Program (DSIP) grants.[4] These grants, alongside SIP grants channeling money directly to provinces, LLGs and now wards, dwarf provincial function grants, and limit the impact of the carefully constructed, equity generating formulae by which provincial funds are allocated. While derided by many as MP slush funds, for others they represent the simple necessity of moving service delivery closer to local populations.

Formal arrangements around the DDAs have all included elements of pro-forma accountability to other levels of government, including Joint District Planning and Budget Priorities Committees (JDPBPC) made up of the MP, LLG chairs, community appointees and the District Administrator. Repeated critiques of the JDPBPC held that it was dominated by MPs and consistently chose poor projects (INA 2016, 55; Kalinoe 2009, vii).[5] Closer observers pointed to its institutional form as a standalone, de-facto authority fusing executive and political power: embodying the personal discretion of the Open MP, and politicizing the key office of the District Administrator.[6] The rise of the JDPBPC also "had the effect of rendering the existing 305 LLGs redundant in any meaningful service delivery programs and projects" (Kalinoe 2009, 6). Under the recent reforms, the institutional vehicle created for creating accountability—the District Development Authority—is institutionally controlled and executed by the same actors.

In sum, despite that DSIP grants enable MPs to respond to local needs directly with services people see and need, the quality of Electorate Development and SIP investments over 40 years has been mixed at best. Creating accountability around these scarce but generous investment funds, and linking them to recurrent budgets, thus remains a considerable challenge for both PFM and PSI reform efforts.

Reform intervention

"Frontline service delivery" and rural development have been central policy initiatives of the 2012–17 O'Neill-Dion government. Integral to this has been an approach to decentralization which, unlike previous intergovernmental reform, has placed the District at the center of service delivery. As above, District MPs have long had constituency development funds enabling them to respond directly to local needs. The new approach to decentralization and service delivery has constituted DDAs as the primary vehicle through which to pursue local development goals.

DDAs were originally legislated in 2004 as an initiative of the current Prime Minister, then in opposition. After the 2012 election, DDAs were prominent among a number of decentralization reforms and reviews promoted by the O'Neill-Dion government. These included a review of the 1995 Organic Law on Provincial Governments and Local-level Governments, establishment of three new city authorities (Lae, Mt Hagen, Kokopo), and the 2016 National Planning Act, with its National Service Delivery Framework.

Despite these reform platforms, the District is still not envisaged as an actual level of subnational government: these roles are constitutionally occupied by the province and LLG. Rather, the role of Districts as levels of administration is envisaged as becoming focal points enabling and directing service delivery, with the active involvement of the Open Member him- or herself. To enable this allocative function, the DDA act institutionalized a number of features of previous JDPBPC, with the MP retaining the crucial chairmanship though as chairman now of the DDA Board, and not of the priorities committee. At the same time, the DDA act made the District Administrator (a provincial official with delegated powers) the CEO of the District Development Authority.

In this double role, the DA/DDA/CEO is responsible for the execution of the SIP, but also with an uncertain but wide-ranging authority over the whole range of government agencies operating at district level, including (at least within the scope of the legislation) human resource and other management mandates. This innovation made the MP/DA relationship crucial to local authority and service delivery: critics say it politicized the role, and made its occupancy by favored MP appointees inevitable. The DA/DDA chair might formally link district to provincial government and even recurrent budgets, but in practice he might equally become the link between official funding and MP business and other clients and partners, his chief incentives caught up in a range of projects and highly discretionary deals. Much would depend on local personalities, but also potentially on the ability of policy leaders to create incentives for the DDA to lead coordination

TABLE 9.2 Acquittals of DSIP/PSIP grants, 2013–17

DSIP/PSIP ACQUITTALSA	ACQUITTED	NOT ACQUITTED
2013	92	19
2014	75	36
2015	36	75
2016	5	101

Source: Department of Implementation and Rural Development, as reported in Courier Post, 31 May 2017.
Note: Actual numbers of provinces and districts, as reported by Department of Implementation and Rural Development (DIRD), Courier Post, Wednesday, 31 May.

and accountability in positive directions. Formal accountability for DSIP expenditure is limited to bare bones acquittals (see table 9.2) with, very low compliance with even this most basic accountability. As elsewhere in polities where political alliances rely on rent distributions, political will to constrain use of allocations has also been minimal (Slater 2010, 10–13).

Central leadership in the elaboration of accountabilities and linkages for the DDA has certainly emerged; how it will work remains to be developed. In 2016, the CACC established a decentralization sub-committee, under the chairmanship of the DPLGA secretary. The DPLGA holds a mandated responsibility for all levels of subnational government, and provides an executive for the Provincial and Lower Local Services Management Authority (PLSSMA), a program focused on monitoring and improving service performance across provincial and LLG.

At the CACC national summit in late 2016, the decentralization sub-committee passed resolutions in support of core decentralization framings, including "performance based power sharing" or "gradative" decentralization (LeLang et al. 2015; Wolfers 2007). Both these concepts refer to the preparedness of the government to let provincial and other authorities enjoy a level of autonomy based on demonstrated ability to deliver services. Selected provinces have already taken a lead in these areas, notably East New Britain and Central province, which are also the sites of the first IFMS provincial and district rollouts.

Concurrently, the DPLGA has developed a "Practice Start-up Toolkit for Frontline Service Delivery and Growth," incorporating the framing of several tiers of policy and service delivery agreements and partnerships. These include an overall Partnership Framework for Service Delivery and Rural Development, Department of National Planning and Monitoring's National Service Delivery Framework (mandated under the 2016 National Planning Act), and DPLGA's Service Delivery Partnership Agreements. The toolkit's authors recognized the necessity to work with the grain (and within the fragmented field) of existing arrangements, including desire for "alternative service delivery" involving the private sector in diverse ways.

Rolled out in 2017–18, the Service Delivery Partnership Agreements are envisaged as enabling subnational governments to share resources and work towards clear service delivery and development outcomes, including the Minimum Standards for Service Delivery being developed under the National Planning Act. Like the minimum standards, the Partnership Agreements are specific to locations, enabling them to include particular projects including the World Bank/ DPLGA Rural Service Delivery Program, and WaSH programs focused on water and sanitation in particular locales. The Service Delivery Partnership Agreements will be further supported by Service Delivery Charters, envisaged as specific commitments and pledges made by local leaders and public institutions to providing frontline services.

Result/Status of reform

Current decentralization is at an early stage, with its DDAs yet to experience serious development; and crucial law reform, based on the Review of the Organic Law on Provincial and LLG, is yet to come to parliament. But some potentially important modalities of reform are about to be unpacked from the "Practice Start-up Toolkit," and rolled out over the 2017–22 term of Papua New Guinea's new government.

Looking to implementation, reformers have several factors on their side. The Organic law review points to a need for change, and has created a potential forum for building consensus within central agencies. Political leadership is highly committed to decentralization focused on provincial and district capacity, and the "gradative" principle restated in the Organic law review and in the Alotau 2 political accord which frames coalition policy. Provincial autonomy, a long tug-of-war process of claims-making and experimentation, is currently back on the agenda. DPLGA leadership have used the previous government term to generate a reform agenda incorporating central agencies (CACC, organic law review processes) and revitalizing existing programs, especially the PLSSMA. On the other hand, the ability of the CACC subcommittee on decentralization and PLSSMA to provide strong platforms for reform is yet to be tested. Remaining to be tested too are platform links with the DPNM National Service Delivery framework, and its local planning and minimum standards processes. Beyond this, two main challenge areas seem crucial: (a) Stronger links and a programmed platform for change involving other central agencies (Treasury, Finance, NEFC) which will lead PFM reforms at subnational levels, and (b) Ability to build service delivery partnership agreements and service delivery charters around the most important emerging "platform level," the District.

Toolkit elements seek to build both a framework and working "shared accountability platforms" or agreements/charters for service delivery partnerships. Basic to this will be reliable, recurrent resourcing, meaning that a core challenge will be aligning them with existing intergovernmental transfers, enacting classic fiscal decentralization concerns with aligning funding, function and mandate. Determination of functions and formalization of funding has been led by the NEFC. As above, their closely considered and legislated annual calculation of function grants for provinces has been a core element in the Reform of Intergovernmental Financing Arrangements (RIGFA). Now, NEFC's admirable technical expertise needs to be harnessed to include funding follows function arrangements at District and City Authority levels.

Working primarily with the District holds a series of further challenges, especially in reformers' ability to bring the right kinds of incentives and expertise to the district context. In each toolkit element, DPLGA is seeking to support District-focused decentralization initiatives, but at the same time to try to create links, co-operation and accountability with other levels of government. These will necessarily respond to MPs' autonomy, and varying commitment to coordination, yet seek to shift the incentives they face to coordinate. They will be framed in specific agreements brokered on a one-to-one basis with district MPs, DDAs, district and through that provincial administration within existing arrangements, and other local government actors.

Of apparent necessity, then, DPLGA are adopting a highly flexible, non-standardizing approach, expecting that individual MPs and DDAs will have specific (perhaps highly alternative) approaches they wish to adopt, and will be able to fund through DSIP. Whether such arrangements can ever be reconciled with recurrent budget funding following defined functions on a national scale remains to be seen (Duncan, Cairns, and Benga 2017).

Whatever adaptive flexibility is necessary or achieved, a range of obstacles remain implicit in current arrangements, and their simple practical capabilities. The DDA, everyone agrees, is not a formal level of government, though the District is a level of administration, operating as a devolved unit of provincial government. The DDA can and does contract out projects, but it has very limited capability in wider administration and technical oversight areas (Duncan, Cairns, and Benga 2017).[7] Currently it is unclear whether the DDA/District could develop the administrative capability to, for example, be responsible for all local roads, school buildings, or health clinics.

Even if it could, it does not simply follow that it should: such capabilities might be much better developed at other levels of government. This expertise exists at provincial level, but DDAs often have limited interest in involving provincial government in SIP-funded projects, and committing to resourcing beyond the project cycle. But without better alignment and designation of provincial and district functions and mandates, DDAs will continue to build facilities and roads without budgets to staff, let alone maintain them. The major outcome of this is poor public investment management, and the de-facto dominance of a build-neglect- rebuild model which is obviously highly inefficient, and sees large amounts of scarce resources wasted.

APPROACH TO REFORM: BEST PRACTICE VERSUS BEST FIT?

Since national independence in 1975, Papua New Guinea has faced a series of major challenges in establishing an effective public sector, one able to support poverty reduction and shared prosperity. Simple costs of delivering services to one of the world's least urbanized, most dispersed, remote and segmented populations and geographies have always been extremely high. Despite considerable endogenous capability in resolving disputes and regulating local markets (Craig and Porter 2017; Craig, Porter, and Hukula 2016), creating capabilities and accountabilities in central, local and urban governance able to coordinate and extend services to remote populations remains Papua New Guinea's core development challenge. Failure to achieve this may well see the country slip further into fragile state territory.[8]

Centralizing tendencies are strong in Papua New Guinea's governance, and central-level capacity has been the focus of much attention and international support over the four decades since independence. Current capabilities in PFM and Public Expenditure and Financial Accountability (PEFA) pillars—including credibility of fiscal strategy and comprehensiveness and transparency—owe something to this long-term investment (Government of Papua New Guinea and Ministry of Finance 2015). While commitments have varied from government to government, and the booms and busts of resource commodity prices have repeatedly led to cycles of voracious spending and heavy cuts, central agency capability in policy and monitoring has been fostered. Central agencies have been able to attract, train and retain highly able staff, and high-quality support to these staff has generally been available through donor programs. Officials are generally appointed on the basis of merit rather than simple political commitment; and highly talented individuals have been appointed to key PS roles.

In terms of the "best practice vs best fit" question that is the focus of this case collection, central agency reform approaches have often followed "best practice" routes, with some success. Achieving orthodox economic and PFM has been a joint project of highly skilled officials with various kinds of ongoing international support, facing changing political commitments. In recent reforms, for example, a highly orthodox best practice PEFA approach has been chosen, along with (orthodox) core legislation and a (standard) IFMS system. Importantly, local leaders had the option to choose orthodoxy, and they pursued it. How effectively this will deal with core PFM issues (and political pressures) around timely cashflow, and use its powers of transparency and legislative reach to bring scrutiny to public investment and procurement remains to be witnessed. But there is expectation that achievements to date mean further reform is technically, administratively and politically possible, and that high-level choices are being made that will support reform.

On the other hand, central agencies have also witnessed strong "best fit" oriented reform, as seen in early 2000s RIGFA reforms driven by the NEFC. Reformers there translated Roy Bahl's classic "best practice" rules for fiscal decentralization (Bahl 1999) deep into Papua New Guinea governance. But at the same time, they relied on some highly creative "best fit" construction of both analytic models and of political consensus, and enabled the allocation of core function grants to the country's 22 provinces to be based on reliable data and a well-grounded sense of what mattered in local variability. The impact of RIGFA reforms has been limited by further fragmentation of Papua New Guinea PFM into a series of vertical transfers, and moves to support very much home-grown decentralization focused on Districts, which political leadership have strongly supported and resourced. But as described above, another round of "best fit" PSI innovation is underway, backed by both political and innovative executive commitment.

Here too, there are choices to be made, and a sense from those making them that there is both space and necessity to pursue real innovation, and choose "best fit" over "best practice." The big challenges now in PFM and PSI reform demand both reliable transfer of funds from central agencies to local levels, *and* finding ways to make Papua New Guinea's unique, homegrown approaches to subnational governance and service delivery work to produce accountability and quality of investment. Here, "best practice" will need to meet "best fit" in some of the most demanding ways imaginable.

Overcoming diversity, distance and fragmentation represents one of two of the country's main governance challenges, which arguably lie beyond the center; or, more accurately, in the core relationships between the center and the remote sites of service delivery. Papua New Guinea is geographically, ethnically, and linguistically among the most diverse countries on the planet. Its population includes 820 distinct cultural-linguistic groups and over 10,000 autonomous tribes, themselves divided into clans, whose boundaries by no means map to political or administrative domains (Anere 2004; Ketan 2007). Papua New Guinea's globally low urbanization rate of 14 percent[9] means most of the population, and most of its political power, is based in low density, dispersed locations, including 600 islands and thousands of isolated mountain and river valleys. Natural resources and their wealth are distributed highly unevenly; and so is the ability of provinces and districts to raise revenues and break dependence on central transfers. A predominantly young rural population—growing 3.1 percent per annum, or 40 percent since 2000[10]—is underserviced by schools and health services, and poorly linked into educational and economic opportunities. Delivering services to small populations in remote villages is vastly expensive. Maintaining transport links to markets and getting teachers and health workers in remote locations is beyond national and local budgets.

Reformers face a geographical, political-economic and institutional legacy they did not create, and which makes subsequent choices more difficult, and more important. These challenges cannot be met simply by a small number of excellent leaders and officials in central agencies, nor simply by choosing or importing best practice approaches or imposing single sets of rules (Pritchett and Woolcock 2004). They require highly dispersed capability, involving local actors capable and compelled to make good decisions and see that resources are well spent, day to day, and location by location. To date, central ability to control what happens sub-nationally, in terms of expenditure and both investment and recurrent budgets, has been highly restricted. At the same time, Papua New Guinea's subnational government has long been the subject of experimentation and "home grown" or hybrid forms of iterative adaptation. But to date, much of this experimentation has failed, and produced more fragmentation between and across levels of government.

At independence, Papua New Guinea inherited a Westminster model which, in the absence of stable political parties and broad-based representation of local MPs, has left all subsequent governments heavily vulnerable to removal through no-confidence votes, and MPs more likely than not to be removed at the next election. Reforms to this have been attempted, but have only partly succeeded; political instability grounded in the fragmented interests of local MPs remains a significant challenge to any Papua New Guinea government. The country in 1975 also adopted an untried system of provincial government, which quickly set national MPs against provincial assembly members. Twenty years later in 1995, it experimented with Organic Law reforms to subnational government which are now universally regarded as failed, and which destroyed local political accountabilities around provincial government, while failing to resolve the basic conflict between Open MPs and the province for resources and authority.

Subsequent attempts to fix subnational government and service delivery in core areas including health have also all been based in experimentation. Most recent decentralization reforms focused on the District level, and described below, are explicitly based on a "best fit" approach. They are very much home grown, expressly relying on what is called a "gradative" approach to decentral-ization, wherein provinces and districts deemed capable of greater functionality and autonomy can achieve that (Wolfers 2007). These reforms reflect diversity and the autonomy of local MPs, and a will to give them more scope to choose development pathways that respond to local needs. But to critics, they add rather than subtract from the overall tendency to fragmentation.

Another key governance challenge emerged from resource based political economy and center-local relationship. Resource wealth is widely seen as a basis for Papua New Guinea's rise into middle income status; yet, as in resource dependent countries elsewhere, this same base provides profound challenges to the country's institutional effectiveness (Auty 2007; Barma et al. 2012). During the recent global "super-cycle" resource boom of 2000–14, increased exploitation of the country's natural resources (petrochemicals and mineral deposits, gold, copper, and nickel), saw a high average annual GDP growth (6.2 percent), and rapid structural dependence on narrow and price volatile commodity base (24 percent GDP, 83 percent exports). The subsequent 2015–17 bust has seen just as dramatic reductions and cuts.

In the absence of own-source revenues at provincial and local levels (and of broad-based taxation across a range of sectors (Moore 2004), Papua New Guinea's central-local fiscal relations have been increasingly oriented to allocating central resource rents to diverse constituencies which each individually need basic infrastructure. These rents have been increasingly committed to both capital investment in infrastructure projects, and especially to district MPs in the form of project-oriented constituency funds, called DSIP grants. By international standards, at PNGK 10 million ($US 3 million) per year, the country's constituency funds are very large.

Together, the various SIP grants at district, province, LLG and ward levels dwarf the recurrent subnational expenditure sent to provinces and LLG, by a factor of nearly three times. In geographically diverse resource economies, such development budget expenditures can quickly become disproportionally significant. During the recent resource boom, and because of the expansion of SIP channels, the ratio of development to recurrent spending shifted from 30/70 percent to 70/30 percent, with much increased spending based on income expectations which failed to materialize.

As a result, the 2015–17 resource bust—driven by construction phase completion of major projects, and a rapid decline in commodity prices—saw huge cuts across public expenditure. Included were cuts equivalent in real terms in 2015 to an improbable 33 percent of the health budget (Howes 2016). Yet risks to political stability saw the PNGK10 million/year SIP constituency funds to MPs preserved, at least up to 2017 elections. Simply, constituency MPs' autonomy and power to bring down the government through a no-confidence vote has led to the increasing and sustained institutionalization of political rents, captured by MPs in these district-level grants. Given the commitment of the new 2017–22 government to District focused, DSIP funded decentralization, there seems to be no reason to expect these allocations to change, even where MPs failed to follow processes that would lead to sound public investment.

Where government formation and stability is based on allocating centralized resource rents to local patrons in this way, such cyclical and sectoral distortions become the norm. The real development challenge, then, is to move beyond the dominance of SIP vertical grants, which reflect their resource-rents basis in their enabling of vertical patronage through grants, de-linked from (but actively displacing) sustained, recurrent budget-funded service delivery in core sectors. It will mean placing more accountabilities around the choices local MPs and DDAs make.

Linking PFM transparency to more equitable, developmental service delivery can be aided by a successful IFMS rollout and a better, more enforceable regulatory framework. And helped too, by tapping the agency and discretionary resources of local MPs. But it also needs to find ways to make core government services less vulnerable to resource booms, busts, and to strengthen visibility and accountability around rent-allocating grant arrangements. To do this, high-level choices need to be made that will make PFM, IFMS rollout and decentralization into mutually reinforcing reforms, together leaning against the dominant tendency of resource revenue-driven institution fragmentation. Whether or not there is space, understanding or commitment to genuinely do this is yet to be resolved.

SUMMARY AND CONCLUSIONS: USING NECESSARY "BEST FIT" INNOVATION TO ACHIEVE "BEST PRACTICE" OUTCOMES IN A DIFFICULT SETTING

In seeking to find solutions to Papua New Guinea's globally difficult governance and service delivery challenges, the country's PFM and decentralization reforms have followed quite different paths. PFM reform is certainly led by leaders promoting global "best practice" concerns: a PEFA review and road map process. DPLGA's decentralization toolkit reforms follow a different route, wherein best practice is replaced by concerns with best fit, and creating cross-agency and intergovernmental adaptation to suit local circumstance. What matters now is both ongoing implementation of these reforms, but especially how these reforms can become mutually reinforcing. For this to happen, leadership in each needs to recognize the potential of the other for enabling sustained reform, and expand spaces where innovation can occur.

While they have achieved considerable momentum, both reforms are still very recent and await full implementation, especially at subnational level. There they will encounter a range of issues, including recurrent funding of subnational level to sustain their working, and ensuring local level commitment to the transparency processes and procedures they introduce. Resistance may come from those enabled by current arrangements to use government money with great personal discretion, who could face new levels of financial and procurement scrutiny. Harnessing the reforms to create greater equity and better quality public investment remains yet one more step, against the wider grain of rent-based project patronage.

Realizing the joint potential of these two reforms—that is, the potential of one to reinforce the value and effect of the other—is an important challenge. PFM/IFMS reform will succeed or fail at subnational level partly around the ways the Districts choose to interact with the new system. The enhanced visibility of transactions the IFMS will bring will need to be linked to surveillance and reporting mechanisms and an ability to spot and react to patterns of malfeasance. But it will also need to be linked to incentives for MPs and staff to comply, and to choose to generate quality outcomes. The DPLGA toolkit will enable new forms of cooperation across government: but unless these can be sustainably linked to visible allocations of funding and function, they risk being both merely local, and heavily dependent on short-term commitments.

Meeting the challenges of proximal and underlying institutional weakness

Papua New Guinea's decentralization reforms have set out to create horizontal and other intergovernmental accountabilities to countervail and regulate current subnational PFM arrangements otherwise dominated by fragmentation and vertical grant systems. The IFMS will indeed change the accountability and visibility game at all subnational levels: exactly how remains to be seen. The proximal measures adopted in the Toolkit are certainly flexible enough, and focused enough on Open MPs themselves, and their use of SIP funds. The kinds of re-incentivizing of arrangements around such funds through provision of matching grants are certainly a step in the right direction.

But this chapter has also argued that addressing underlying drivers of institutional weakness requires more than proximal measures. It requires a critical awareness of the natural tendencies of resource-cursed institutional formation, and the ways it is likely to shape and undermine institutional capability. It requires long-term commitment, for example, to broadening the tax base, and to the kinds of macro-policies in areas like urbanization that could support wider diversification of both the economy and of political arrangements. It involves maintaining a healthy critical stance about the virtues of combining executive and political power, and of trying to do "service delivery" through creation and expansion of vertical grant arrangements de-linked from salaries and operational budgets. It requires ongoing countervailing of developments that see more control of rents centralized, further empowering elite actors at central and district levels, and making their decisions at once more important and less well informed or scrutinized.

Clearly there will be ongoing necessity for "best fit" innovation, especially, perhaps, around ways to make most of the "best practice" IFMS reforms, and around ways to enable best practice to support best fit in local service delivery pacts and commitments. But the wider strategic and policy orientation needed to address Papua New Guinea's institutional challenges is not necessarily present in either "best fit" or "best practice" approaches, and their relation to the main historical, place based and political economic drivers of institutional weakness. Both risk disappointment, whether in the capabilities of either central controls or local agency; both too need an analytic and strategic fulcrum outside of the immediate policy and operational context.

NOTES

1. These observers characterized much of the report as "a damning indictment of financial administration: control over budget execution is weak; there are high levels of variance between budget and expenditure; expenditure control is weak; project implementation is weak; budgets contain insufficient analytical detail; many bank reconciliations are not carried out in a timely manner and contain significant unresolved items; the coverage and classification of in-year data does not allow comparison with original approved budgets; many state-owned enterprises receive very poor audit reports; there is no overall PFM reform strategy." http://devpolicy.org/pngs-financial-management-can-it-be-turned-around-20160112/

2. While Department of Treasury is responsible for macroeconomic functions, including the budget.

3. A review of SOE, Statutory Authorities and Trust Accounts has commenced. This will result in revised legislation to bring them into line with the PFMA and force operation of Trust Accounts into IFMS (or accounts will be closed and funds sent to the consolidated revenue fund).

4. There are now SIP grants at every level of government, including the local ward. But it is at the District level that SIP investment has been greatest.

5. Then-Treasurer Don Polye's candidly remarked in 2013 that "our monitoring and evaluation systems are non-existent." http://devpolicy.org/reflections-on-the-png-budget-forum-can-devolved-funding-be-effectively-utilised-2013040/.

6. 'It would seem a fair observation to make that the JDPBPC is a standalone institution created by the OLPGLLG that is rather disjointed from the governance structures. 'The DA is at a serious risk of being mistaken for a political staffer of the MP concerned and radiating as the "Member's Servant" rather than a "public servant" and this is bound to undermine the office of the DA' (Kalinoe 2009, 165).

7. For DDAs to be successful, they will require the right staff at the right location to coordinate and implement district and local-level service delivery programs and development activities. Staffing gaps are evident. Some districts have commenced reviews of their staffing establishments and some have submitted proposals for staffing changes. The fiscal

viability of these proposals will be important, particularly in the current fiscal context with salaries, wages, and administrative costs making up more than 70 percent of total expenditures, leaving little for operational expenses such as transport. The hiring of new staff and/or relocation of existing staff will have significant non-salary implications, including the need for housing and leave entitlements.

8. Papua New Guinea's CPIA score moved from 3.2 to 3.0 in 2015–16.

9. This is likely to be an underestimation: figures closer to 20% are accepted by Papua New Guinea urbanization leadership.

10. https://www.nso.gov.pg/index.php/population-and-social/other-indicators.

BIBLIOGRAPHY

Andrews, M., L. Pritchett, and M. Woolcock. 2013. "Escaping Capability Traps through Problem Driven Iterative Adaptation (PDIA)." *World Development* 51 (11): 234–44.

——. 2017. *Building State Capability: Evidence, Analysis, Action.* Oxford: Oxford University Press.

Anere, R. 2004. *Ethnic Structure, Inequality and Governance of the Public Sector in Papua New Guinea.* UNRISD. Port Moresby.

Auty, R. 2007. "Patterns of Rent-Extraction and Deployment in Developing Countries: Implications for Governance, Economic Policy and Performance." In *Advancing Development: Core Themes in Global Economics,* edited by G. Mavrotas and A. Shorrocks. London: Palgrave.

Bahl, R. 1999. *Implementation Rules for Fiscal Decentralization.* Georgia State University International Studies Program Working Paper 99–1. School of Policy Studies, Georgia State University, Atlanta, Georgia.

Barma, N., K. Kaiser, T. Le, and L. Vinuela. 2012. *Rents to Riches? The Political Economy of Natural Resource Led Development.* Washington, DC: World Bank.

Cherotich, A., and O. W. Bichanga. 2016. "Factors Affecting Effective Implementation of Integrated Financial Management Information Systems by the County Governments of Kenya." *International Journal of Economics, Commerce and Management* 4 (4): 1049–1068.

Craig, D., and D. Porter. 2017. *There Is Security from this Place: Promoting the Safety and Economic Vitality of Port Moresby's Local Markets.* Policy Note, Justice for the Poor. Washington, DC: World Bank.

Craig, D., D. Porter, and F. Hukula. 2016. *Come and See the System in Place: Mediation Capabilities in Papua New Guinea's Urban Settlements.* Port Moresby: World Bank.

Duncan, R., A. Cairns, and C. Benga. 2017. *Papua New Guinea's Public Service Delivery Framework at Sub-National Levels.* NRI paper 154. Port Moresby.

Government of Papua New Guinea. 2016. *Budget.* Vol. 1. Ministry of Finance, Port Moresby.

Government of Papua New Guinea and Ministry of Finance. 2015. *Public Expenditure and Financial Accountability Road Map 2015–2018 and Assessment.* Ministry of Finance, Port Moresby.

Howes, S. 2016. *Where Has All the Money Gone?* DevPolicy Blog, April. http://devpolicy.org/pngs-fiscal-woes-where-has-all-the-money-gone-20160408/

Hughes, C., S. So, E. Ariadharma, and L. April. 2017. *Change Management that Works: Making Impacts in Challenging Environment.* Policy Research Working Paper, World Bank, Washington DC.

INA (2016) *PNG at 40 Symposium: Learning from the Past and Engaging with the Future.* Port Moresby: Institute of National Affairs.

Kalinoe, J. ed. 2009. *Review of the Implementation of the OLPG and LLG.* Port Moresby: CLRC, 165.

Ketan, J. 2007. "The Use and Abuse of Electoral Development Funds and Their Impact on Electoral Politics and Governance in Papua New Guinea." CDI Policy Papers 2007/2, pp. 14–15. Canberra: Centre for Democratic Institutions, The Australian National University.

——. 2016. "Good Governance Is Essential to Building the Nation State in Institute of National Affairs." mimeo, Papua New Guinea.

Lelang, J., G. Linge, A. Marat, J. Komal, W. Longgar, and M. Matui. 2015. *Final Report. Provincial Consultation Report on the Inquiry into the Organic Law on Provincial Governments and Local-Level Governments.* Volume 2. Constitutional and Law Reform Commission, Port Moresby.

Moore, M. 2004. "Revenues, State Formation, and the Quality of Governance in Developing Countries." *International Political Science Review* 25 (3): 297–319.

Pritchett, L., and M. Woolcock. 2004. "Solutions When the Solution Is the Problem: Arraying the Disarray in Development." *World Development* 32 (2): 191–212.

Rodin-Brown, E. 2008. *Integrated Financial Management Information Systems: A Practical Guide.* Washington, DC: USAID.

Slater, D. 2010. *Ordering Power: Contentious Politics and Authoritarian Leviathans in Southeast Asia.* New York. Cambridge University Press.

Wolfers, E. 2007. "Bougainville Autonomy—Implications for Governance and Decentralization" *Contemporary PNG Studies: DWU Research Journal* 6: 92–111.

World Bank. 2017. *World Development Report 2017: Governance and the Law,* chapter 7. Washington DC. World Bank.